the Walker Brothers

No Regrets

the Walker Brothers
No Regrets
OUR STORY

JOHN AND GARY WALKER

JOHN BLAKE

Published by John Blake Publishing Ltd,
3 Bramber Court, 2 Bramber Road,
London W14 9PB, England

www.johnblakepublishing.co.uk

First published in hardback in 2009

ISBN: 978-1-184454-815-6

British Library Cataloguing-in-Publication Data:

A catalogue record for this book is available from the British Library.

Design by www.envydesign.co.uk

Printed in the UK by CPI William Clowes Beccles NR34 7TL

1 3 5 7 9 10 8 6 4 2

Papers used by John Blake Publishing are natural,
recyclable products made from wood grown in sustainable forests.
The manufacturing processes conform to the environmental
regulations of the country of origin.

Every attempt has been made to contact the relevant copyright-holders,
but some were unobtainable. We would be grateful if the
appropriate people could contact us.

This book is dedicated to our loyal fans and friends all over the world, and to all those who have kept faith with us since the sixties.

CONTENTS

AUTHORS' PREFACES

If you're thinking of writing a book, my advice would be don't! Unless you want to expose yourself to public scrutiny and take the consequences. That's a risk I feel I must take, because mine is a story that has to be told. I have been privileged enough to have the most extraordinary life as a member of one of the most famous pop groups in the world. It has been quite an experience reliving the past and revisiting all the ups and downs, the good things and the bad, the happiness and sadness, and I have long wanted to counteract the many falsehoods that have been written about The Walker Brothers.

I want to say a very special thank-you to my wife Barbara, my son Michael and Barbara's family, who have become my family. To Sue Walton for all the time and effort spent on my website and for backing me. A thank-you to Sue Hadley for her part in assisting her. To Pete Weller and his dear late wife Pam, great friends over many years; Jean and Colin Timcke; Dean Gerard (my spiritual brother), with whom I grew up with from the age of two; Mike Williams, whose parents let me stay at the Old Bull & Bush pub when I had nowhere else to go; John Blake, Lucian Randall and their colleagues at John Blake Publishing; Scott Walker and John Walker; Dave Oddie for his direction; and Gary's Girls – they know who they are! I would need a whole book on its own to thank everyone I want to, but I must add a huge extra-special thank-you to the author and historian Alison Weir, for her professional guidance and for

mentoring and editing this book, and her husband Rankin, for all the generous hospitality and wonderful meals. Last, but certainly not least, I also want to say a huge thank-you to all our fans, without whom none of it would have happened.

It has been an incredible experience recounting the story of my life. It is my privilege to share it with you.

GARY WALKER

www.gary-walker.net

I've been asked over the years to consider writing a book about being part of the Swinging Sixties – beginning in Hollywood and finally landing in London at the height of the British pop explosion and the meteoric success of The Walker Brothers. Those of us who lived through that time know that it was unique in history: a revolution in music, art, clothing, lifestyle and social changes – and also more than just a sentimental journey for many of us. I was lucky enough to be in the middle of that phenomenon and I think there are lots of folks out there who would enjoy knowing about what it was like for me, an American, getting caught up in the whirl of success as a young man, and the ups and downs of an artist's life.

Over the years, the public has been subjected to countless stories, articles, books and interviews about us that are based on false or misleading information and half-truths. Many accounts are just complete figments of their authors' imagination, the most outstandingly offensive being *A Deep Shade of Blue*. It has been my pleasure to set the record straight as far as possible about The Walker Brothers, individually and as a group.

I'd like specially to thank my wife, Cynthia, for her support in not only writing this book, but also for her unwavering assistance in keeping me on track with my endeavours; thanks to my sister Judy, who has watched my life unfold – and kept track of many facts; Alison Weir, historian and author, for mentoring the project; David Oddie, Ann Gwilliam, Joy Ryan, Jamie Andersen and the staff at John Blake Publishing; Gary and Scott – and, of course, our fans, who have shown fantastic support over the years.

Writing this book forced me to look back over my life, recalling it in great detail. During the process I experienced a mixed bag of emotions and mental challenges. I hope the end result is enlightening and entertaining for all of you.

JOHN WALKER
www.johnwalkerinternational.com

CHAPTER 1

OUR EARLY YEARS

A VERY SPECIAL TIME IN OUR LIVES
GARY WALKER

Of all the towns and places to be born, Glendale, north of Los Angeles, was one of the best. I was very lucky. California has permanent sunshine and within an hour or so you can get to the desert, the mountains, or beaches with miles of golden sand. It's a paradise; there is no other place like it in the world. It has everything you need for the good life.

Glendale is the ideal American town: it's the kind of place where you might expect to bump into Mickey Rooney or Judy Garland, or star in a movie with them. The famous director Stephen Spielberg uses Glendale and its surroundings in his movies because it has a feel-good atmosphere and is visually appealing; he filmed *E.T.* at a house in nearby Sunland Tujunga, where I lived for most of my life, although by then it had changed so much over the years that I didn't even recognise it when I saw the movie.

Glendale enjoys mild weather, with the sky always brilliant and clear. It has several claims to fame. Number one would be John Wayne; number two is beautiful Forest Lawn, one of the most famous cemeteries in the world, known for all the movie stars buried there. When I was a teenager, I would take my lunch up to Forest Lawn, and I'd sit and eat it next to WC Fields and Errol

1

Flynn. When I returned, years later, I would discover a little stone statue of a fairy sitting on a rock, which marked the resting place of Walt Disney. It was the final time that my path would cross with his.

The third most famous thing about Glendale is that I was born there: 'Glendale Memorial Hospital proudly presents live at 2:10 am on 9 March 1942, Gary Lee Gibson!'

My father's name was Don Gibson. He came from the Great Plains, a region best known for ranching and farming. My mother's name was Violet Irene Bowen. She hailed from Oregon, and was to have a big influence on me. She had an hourglass figure, dark hair and brown eyes. To me, she looked like a film star, a cross between Jane Russell and Rita Hayworth. Everybody liked my mother; she was very friendly and outgoing, a strong, confident person with high principles. All she ever cared about was that I would have good health and great manners, and she taught me those well.

We lived in a white bungalow, a small, timber-framed house, quite plain compared with many others, but we were happy there. My mother's family was very close-knit; its members all lived together in one house and were very supportive of one another. There were my father, my mother and me; my grandmother Helen ('Mama'), who very strict; and my mother's sister Joyce, nicknamed 'Ant', whom I could talk to in a way I never could to my mother. Ant was married 11 times but she could never have children, so, in time, I effectively became her child and she had a strong influence on me. Later, because of her marital difficulties, she became an alcoholic. My mother was teetotal, which led to my aunt's departing in acrimony. They didn't talk to each other for 15 years.

I was very upset, as I really liked my aunt. When I was about 16, Ant called in a drunken stupor from her home in San Bernardino and told my mother that she had slept with me. It was untrue, of course, but that did it for my mother, even though Ant was drunk. But they say that time heals all things, and it did in this case. When my aunt genuinely quit the drink, with the help of Alcoholics Anonymous, they got back together again.

Don, my father, owned a shop and sold doughnuts. He liked girls, and was not the family type. They split when I was too young

to be shaken up by their divorce and the reason for it was never discussed. My mother then married an Italian guy called Phil Baloumo, a Glendale taxi driver and a very nice man. That's when we took a small house in Burbank, and when I first became interested in planes. Grand Central Airport was near our house and I would go stand at the end of the runway to watch the bombers coming in to land, passing just above my head. I loved the airport and the planes, and eventually everybody at the airport got to know me. They let me sit on the planes because Phil was taking flying lessons there. But that marriage lasted only a year and I have no idea what became of Phil.

To compensate for her two divorces my mother went to great lengths to make me happy. We used to go bike riding together or play baseball, but she was always overprotective and became obsessed with my health. As I grew older her possessiveness became a problem. She never really liked any of my girlfriends, thinking none of them were good enough for me. Nor did she like my being away from home for too long and all her life she would constantly call, trying to blackmail me into coming home, saying she wasn't well.

After my mother's second marriage broke up we moved to a bigger house in Glendale. She went out to work as a switchboard operator for the Ritter Corporation and met Jack Charles Leeds, a wonderful man who was to have a deep and lasting influence on me. Jack was a chemist who would eventually become general manager of the company, and he helped to develop the Dr Pepper soft drink. He looked like David Niven, with a thin moustache and blue eyes. He was very intelligent, with a good sense of humour, and he'd tell stories with a lot of gesticulation, like Walt Disney. Jack came from New York and had quite a rough childhood, which he never talked about. He was a highly principled man, warm and kind, and you would never have known that I was not his own child.

He came out of the United States Coast Guard after World War II and bought a motorboat, which was moored in a marina at San Pedro in California. Next to it was one belonging to Humphrey Bogart and on the other side was Orson Welles's boat.

Jack would tell me what happened when Bogey went sailing with his then wife, Mayo Methot, a well-known movie star in the

thirties and forties. They would speed out about two miles in their boat, called Sluggy after Mayo's fiery temper and her ability to hit Bogey hard. My father said you could hear them, arguing, screaming and throwing stuff, fuelled by alcohol. They were well known as the Battling Bogeys, and divorced in 1945.

Orson Welles was the idol of my future fellow Walker Brother, Scott Engel. Both men liked my father because he shared their love of boats and they would throw garbage at each other for a laugh when they were all cleaning them at the same time. When studios invited guests on board Welles's boat for a party, he'd sneak away and hide on my father's because he didn't like those Hollywood party people. Bogey was the same. I didn't realise when I first heard these stories that Humphrey Bogart, like Walt Disney, would feature uncannily often throughout my life.

After Jack had been around for about a year, we had to go and meet Don, my real father, at a motel to sort out some things about the divorce. I was about five then and I was afraid of Don's new girlfriend, Mildred, who had black hair and looked like Olive Oyl in *Popeye*. I'd asked my mother why Don wouldn't come back to us.

'Mildred's got a gun,' she replied, 'and, if he tries to leave, she'd kill him.' So there I was, cowering on the floor in the back of the car while Jack went to talk to Don and my mother tried to calm me. I was really scared. I couldn't figure it all out.

Don married Mildred and moved back to Nebraska. It was hard going to stay with them on their farm for the summer. Mildred was more of a tough cookie than my mother and I remember that on one car journey, when I needed to go to the toilet, Mildred said, 'No, you can wait a bit longer and don't be such a baby.' That was unkind.

Don and Mildred had a large white house; it was exactly like the farmstead in *The Wizard of Oz*. There were corn fields and wheat fields stretching for miles with dirt roads leading to the country stores and the supply shops. Don took me fishing at a nearby lake and bought me new fishing gear. I was the only kid there with good equipment – and the only one not catching fish. Don bought fish from some of the boys which we told Mildred we'd caught ourselves. She told me to clean the fish before she cooked it, but I wasn't sure I'd like doing that so I deliberately cut out its eyes.

Deep down, I think I was trying to make her sick, although it didn't bother her at all.

On 4 August 1950, Jack married my mother and he proved to be the best stepdad ever. His presence had a major effect on me: I knew that they both loved me totally and I felt a lot more secure than I had been. Jack would explain things and help me figure them out. I particularly loved to watch and help Jack cooking. He was very good at it and that's probably why I love to cook many different kinds of foods from different cultures and find it very relaxing and rewarding.

I had a vivid imagination and I didn't need entertaining as I was always able to amuse myself while my mother was working at Ritter's with Jack. Grandmother Mama took care of me when they weren't around. Times were tough and they needed extra money, so they took a job managing an apartment house at 311 East Cypress in Glendale, which became my home until 1954. It was owned by a Mrs Grosse. She was a genuine, immensely kind soul with a huge smile. She just loved our family and made a great fuss of me. Her dog, Pal, had starred in the *Lassie* movies.

The first elementary school I went to was Horace Mann in Glendale in 1948. I was good at art, drawing and sports, but terrible at maths and English. It was there I first learned to perform in public. I was elected business manager, to my shock, and had to stand on stage in front of the whole school and talk about picking up waste paper and keeping the yard clean. It was torture because I was very shy. My friend Dean Gerard was sitting in the front row, making me laugh, which got me into trouble, but it was better than being frozen stiff on the stage. I knew I had to conquer my fear of being on stage and kept forcing myself. The first time I enjoyed it was when my friends and I put on a puppet show, which had all the other kids laughing and cheering, especially when the blanket fell down and you could see us holding the puppets.

Dean Gerard was my best friend and we grew up together from when we were toddlers. We did everything together. Dirt road alleys ran behind the houses and we would play up and down them all the time. Life was just one big adventure after another and there were no limits to our imagination.

I was in the third grade, just eight years old, when I got my first girlfriend, which was quite unusual. Most people didn't have girlfriends until they were about 15 – certainly no one else in my class had one. Her name was Barbara Stump and she was a giggly little thing with dark, curly hair. I made her play kickball (a bit like baseball) among other sports. She was the first girl I kissed. This kissing was very exciting and made us laugh and giggle because we thought we were getting away with something naughty. It seems hard to believe, the way things are nowadays, how innocent we were, though I did talk her into taking her panties down and showing me her body. We boys had heard that girls differed from us. She and I were scared of being caught but, even so, time seemed to stop as I tried to take in what I was seeing. It was all over in 15 seconds, but the memory would stay with me for ever. It was my first encounter with sex.

Then there was Karen Weaver, who I met when I was about 12. She was a chubby little thing with light-blonde, wavy hair and the best smile in the school. I think we went around together for about six months. All we did was laugh. We couldn't stop! She almost got me expelled from school. When we moved classes we were split up – deliberately, I'm sure. But by then I was then becoming more interested in sports than girls.

I was very fast at running, but never big enough for American football, although I did play really good baseball. Everybody was a big baseball fan and when the children's Little League Baseball teams came to Glendale, I would go with Jack. I played for a team called Krieger Realty. When we got to the last games of the summer series and were ahead of the other team for the first place in the league, 12–11 in our favour, it was I who caught the winning ball. The crowd went wild: people jumped the fence and ran screaming and yelling at me, they picked me up and carried me across the field with everyone cheering. It was my first taste of stardom. My mother and dad were so proud.

My other developing interest was in music. Jack had a lot of big-band and jazz records, and I would listen with him to these and a lot of tunes from shows such as *Oklahoma* and *Carousel*. He used to have his own group of musicians and played the trumpet. I still have that trumpet. He said it was fine if I wanted to do something with music later, when I was older, so long as I got a good education to fall back on, or some sort of trade.

For us kids, Saturday was the best day of the week. It was the day we got to go to the movies. This was when my imagination started running riot big time. Those movies had a huge influence on me. Our local theatre was called Cosmo's, and it showed all the films we liked: *The Lone Ranger*, *The Rocketman* and *Hopalong Cassidy*. They also ran serials such as *Superman* and *Batman*, shown over several weeks and always ending on a cliffhanger. In 1949, my mother went to work at the Alex Theatre in Glendale, taking tickets and serving popcorn and other treats. I knew Bob, the manager, very well and the girl at the booth would let me go upstairs to see him so I didn't have to pay for a ticket. Once he was up there talking to a man I learned later was Walt Disney – the first time our paths crossed. Walt showed his cartoons in the theatre to check the colour and the reaction to them. I'd often sit near him.

The Alex Theatre staged premieres and the stars would come and sign autographs. In 1949, I met Lou Costello of Abbott and Costello when they showed *Africa Screams*. He patted me on the head. I got another pat on the head from Jane Russell when I gave her directions to an air show at the Glendale Grand Central Airport. My mother was a big fan of the movie stars. I suspected that she loved those stars more than me and I reasoned that if I were famous she would like me a lot more. I couldn't think of anything better than playing a cowboy or an Indian.

My mother's favourite was Lana Turner, famously discovered – or so it was thought – sitting at the soda fountain in Schwab's Drug Store in Hollywood. It later emerged that she had actually been discovered at a malt shop about a mile away called Top Hat Café, across the road from Scott Engel's school – he must have gone there all the time. Mother took me to the church when Lana Turner got married for the third time. We followed her and the wedding crowd to her house in the Hollywood Hills where she came out in her wedding gown to wave to the crowd screaming her name.

Away from the cinema, one of the most exciting annual events was Hallowe'en, when we would go out to play trick-or-treat and collect candy. We were all dressed up like the little monsters we were and as we got older the trick aspect got a bit out of hand. We got bored with soaping windows or ringing the doorbell and

running. I remember an old man who seemed to hate all us kids. We got a brown paper bag, put some dog muck in it, took it to his front door, set it on fire, rang the bell, then ran and hid. It was dark and we knew he would never see us, let alone catch us. He came to the door and of course he saw the bag on fire and started stamping on it, only to get dog muck all over his socks.

Another Hallowe'en, my mother made me go dressed as a Disney Mouseketeer around the stars' houses in Hollywood. It was the only time of year you were allowed to knock with no one trying to stop you. Part of the deal was that I would get to go to Walt Disney's house but it was only the maid who answered the door. Lana Turner's house off Sunset Boulevard was a must and her husband, Lex Barker, who played Tarzan in a couple of movies, came and gave me some candy. They were directly across the street from Jayne Mansfield's house, which Engelbert Humperdinck later bought. At Judy Garland's home, a bubbly little girl answered the door. We struck up an instant rapport and I asked her to come out with me. Someone indoors told her that she couldn't – later I realised that the little girl was Liza Minelli.

The last house was Bing Crosby's. There were big gates and I rang the bell but nobody answered. At the time it was a bit of a disappointment not to see wholesome family icon Uncle Bing, though I got a different view of him years later. Bing's son Gary Crosby came to see The Standells when we played at the Peppermint West club in Hollywood. He told me – to my disbelief – that Bing never gave him any money and never took him anywhere. He felt that his dad didn't love him, that he was a creep and a terrible father.

I awoke one school morning around 3am to find the bed covered in blood: it was my first and last nose bleed. I went to the bathroom to clean up but, as I was looking in the mirror, it started to judder a little and then the juddering got more violent. This lasted for about 30 or 40 seconds. It was the first – but very far from the last – earthquake I experienced. They got to bother me so much that it was no small part of why I later moved to England.

I was sick for most of my childhood. I would catch everything. I've often wondered, reflecting on how life balances out, whether the phenomenal success I enjoyed in the sixties was a

compensation for missing out on so much in my childhood through illness. When I was two or three, my tonsils were taken out, but they left my adenoids alone and through most of my school years I would be sick. Nobody could figure out why I used to get such sore throats and very high fevers; they'd give me penicillin to clear them and I would be better in two weeks. But within a month or so, the problems would invariably return.

When I was about four or five, my legs began aching at night and I later discovered that I had a mild case of polio. Fortunately, it was limited to my growing up with my legs a little thinner than my upper body. At the age of seven, I developed a temperature of 104 degrees and was taken into the Glendale Sanatorium, a Seventh Day Adventist hospital. I kept drifting in and out of consciousness, but while my eyes were closed I could see a wall of light that became increasingly dazzling until it was almost like looking directly into the sun. Then it just disappeared in an instant. Maybe that was the breaking of the fever, but I wonder also if I had a near-death experience?

There was no doubt about how close I came to the end in my teens. I thought I had a sore stomach, which my mother didn't believe. I endured about three or four hours of pain before she finally called the doctor, who made me go to the hospital for a check-up in case I had appendicitis. Later that night I had surgery, because they thought there might be some risk of an eruption – they told me afterwards that I was about two hours away from death.

I lost a whole year of school due to sickness. Mrs Grosse owned a house in Lake Elsinore that had belonged to media evangelist Aimee Semple McPherson. Knowing I was ill and that I would benefit from a change of climate, Mrs Grosse kindly asked if my parents wanted to stay there and look after the place for her. It was a castle! We lived there for almost six months in 1952, with Jack coming down at weekends. The house was on top of a mountain that overlooked Lake Elsinore. From that vantage point, you had a breathtaking view of the lake and all the surrounding area. You would get up early to look at the lake, but you couldn't see it because the house was literally above the clouds and it was as if you were floating on them.

The interior was striking as well. The house had been built in the

1930s and had amazing features that most people would never have seen before. There was a central indoor fountain by the living room and a sliding roof through which you might get rain in the centre of the house. Aimee had decorated the whole dining room in black velvet and at the very top of the house she had a prayer room. A tunnel led from the basement to another house lower down the hill. I absolutely loved this tunnel: it was built like a long, narrow, plaster cave and was lined with coloured lights. But the house was also isolated and it got really spooky. Sometimes at night we would hear odd sounds outside.

We returned to Glendale when I felt better and soon afterwards we moved north to Sunland-Tujunga in the mountains. Because it was high up, it was ideal for me. We bought a cantilever house on stilts built by Vic Seese, an up-and-coming architect of the time, and it looked like a tree house, so that was what I always called it.

Between 1952 and 1955 I attended Mount Gleason Junior High School in Tujunga, where I made a lot of friends and was about average at lessons. My biggest influence at this time was James Dean. Everybody liked the way he looked. He had this red nylon windbreaker jacket that we all wanted, and I eventually got myself one from the same store where he bought his, Mattson's in Hollywood.

When I saw John Wayne's *The High and the Mighty*, in which he played a heroic pilot who saves his plane from crashing, I decided I wanted to be a pilot. I was 13. Three years later, my dream came true when I started lessons at Whitman Airport, near Burbank, with Hank Coffin's School of Aviation. The aeroplane that I flew was a Cessna 150.

Learning to fly came easily to me, and I was flying solo after only seven hours of flight instruction. I am quite proud of that. I remember taking my mother and father up in the aeroplane for a short trip. I intended to fly over our house in Sunland-Tujunga but my mother hated all the bouncing, as it was rough weather.

I soon qualified as a pilot in flying hours, went to Glendale Collage to study aerospace technology and got the licence as soon as I was old enough at 18. After that, I would take a plane up now and then to build up and maintain my flying hours.

My last significant memory of the Alex Theatre is of going in 1955 with Dean Gerard to see the film *Blackboard Jungle*,

featuring Bill Haley and His Comets playing 'Rock Around the Clock'. Everybody was jumping from their seats, dancing and clapping their hands. Elsewhere the movie had provoked vandalism in cinemas, so they stopped the movie because they thought we were terribly badly behaved. I was a big fan of Bill Haley; I used to roller-skate in the park to his songs but I never thought that as one of The Walker Brothers I would one day be on the same stage with him in Paris (when, incidentally, he stole the show).

Whenever I returned home from the Alex Theatre I would start listening to Jack's record collection, especially drummer Gene Krupa. I liked the way he played and I thought to myself, I can play like that. I would slap my legs and mimic the rhythms; it came very easily. My first proper kit was a very old set framed in red wood that we bought out of a newspaper for $75 in 1950. I got it without thinking that people can hear you practising miles away. The neighbours stormed, 'Either he goes or we go!' Boy, was I in trouble! The only time I could practise, I finally realised, was when I was on stage. It took me about two years to become proficient.

Sometimes I went to visit Nana, Jack's mother, in Hollywood. At one o'clock in the morning on a weekend, I'd sneak out of the bedroom window and go down Santa Monica Boulevard to a shop that sold only drums. I would just stand there and gaze. In that window there was a complete set of sparkling blue drums and I promised myself that one day I would have a set just like those.

But first I had to get through high school, which I started in 1955. I went to Verdugo Hills High School in Sunland-Tujunga and it was probably one of the best periods in my life. We just had so much fun there – it really was like being in the movie *Grease*: the dances, the football games, the basketball and the social life, all shared with good friends who really cared about me.

My behaviour wasn't always angelic. They brought us sheep heads to dissect in our science class. We cut out an eye, attached it to a piece of string and hung it in the centre of the main door to the school. Then we stood at the side, watching to see what happened. The bell rang and a lot of students walked by. The eye slapped into the faces of two hapless girls. They started screaming and one almost passed out, so a teacher took her to the drinking

fountain to get some water to splash on her face. However – and this was the wickedly brilliant touch – I had put the other eye in the drinking fountain and when this girl got there and saw it staring up at her, that did it!

I met Charlotte McSwain at Verdugo Hills; she was a hot little number with bobbed, blonde hair. She and the other girls would wear dresses that had three or four petticoats underneath although the guys preferred it when they poured themselves into skin-tight skirts and clinging sweaters. We boys mostly wore Levi's jeans, Ben Sherman shirts and nylon windbreakers. If you were caught wearing a leather jacket at school, they would make you take it off, as the boys who wore them were usually troublemakers and got into fights all the time. The main thing for us was music and dancing: the girls dancing were heaving bosoms and bums and that's all we cared about.

We were all looking for the right person and it was not uncommon for a boy to go with one girl one week and with someone else the next. The big deal was 'going steady' and you could prove it by buying a giant ring that your girlfriend could wear on a chain around her neck. It was like an engagement ring and it let everyone know that she was taken.

Sex was never discussed in our family and people in general didn't talk openly about it. You were taught to respect girls and sex was for married people, so we found out about it through gossip and experimentation. The worst thing that could happen (after getting thrown out of school) was getting a girl pregnant, but no one talked about being careful, so people took chances. If it did happen, you were expected to marry the mother.

At high school, aged 13 and a half, I started going out with an Italian girl named Ann Conti. She was a year older, but shorter than I was. Ann was going though a tough time when we met: her boyfriend had passed away with leukaemia. I was the school clown and Ann liked me because I made her laugh and because I was a brilliant dancer. I loved to dance as much as I loved to play music. Ann and I were two of the best dancers at the school. During lunch breaks, anyone could go into the gym and dance to Chuck Berry and Little Richard records, and she and I would make up jive steps. The teachers liked our moves and would ask us to demonstrate them to the whole school.

Ann's parents weren't crazy about me because I wasn't Italian or Catholic, but this didn't matter to us as we liked each other an awful lot. In turn, my mother didn't like Ann because she wasn't a typical American Protestant. She felt I was spending too much time with Ann and feared that Ann, being older, would have her wicked way with me. But we were mad about each other. We talked about love and were very romantic, kissing and hugging, though I was jealous to the point of destruction, something I would have to deal with all my life in regard to women. We were together for about three years until Ann found somebody older and left school a year before I did, in 1960. I was hurt beyond words and never thought I'd get over it. I made up my mind that I would never let myself get involved like that with anyone else.

I had joined the high school band as soon as I could, and the classical orchestra. Then I formed a rock'n'roll band, The Beltones. The line-up comprised Tom Bronheim on guitar – he later went on to perform in Las Vegas – myself on drums and Randy Thomas, an excellent piano player who later played in surf group The Hondells. We loved Jerry Lee Lewis and played his songs. The manager of a club on Sunset Strip allowed us to watch him one time. We were five feet away and he was absolutely incredible.

Another record that made a big impact on me was 'Sh-Boom', recorded by The Crew Cuts in 1954; and the King was inevitably a huge influence: I loved 'Don't Be Cruel' and 'Hound Dog'. Frankie Avalon was one of the many Elvis-alikes and he'd play in amusement parks. I liked the way the girls screamed at him and I thought that I'd like to become famous and experience something like it. But I never dreamed it would really happen for me too – and in a far more spectacular way.

By 1957, The Beltones had split up, but I continued my drumming in a band called The Biscaynes. Randy Thomas was on piano again, a guy called Mike played the bass and there was a saxophone player called Tom Funk. We recorded a surfing-type record called 'Blue Skies', which was a minor hit in San Bernardino. In Riverside County we did a show with Bill Medley before he became a Righteous Brother. He was with a group called The Paramours and we'd never heard anything like the sound they made, except from black singers. They called it blue-eyed soul.

Paul Anka was to be on the same show, but he never showed up. He'd gone off with this girl. Evidently, he was a little bit girl-crazy, even though he was only 15 or 16 at the time – we were a bit shocked by it back then.

It was important to have a car at school. You could go to a drive-in movie and be alone with a chick. I was one of the only teenagers at Verdugo Hills who didn't have one and I had to ride a bike, which I would hide at a friend's house near school. Jack told me I'd have to save up enough money myself and it took me two years. It was worth it, though, because a lot of new girls were on the scene.

In 1961, when I graduated, my close friends Joe Borskin, Bob Strickland and I went to Bob's Big Boy Restaurant in Glendale. I took my snare drum, Joey took his saxophone and Bob had his guitar. We were playing a song called 'All Night Long' as we cruised through the drive-in, feeling absolutely great because we had just graduated. We also used to love cruising Hollywood Boulevard, which was packed for about two miles with people driving up and down, waving and beeping their horns. That became quite the thing to do on Friday and Saturday nights. People came from all around; guys and girls were in their cars, screaming and yelling, playing radios at full blast and having a lot of fun. There wasn't any drinking involved, just sheer enjoyment. It was a very special time in our lives.

Tom Funk and I visited a magic shop called Blackstones, on Hollywood Boulevard. There were some brilliant masks but they cost about $30 – and that was really big money for us. But Tom and I managed to buy a werewolf mask just as good as the ones they used in the movies and went to our friend Danny's house with bass player Mike when it got dark. I went to the door with Mike and asked Danny if we could have some water. He said, 'Yes, fine.' We all trooped into the kitchen and found that the window was open so that you could see out, as we had hoped, to where Tom was hiding.

But then the phone rang and Danny left, leaving his younger brother and sister with us in the kitchen when Tom popped up with this mask on. These kids just screamed the place down. Dan ran in, yelling, 'What is it? What is it?' We said we weren't sure.

He ran outside and we followed. We could see Tom running away and I said something like, 'We'd better be careful here!'

The kids were crying, 'It's a werewolf!' But Danny didn't believe it. He knew something was up, though, and called the police. They asked for a description of the werewolf and suddenly it was on the radio and in the paper. People were coming from all over LA to see where the werewolf had been sighted and they had to have police cars on the beat there.

Tom had another go with the mask when we all went down to the local laundry and that also made the papers. So now it really had got out of hand; three or four days of this and we were on the front page of the *Los Angeles Times*. They printed this terrible picture of a werewolf, which was nothing like our mask.

At this point we decided we'd better own up because more police were being deployed and no one knew if some nut was on the loose. We went to the police station and said, 'We have to tell you it was us.' Of course, nobody believed us. They said that the police were covering up because they didn't want people to panic. Everybody wanted to believe it – including me! The crowds were having so much fun, coming up to look for the werewolf. We had to give the police the mask that we had spent $30 on – but we never got it back.

I made something of a major move in joining my third group, The Standells. They were formed in 1962 by piano player Larry Tamblyn, a nice guy and brother of the actor Russ Tamblyn. Tony Valentino, the guitarist, came from Sicily. The name came from standing around for ages at the agent's trying to get some work. They were eventually hired by Mac McConkey, who also represented a local group called John and Judy – John Maus and his sister. It was through this agency that John, Scott and I would all come to know each other.

The Standells had Gary Lane as bass player, also from Sunland-Tujunga. For the next couple of years, we performed in nightclubs in California. By 1962, I was attending Glendale Junior College, taking a degree in aerospace technology. At night I would play the clubs with The Standells to make some money. We were the resident band at a club called the Peppermint West at a time when there was a new dance craze called the Twist. The Twist kept me out of the military.

I was one of the few who wanted to enlist, as flying was my first love, and I thought I would be able to further my flight training for the Air Force, then go on to work for an airline. Most people were trying to get out of it because we were all only 18 and wanted to have fun. None of us really wanted to crawl around in the mud, get up at four in the morning and – worst of all – have our heads shaved. What we didn't know was that the draft board were quite choosy and I had once got carried away demonstrating the Twist to my mother, breaking the cartilage in my knee. That was the end of my Air Force ambitions. It changed the course of my life.

The Peppermint West was like a disco and all the stars would come in on Thursdays. I met Zsa Zsa Gabor and Tony Curtis. The place would be packed to hear us play our stuff. There was a new British group on the scene called The Beatles and we had to learn such smash hits as 'I Want To Hold Your Hand'. One night we ended up playing it to George Martin, The Beatles' producer. He had come over to America ahead of their first tour and I got talking to him. He told me he thought our group was very good; I thanked him – and never forgot it.

The Standells also worked as one of the two house bands at a place called PJ's in Hollywood; this was a more flashy club, like some of the London clubs I would soon get to know, and to get in you had to be a member and somebody with a name. A lot of stars would come in, among them Frank Sinatra himself and Doug McClure, but the person who stood out for me was Judy Garland. She arrived at PJ's club with these strange minders, but she was really drunk – and that is an understatement. She was swearing and making a fool of herself. They eventually had to ask her to leave. I felt really bad about seeing her like that, because I never drank or smoked a cigarette until I was 22, and – to me – she was still Dorothy from *The Wizard of Oz*.

A better-behaved customer was Tony Bennett, who was pretty slick. He and Tony from The Standells both came from Italy and used to talk together in Italian. I got along with him famously too. He too was kind enough to say he thought we were good.

I started to see Ginger Blake, from a fellow group called The Honeys, who had done lots of session singing. Ginger was the only one of my girlfriends whom my mother approved of, probably because she wasn't that special to me – I was seeing a couple of other girls at the time. Ginger would call up my mother and they would conspire against me, while my mother would tell me every other hour how great Ginger's sister Marilyn was (she later married Brian Wilson of The Beach Boys, who were just getting big at the time).

Janet Havilland was a more serious girlfriend. She was an air stewardess from Connecticut who worked for American Airlines. I had a Beatle haircut when I met her while playing with The Standells at the Peppermint West in 1963. Janet was tall and thin, with her short black hair cut in a Mary Quant style, and she was extremely pretty and trendily dressed. There were a lot of girls throwing themselves at us at the Peppermint West, but I've always been a one-woman guy. Along with my parents, I think Janet had the most faith in me.

Janet and a fellow stewardess moved into an apartment on Clark Street in West Hollywood, not far from the Whiskey A Go-Go and close to PJ's, and Larry and I later moved in with them. This was one of the best times for me, growing with the band, learning about life, and being away from home and my parents. But Janet was away a lot, flying – it was hard to hold it together. Sometimes we had some fights.

In late 1962 I met PJ Proby through Mac McConkey. PJ was from Texas and would usually wear his cowboy boots or buckskin jacket and look the part. Many people said he resembled the actor John Derek. I'd always ask PJ to the clubs in Hollywood where we were playing and have him sit in and we'd pay him in kind with free drinks – a lot of them! He would steal the show. A good singer and a good mover, he was absolutely great on stage. It was through Proby that we ended up playing football in the park with Elvis in Bel Air in Beverly Hills. It was quite startling for me to meet the King. He was wearing just blue jeans and a white T-shirt, but all I could see was this three-dimensional, larger-than-life, almost Technicolor person.

'This is Elvis,' PJ said.

'How do you do, Mr Presley?' I replied.

'Elvis, son,' he corrected me.

He was very well mannered and put me at ease quite quickly. He said, 'Let's play some football.' Eventually the fans found out about it, as fans do. If governments could use fans as spies, they'd find out everything they needed to know! I remember when we were in England and Scott had to move because of problems with the fans. We did all of it at three or four in the morning – and the next day the fans found him. Not bad. Just as they had found the King, which put an end to the football game.

The Standells got kind of fouled up for a while. Larry was more the family type and he left for a regular, secure job. I flew to with PJ Proby to England, but the band did find Dicky Dodd from the Fame Academy in Hollywood to drum and sing. The Standells went on to have quite a few major hits in LA and the Boston Red Sox picked their song 'Dirty Water' as their unofficial theme tune.

For me, though, England beckoned!

A PASSION FOR MUSIC
JOHN WALKER

My mother, Regina Rosalee Prohaska, one of 14 children, was born on a working farm in Standish, Michigan, which had no indoor plumbing or electricity. Her ancestors were Slovakian, Czech, Austrian, Polish, English and Dutch. Her parents spoke little or no English. All the children were bilingual, and spoke a form of Czech. My grandparents were tall, light-eyed, and had very strong, chiselled facial features typical of people from Eastern European countries. I inherited these physical characteristics.

Throughout her life, my mother ran the show without being overdemanding. She didn't want my sister Judy or me to go through the hardships she had gone through. She was very gentle and extremely protective of us both. Even when she came to see us perform as a duo, it was more to make sure that nobody would harm us.

Mother did not believe in waste or extravagance – a trip to a restaurant was a rare occasion. I remember her getting angry with me when I became successful because I took my family and friends to a beautiful steakhouse in Laguna Beach; she refused to order anything because she said it was a waste of money. She had a plain, functional wardrobe with just a few nice dresses or suits for church or special occasions. It didn't change much over the years. She and Dad were Catholic and we all attended Mass every week. Ours was a typical, old-fashioned upbringing.

When I was very young we went to the Prohaska family farm in Michigan. The men in the family had all been farmers and I always admired their quiet strength, particularly that of my grandfather. Grandpa, whose English was quite limited, called me 'Janco' and exhibited what I thought to be great courage in dealing with some of the farm animals. There were plenty of them for me to watch and to play with, though I'm ashamed to admit I took an exception to one of the cows and slapped it around the face. Ever since I've made up for that by going out my way to be very kind to cows. Apart from that, I loved it out there. When it came time to go home, I covered the car wheels in snow, figuring we wouldn't be able to drive out of it.

My father was John Joseph Maus and had been born in New York City. His father was an English-speaking German, and his mother was Irish. My father played the harmonica and loved the popular music of the day. He was a sharp dresser and preferred Italian-cut suits worn with the correct tie; he taught me how to tie a full Windsor because he felt that was the only knot a gentleman should wear. He was a real stylish dandy, a New York dude, yet streetwise as well.

My father liked Tony Bennett and Dean Martin and listened to the radio a lot. In the fifties he actually began liking some rock'n'roll and often correctly predicted which songs would become hits. He knew the geography of New York City and worked as a cab driver and private chauffeur for several years. He also worked as a machinist at North America Aviation in California on the Atlas Rocket programme and the experimental rocket plane XB-70. It was a highly secret operation and I don't know to this day exactly what my father did.

Dad never, ever, missed a day of work. He told me some very grim stories of his childhood spent growing up with his alcoholic father: the family never knew if the rent would be paid or if there would be food on the table. That must have influenced his very strong work ethic. I never knew any of my father's side of the family. He was my biggest influence and supporter. He had a store of wise sayings such as, 'Figure out a way to use your brains and not your back.'

He would hold up a dollar bill and ask me what it was, and I'd say, 'It's just a dollar,' and he would reply, 'No it isn't, it's the *almighty* dollar, and never forget it.' He loved cars and driving, and we both took care of the family car every Saturday for years. When I started playing music, he became my self-appointed roadie. He taught me that if I wanted something bad enough it was more effective to earn it and make a grand effort to get it.

As a young woman in her early twenties, my mother went to New York City to escape the unglamorous life of farming. She met my father at a party. Dad thought she was 'a real babe', and throughout their marriage he used to call her 'babe', like a true New Yorker. She called him 'Johnny' and I was 'Johnny' also. By the time Judy and I came along, Mom and Dad had settled into a conventional family life. The move from New York City all the way to California in 1947 was definitely their last big hurrah.

I was born on the morning of 12 November 1943 in St Elizabeth's Hospital in New York City, weighing in at seven and a half pounds and almost two feet long. I had to have my tonsils removed when I was only 22 months old – dangerous surgery for a young child at that time. My older sister, Judith Carol Maus, had been born on 20 January 1941. Our first home was a small New York City apartment. I remember playing with alphabet blocks with Judy in this apartment, and being bundled up for our daily walks in Central Park, with me in the giant pram. When I was around three or four, I would climb down on the rocks by the Hudson River, watching my mother put pieces of meat in the crab traps, catching crabs out of the river and taking them home for dinner. We ate a lot of Hudson River crabs, unheard of nowadays.

In 1947, our parents took us on a one-way trip from the East to the West Coast. Mother had decided it was time for the family to move to California to get away, once and for all, from the cold weather. Dad didn't want to go – he loved New York. Neither of my parents had ever been to California, but Mother's friend Bea Roth, whom she'd worked with in New York, had since moved to Venice, California. She loved it there.

The car was jam-packed with our belongings and it took over a week to reach our destination. I remember leaving the cold behind and feeling increasingly intense heat as the family got closer to California. I have memories of a desolate desert with weirdly shaped Joshua trees, cactus and other desert life – with no sign of civilisation in sight, it seemed so strange. It felt as if we were

pioneers, except that, instead of having a horse and wagon, we had the old Plymouth and took Route 66 straight across the country. Indiana was freezing; St Louis, Missouri, struck me as being the poorest city I could possibly ever see in my life, while Flagstaff, Arizona, was beautiful with lots of cool, fresh air and mountain forests.

The first time we saw the Pacific Ocean was by accident, when we got lost trying to find the Roths' house in Venice. Some days later we went looking for the ocean again and, when we got out of the car and actually walked on the beach, I was awestruck, as I had never been to a beach or seen an ocean. But I did not enjoy our time in Venice, where we stayed with the Roth family, as their son Johnny was a big nasty kid who loved to bully me and beat me up; even Judy was afraid of him. He cut her eyebrow when he threw a rock at her and she still has the scar.

A few years later, when the Roths were having Sunday lunch at our own house, I finally beat the shit out of Johnny. In his usual bullying manner, he came over and just grabbed some toy cars from me, daring me to get them back. Even though he was a lot bigger than I was, I'd had enough of Johnny Roth and chased him around the yard. He was screaming at the top of his lungs – much to the delight of my father and the dismay of Johnny's. I finally caught him and punched the hell out of him everywhere I could reach before he escaped from me indoors, where he hid behind his dad, still screaming. No one said a thing to me, but my dad had a big smile on his face for the rest of the day.

Around 1947–48, my parents purchased a house in Redondo Beach, having stayed with the Roths for months, all in one tiny room. It had been torture for Judy and me and it had to have been rough on my parents, too. Our own place was in a farming community, completely rustic and wild. There were no sidewalks and few street lights, just barren fields in every direction and overgrown plots of land that were completely uncared for; no trees, no greenery, just straw-coloured weeds and scary tumbleweed. The nearest good-sized town was at least five to ten miles away, so we felt very isolated in our little residential community with its few stores. Our house stood on a third of an acre of land, a small, wood-frame, two-bedroom home.

When I was five or six, I started collecting keys and soon had a

prized collection, which Judy threw on the roof in the middle of an argument. I climbed up a ladder and got the keys but tumbled off the ladder and cut my chin wide open. My father helplessly watched me fall off the roof from down the street where he was talking with our neighbour. He rushed over afraid he'd find me dead. I was unconscious and Dad later told me he'd found me lying in such a great pool of blood that initially he thought my head was cracked open. He and the neighbour carefully picked me up with my father holding my jaw in his hands in transit and they got me to the emergency room, where my chin was stitched up. That really hurt and I have the scar to this day. I still like to collect keys, though.

Mom and Dad bought a parcel of land down the street and began building a larger house. Our neighbour built it by hand with my father assisting, as he himself was not great at construction. The new house was a lot bigger, though there was still no bedroom for me. When I was very young I shared a room with Judy – now our parents had one bedroom and Judy the other, while I had to sleep on a pull-out Riviera sofa-bed in the living room.

Around 1948, when we moved into the house on Carnegie Lane, I started going to Grant Elementary School. My sister and I had developed a close bond because of moving to different neighbourhoods and going through various family crises together, and we stuck together loyally. While I was generally quite reserved, Judy was much more outgoing. I was painfully shy – quite afraid, actually – when I started school, but Mom felt confident that Judy would look after me there and walk me to school and home afterwards. She was a tough, no-nonsense little girl and if anyone bullied me at school she would hit them with her lunchbox, often specially packed with rocks. Being older than I, she has always been in charge.

I first began performing at elementary school. I took my first music class of any kind there, studying alto saxophone at first, then eventually switching to clarinet, because the sax was just too heavy to tote back and forth from home every day. In the fourth grade, when I was nine or ten, I ran away with two friends to avoid the dreaded square-dance class. We climbed over the school fence and just started walking. We ended up about five miles away near the beach and when it got dark we began to be afraid. We put our

thumbs out hoping to get a ride home and – fortunately for us – we were picked up by a man who made sure we got back safely while lecturing us about the dangers of hitch-hiking. Just to be on the safe side, though, Michael kept his hand on the door handle of the car in case the three of us needed to make a quick escape. Of course, my parents let me know in their own way that what I did was very wrong and the punishment inspired me to behave for at least a month, but I still refused to attend square-dancing. It would be five or six more years before I tried to run away again, by which time I would be in Redondo Union High School.

Three of us decided we'd had enough of Southern California and carefully thought out a plan to escape to Washington State and live there. I can't remember why we chose Washington State or, for that matter, why we disliked Southern California. We were to buy a car with my dad's driver's licence, as his name was exactly the same as mine. All of us stashed away canned food from our various kitchens. But it all fell through when the dealer wouldn't sell us a car because we were all underage – and life resumed the next day as usual.

My fourth-grade interest in playing and performing developed when I was cast as Prince Charming in a school play of *Snow White*. A girl called Sandra Kearns played Snow White. During the first performance, I gallantly rode out on my broomstick horse and kissed her on the hand as directed, breaking the evil spell and riding off together; but I became a bit bolder in the second performance and kissed her on the lips. A few days later, she came down with the measles and I followed about a week later. That should have been lesson number one.

When I was ten years old, the family moved again, this time several miles away to Loma Drive, Hermosa Beach. Though the new home was smaller, the area was much more desirable and it was only seven blocks away from the Pacific Ocean; by now the entire family had come to love the beach. The house had two bedrooms and, after moving in, Dad immediately had another reception room added on to the house. Judy got the large master suite with the shower and her own private entrance – but I still had to sleep on the Riviera sofa in the family living room.

I started attending nearby Valley Vista Elementary School as a fifth-grader. I wasn't concerned about being popular because I was already embarking on an acting and singing career and just didn't have much in common with the other students. But I really enjoyed school. My parents never had to remind me to do my schoolwork because I had my own routine, getting it done as soon as I got home.

I met three girls who used to take me home with them and kiss me a lot. It was strictly their idea but I went along with it and thought it was quite wonderful. I rarely missed an afternoon with them until I went to junior high school. I did get into a little trouble at home for staying out too late – but it was worth it. It was nothing more than kissing on the cheek and on the lips – but there was a lot of it.

My best friend in Hermosa Beach was Ted Jones, and he lived just down the street. We skateboarded and surfed – and we lived close enough to the beach to surf a lot. We also loved comic books such as *The Fab Four*, *Spiderman* and *Tales of the Unexpected*. I amassed quite a collection of comic books – hundreds of them – and when alone would act out the role of some of the characters as if I were putting on a dramatic performance. I was also acting properly, in plays, television and commercials. My mother found an agent for me, at the urging of my elementary school principal, and I started competing in talent contests as a singer. I won several and ended up singing in television and radio shows and for different school and community functions. I also modelled, but it was my acting career that really took off. My parents had promo photos taken of me by Hollywood photographer John Reed. I began getting parts in plays and commercials.

For three weeks, I was in a play by William Berney and Howard Richardson called *Dark of the Moon*, at the Ivor Theatre in Hollywood. I played the part of Floyd Allen, the brother of Barbara, who has been seduced by a warlock and gives birth to his demon child. I had to sing 'Down in the Valley' while playing guitar. The play got quite a bit of attention and publicity for its adult topics and, for the first time, my picture started appearing in the local papers. Director Lamar Krask took particular interest in my career and set me up for a lot of auditions at which another boy my age named Dicky Dodd would – without fail – show up with his a tuxedo, patent-leather shoes, formal shirts, perfect hair

and show mom. He really bugged me but, the last I heard, Dicky Dodd was playing drums in a bar in Laguna Beach. I don't know if that's true, but I like to think so.

My first television appearance came when I was 11 and won first place in the *Chef Milani* talent show, singing 'I'm Gonna Live Till I Die'. The prize included my first go in a real studio, Goldstar in Hollywood, where I recorded a demo of the same song accompanied by accordion player Jimmy Haskell.

I also performed in a TV variety *Christmas Special* hosted by singer Eddie Fisher. I was in The Mitchell Boys' Choir, who that backed Fisher after six weeks of rehearsals, but I preferred popular music to the choral music and hymns, so dropped out shortly after.

I appeared in some popular television shows such as *Peck's Bad Girl* and it was when I was playing my guitar while waiting to be called to set to play an extra in *Playhouse 90* that Scott Engel walked up. He asked me if he could play something too and did some uptempo rock song. I thought he was posing a bit too much and taking himself too seriously, generally overdoing the cool-kid act. After the show we went our separate ways and wouldn't meet again for a few years.

My bit parts continued in such films as *The Eddie Duchin Story* (1956), with Tyrone Power, and *Missouri Traveller* (1958), starring Lee Marvin. Along with TV shows and films came some commercials and modelling jobs. An Ovaltine commercial that I appeared in with the racing car driver Pat Flattery turned out to be my biggest pay-off financially, though Flattery himself died the following year in the Indy 500 car race.

The theatrical world was a less inhibited environment to grow up in and I felt quite a bit more worldly than my schoolmates. Singer and actress Betty Hutton, for example, completely unbuttoned her blouse in front of everyone without a second thought, because the lights made the set so hot.

In 1955, aged nearly 12, I went on to Pier Avenue Junior High School in Hermosa Beach, within walking distance of home. I had begun to notice that girls were starting to look way different from guys and, when we had to take showers after gym for the first time, all us boys tried unsuccessfully to peek into the girls' shower room. My upbringing in a strict Catholic household of the forties and fifties affected my attitude towards sex and girls. I thought that women were special and should be treated with a great deal of respect. All the guys knew about the girls who were sexually active and always available, but I never wanted to get involved with them. I wasn't a prude, but I believed for years that sex was reserved for older, married couples.

I became afraid of having intercourse because I felt inexperienced and awkward whenever it got to that point. Curiosity still got the best of me, though, and I never felt the slightest bit awkward in sneaking off with my various girlfriends and finding out what secrets lay beneath their blouses and skirts. My first serious rival for a young lady's attention was Jeff, an average fellow the girls all seemed to like, although I couldn't figure out why. We both fancied a girl named Sheri. She had just moved from Alaska, which seemed fascinating and exotic to me. She had blonde hair in a ponytail and a much more interesting and developed figure than the other girls. I followed her around a lot but had no success in wooing her because she preferred Jeff. I moped around when I realised there was no hope with Sheri.

I starting attending school dances at the local sports stadium each month and loved the music as well as dancing with the girls. The dance bands had at least seven to ten players with lots of brass, drums, bass and keyboards, and they played the big-band music of the fifties – no rock'n'roll. Rarely was there a singer or guitarist. There was always a dress code – girls in nice dresses and guys in proper attire. And of course they were chaperoned by the community organisation that hosted them.

Kids would sneak outside to have a cigarette. I started smoking when I was 15 or 16 and my friend, Ted Jones, and I took some of his mother's Benson and Hedges. I later switched to Marlboros because all the cool surfers smoked them. Back then a lot of teens and adults smoked everywhere – there was no stigma attached to it as there is now. Quite the opposite: smoking was considered sophisticated. It was, for me, a habit that continued for over 30 years.

The school dances were my first big exposure to live music. My family always watched a country music programme on television called *Town Hall Party* and sometimes we got *Grand Ole' Opry* from Nashville, Tennessee, on TV, but we didn't go to live shows. I listened to the local Los Angeles pop music radio station,

KFWB. Elvis Presley was just starting to make a name for himself and of course I thought he was great; I liked everything he did musically, but especially 'That's When Your Heartaches Begin'. I also loved Johnny Cash, Rick Nelson and The Platters. 'Sail Along Silvery Moon', performed by Jimmy Vaughn's orchestra, was a favourite. I was really impressed with the arrangement featuring the saxophones.

Around 1954, I started playing Little League Baseball. I could throw the ball farther than anyone else with great accuracy and was also a fast runner with the ability to catch any ball that came within my area. In my first year I made the All Star team as a centre-fielder and, after being scouted for promotion to the next level, looked forward to a promising professional baseball career. I got my informal training from my father. He used to come home from work each night and we would go to the stadium, conveniently located behind our house.

I also enjoyed American football. A bunch of us used to play without any padding or protective gear down at the stadium until I sustained a serious knee injury in 1956. It ended all my athletic ambitions and hopes of a sporting career. I was tackled by a huge guy who weighed at least 200 pounds. I was still rather small – maybe 120 pounds – and ended up being carried off the field with a ruptured cartilage and ripped tendons. The injury kept me in a cast and out of school for six months.

While I was still on crutches, I was cast as Betty Hutton's son in a television series called *Hey Mom*, but she backed out. I was also up for the part of Little Luke in *Rifleman*, starring Chuck Connors, but because of the *Hey Mom* contract I wasn't free to accept. It was a terrible blow for me to lose both shows, which had seemed such sure things. That was my first taste of crushing professional disappointment and I'd got to the age when nobody wanted to cast me – because I was too young or too old – so my acting career was put on hold for a while.

Because of the knee injury and the cast on my leg, I was cloistered at home with only schoolwork to occupy my time. I had started playing steel guitar, but I couldn't get under it with my cast, and my parents bought an Epiphone six-string acoustic to encourage me and keep me busy. I had nothing to do but practise for hours and hours every day, copying the records that Judy

brought home, starting with Johnny Cash's 'I Walk the Line'. I just played it over and over again.

Judy joined in, adding harmony, and we began singing together in talent shows, our first songs being Harry Belafonte's 'Marianne' and The Everly Brothers' 'Bye Bye Love'. We billed ourselves simply as John and Judy and our backup band was whatever was provided at the time, or we mimed to our recordings. Our popularity grew as did the publicity. We won the *Squeekin' Deekin* radio programme talent contest at Riverside Rancho, California. I was often nervous and overwhelmed on stage, even to the point of forgetting what I was doing. For many years I relied on Judy to protect me from everything but, by 15, I had gained more and more confidence as I put our bands together and took responsibility for all the business decisions. But my onstage confidence developed last and still comes and goes with each performance.

Judy and I also appeared on an important talent show called *Rocket to Stardom*. Being on television then was quite a big deal, but there were more exciting things to come. Around 1957–58, Judy and I met Fran Whitfield, who lived in Hollywood and was known for developing new young talent. She got us hooked up with Aladdin Records – surprisingly an all-black label – and we recorded our first single, 'Who's To Say'. We had a really nice orchestral accompaniment with backup vocals.

The owner of Aladdin suggested that I start writing my own songs, which had never occurred to me. Luckily, a number of my initial efforts were good enough to be recorded: in 1959 we did 'Hideout', 'Lovebug', 'Why This Feeling' and 'Tell Me' for Dore Records. In 1961, we signed to Arve for 'Live It Up', 'You Can't Have My Love' and 'Oh, No No'. Then, in 1962, we got a contract with Admiral and recorded 'Yes, We're Moving' and 'When You Are Lonely'.

Judy and I also did an embarrassing country-music spoof for KRLA radio with a popular DJ, Sam Riddle, as The Buckshots, recording 'Animal Duds' and 'The Letter'. We promoted these last two, but thankfully there was no success and the project sank into much-deserved anonymity.

When I was around 14, I saw a Carvin electric guitar in a music magazine, and decided I had to have it. It cost $139. My

after-school job at that time was painting all the trim of a neighbour's house bright red, and gardening for her; this was how I earned my first electric guitar. Dad said that, if I bought the guitar, he'd buy the amp. He bought me the coolest amp possible – a '57 Fender Bassman.

I started attending Redondo Union High School right after the Carvin guitar purchase and, for the first time, I started having difficulty fitting in with my peers: my hair was long, I dressed a little differently, and I didn't get involved in the school cliques and activities. I guess you could say I had a bit of an attitude. Consequently, I got into several fights because I must have been perceived as an outsider, and didn't take much interest in what the other kids were up to.

It was at Redondo Union High School, when I was 15, that I met a girl called Sharon, of Scandinavian descent with reddish-blonde, short hair. She was very popular at school and of course all the guys followed her around. Fortunately, she liked me. We went to football games and made out passionately behind the stands, having to find out who had won the games before we got home in case our parents asked. Up to this point there was just a lot of kissing and petting going on – nothing too sexual.

In 1958, Judy and I saw Ritchie Valens performing 'Come On, Let's Go'. We actually met Ritchie through a friend we had in common, Gail Smith, at a record hop; then we met him again when he was performing at an assembly at Pacoima Junior High, his former school. That day, Ritchie Valens unwittingly became my mentor, inspiring me to form my own band so that I could play live instead of having to mime to my own records at dances, functions and shows. We became friends, and he taught me new guitar techniques. Along with Buddy Holly and Eddie Cochran, he began to influence my writing. When I saw him perform on stage with his drummer, I decided right then and there that I wanted a drummer to complete my act.

I remember two weird things associated with Ritchie Valens. In 1957, when he had been a student at Pacoima Junior High School, he missed a day of school, the day that a plane crashed into the playground killing several kids. Because he was home attending a funeral he was miraculously saved.

Not long after this incident, when Ritchie had left school and we had begun our friendship, he went away. I was really looking forward to his return, because he had promised he would show me more guitar skills and techniques. Sadly, before he could do that, he was killed – ironically, in a plane crash – along with Buddy Holly and The Big Bopper on 3 February 1959. He was just 17. Mysteriously, I began to play the guitar with much more agility and flow immediately after his untimely death.

I heard about the crash from an asshole at school who offhandedly, and in a mocking sort of way, remarked to me on the bus drive home, 'Wasn't Ritchie Valens your friend? Well, he's dead.' I didn't believe it until I got back and heard the details from Gail Smith, and on the radio. I didn't want to believe it, and, when I did, I was quite upset and stunned for a long time.

I was an honorary pall bearer at the funeral in Pacoima. A week or so after the service, my family and other friends and relatives gathered at the house of Ritchie's mother, Connie. I wanted to play the guitar, so Connie told me I could use Ritchie's amplifier, which was up in his room. Ritchie had told me about a song he was writing called 'From Beyond', and he had taught me the song as far as he had got with it. I remember that it was very eerie and had a lot of tremolo. I went up to his bedroom and began to play 'From Beyond' – and he appeared. He was standing before me with a big smile on his face, wearing a shirt with black and white stripes and square gold buttons, buttoned all the way up to the neck. It was freaky; I could feel myself turning as white as a ghost.

I went downstairs and told everybody. Connie started to cry, and everyone thought it was awful that I had come down to tell them about this strange event that seemed so real for me, but which they saw as an overdramatic figment of my imagination. But, when Connie told us that the shirt I described was the one Ritchie had been wearing when the plane crashed, there was a stunned silence in the room.

I'd had trouble fitting in with the other students at Redondo Union High School, but that all ceased when Judy and I finally appeared at an assembly in our high school auditorium, and played some rock'n'roll. The others now seemed to admire me, and I became the token Redondo Union rock star. I covered a lot of songs by Buddy Holly, Rick Nelson, Eddy Cochran, Little Richard, Chuck

Berry, Larry Williams, Elvis Presley, Dion And The Belmonts, The Coasters, The Olympics, Ray Charles (who was later to influence my writing) and, of course, Ritchie Valens and other popular rock'n'rollers of the fifties.

Around 1958–59, Judy and I toured with The Masked Phantoms on a legion stadium tour circuit that featured R&B artists like The Coasters, Eddie Cochran, The Olympics, Donny Brooks, Don and Dewey, and other black artists. We were among the few white artists on the tour.

By 1959 John and Judy had started performing at a lot of USO (United Service Organizations) shows with me on guitar and both of us singing in harmony. Being exposed to the military bases and way of life, I decided to take a Reserve Officers Training Corps military preparation course at school, and hopefully go into the Air Force as a second lieutenant after graduating from high school. Unfortunately, the knee injury prevented me from passing the physical, so I abandoned the whole idea.

I continued to do well in high school, and took college prep courses. Not knowing if or where my music career would take me at the time, I considered either getting into a career involving technical drawing, which I excelled in at school, or becoming a history teacher. I loved to read about history and had a teacher who brought the subject alive for me. Political science and psychology courses also kept my interest.

Then, in 1959, we moved again so that my father could be closer to work. Our new home was at 637 Inglewood Avenue, Inglewood, near Los Angeles International Airport. I had started my sophomore year at Redondo High and, having moved in the middle of the school year, finished it up at Inglewood High School, which was over 25 miles from my former neighbourhood. Once I moved to Inglewood, I gave up surfing and started getting a lot more jobs playing music.

I had to go through the same old crap at the new high school because, again, I really didn't fit in. I had very long hair for the time, and wore jeans and white shirts. I was now consciously creating an image and loved great clothes. At the time there were no hair stylists for men, as we know them now, so my mother trimmed my hair. The student body generally looked much better at Inglewood High than the Redondo High School crowd, and also

came from wealthier families. The girls looked great: a tight-fitting dress called the chemise was popular, full skirts were 'out', and the guys loved that. These girls wore their hair in ponytails and they all seemed to be copying Annette Funicello, Sandra Dee and Debbie Reynolds. Everyone appeared very well groomed and stylish. The guys all had pomade in their hair and crew cuts.

There was a guy named Joe who threatened me with bodily harm if I didn't get my hair cut. He fancied my sister and when I told her about his threat she straightened him out real fast. Not too long after starting school I was called into the office to see the boys' vice principal, who wanted to discuss my hair. Bleached hair like mine was not allowed, and neither was long hair permitted. I simply told him that I was a rock'n'roll singer and that this was my image. He let me go without making a decision one way or the other. I immediately got in touch with the entertainment director at the school, and volunteered my band for a guest appearance at the next dance. We played the dance and won everyone over, including the vice principal. It meant a lot to me to have him agree that I was indeed a rock'n'roll star.

I had become friendly with a guy called David Marks. His mother, Joanne, and Judy knew each other, and Joanne told Judy that David wanted to learn how to play guitar. He had seen me play at the Biltmore Hotel in Hermosa Beach, and asked if I could be his teacher. Judy volunteered me for the job.

David introduced me to his neighbours, the Wilson brothers, who were also starting to get into music. Carl Wilson, unlike David, already played some guitar, but he also signed up for lessons with me. I was a few years older, so I managed to stay one step ahead in our lessons. David and Carl were both very serious about developing as really good musicians. I taught them chords, riffs and how to play lead. David impressed me as being particularly tenacious; he practised a lot. Although we lost touch for several years, I'm happy that we've since rekindled our friendship and get together whenever possible.

As Carl progressed, I had him play guitar in my band at the college jobs once in a while. His brother, Dennis Wilson, and I became good friends because we both loved fast cars and the beach. I remember Dennis driving over to my house to show off his 1959 Chevrolet, which had a Corvette engine. Brian Wilson wasn't

around the house much while I was giving lessons, but I believe he attended a community college as a music major and played the organ – there was a Hammond organ in their living room.

In my junior year, I took up with a hot senior called Kathy, whom all the guys were chasing around. She was a year older than I, a tall, great-looking model type with light-brown hair and a curvaceous figure, much more voluptuous than the other girls'. She and I kept catching each other's eye in the school halls, and my friends dared me to go over and say hello to her. Even though I was terrified, I somehow got the courage to do it and, before long, Kathy and I became an item. She was the first girl who aroused serious sexual feelings in me. She was kind of quiet – a trait I found that I preferred in girls, as opposed to the talkative, overbearing types. She was also more mature than I, which sometimes made things uncomfortable for me, as I was still very inexperienced around girls, while she was more sophisticated.

Kathy and I went regularly to David Marks's house in Hawthorne to attend his mother's book reviews, but somehow these occasions always turned into petting sessions between Kathy and me. How we managed that without Mrs Marks catching us is still a mystery to me. Our relationship ended when Kathy graduated from high school and I still had one more year to go.

Even with the move to yet another house, I still never, ever had my own room. Judy always had her own bedroom, while I always had to 'make do', right up to the time I left for England – I was 21 by then. This arrangement always bothered me, even though I never consciously questioned the living arrangements. Yet I never felt deprived, or like an 'extra' or an afterthought in the family, and I had no resentment because my parents were always supportive and loving towards me and Judy.

Still, I never understood why I couldn't have my own room. My possessions, big and small, became my personal space. Sometimes things got a little neurotic. For example, if anyone used my pens or writing pads, I wouldn't use them any more. I'd go out and buy new ones. In 1961, I even put a record player in one of my cars so I could listen to my albums in privacy. I became a very possessive person – what's mine is mine – and I wasn't happy to share what was mine with anybody. Over the years I've been told countless times, by women in particular, that I am indeed possessive.

I remember sleeping on the Riviera when I was a teenager, after playing late-night music jobs several nights a week – and Judy and her girlfriends would continually socialise in the living room while I was trying to sleep. By then, I had taken to sleeping in the nude, and after getting really annoyed and frustrated with the constant lack of privacy, I shocked the girls one night by pulling the sheets off, getting out of my 'bed' and walking buck-naked to the bathroom. They never came into the living room when I was sleeping there after that incident, but I apparently so impressed one of the girls that she took a real fancy to me. She kept hanging around the house a lot after that, and we ended up in her car, getting to know each other sexually – with me backing off from complete sex. I was still afraid at that point, and didn't know what to do.

When I was 16, I built a loft in the attic area of the garage at our home on Inglewood Avenue. It measured about ten feet by nine, and had a difficult and dangerous access by ladder only. That was my first private space where I could finally keep all my earthly possessions.

I started to develop some really good friendships during my junior year, when I was around 17. My best friend in Inglewood High School was Cody Vaught. Like me, Cody was different from the other kids, and we gravitated to each other. We both liked great clothes like 'continental' pants and Cuban heels, which weren't always available in Inglewood, so we went to Mattson's in Hollywood and Scotty's in Inglewood. I formed a doo-wop group with Cody, Dale Lundburg and Tom Alu, with the sole purpose of picking up girls as we cruised Hollywood Boulevard, singing in the car. Dale drove his '48 Mercury, I sat in the front seat and played acoustic guitar, and Tom and Cody were in the back seat singing away. We got a lot of attention, and of course lots of invitations to parties, where we all smoked and drank too much, and miraculously stayed out of trouble with the law.

I think there was a lot of dope around at many of the parties in the Inglewood and Hawthorne area, but I never got involved with that; I wasn't the least bit interested, and no one offered me any anyway. The drug scene was new at the time, and I saw a lot of kids spaced out but not drunk, so I knew they were doing something different from drinking. We four showed up, sang,

drank a lot, and tried to score with the girls. We usually left when the parties began to get very loud and spill out onto the street, and we often escaped just in time, passing the cops coming down the road.

After breaking up with Kathy, I wasn't particularly looking for another girlfriend. Instead, I got more into my music, and became fascinated with engines, speed and cars in general. I had started going to drag strips to watch the cars race the quarter mile. At 16 I purchased my first car, a very cool black 1946 Ford Coupe. I. During my teenage years, I bought many cars, including a 1948 Mercury that I had painted a silver blue-green and completely customised; I got this because I was starting to play more and more musical engagements and needed reliable transport. Over the years I drove a 1957 two-tone copper Plymouth Fury; a 1955 powder-blue Thunderbird with a white roof, which was one of my favourite cars; and a 1961 powder-blue Plymouth Valiant. My first luxury car was a 1961 white Chrysler New Yorker. I also had a 1957 black Thunderbird into which I dropped a 350bhp Lincoln engine and had the transmission beefed up for racing – it reached 150mph at Dan Gurney's test track.

In 1959, Judy and I were recording 'Hideout' at Goldstar Studios when Phil Spector came into the control room. He asked me to help him out in the next studio, where I ended up playing guitar for a Teddy Bears recording that same day. I can't remember the song. There weren't a lot of session guitar players around at the time, so it was common to be asked to sit in on somebody's session. Phil was three years older than I; he had a college-kid look, conservative and clean cut with a great head of hair. He was still an up-and-coming producer and singer at the time, and was yet to establish himself with his signature Wall of Sound.

Around 1959–60, I heard Ray Charles sing 'What'd I Say' on the radio, which blew me away. I thought he was the greatest singer in the world at that point. For the first time, I started collecting albums, digging up everything Ray had recorded that I could get my hands on. As I grew older, Ray Charles became a huge influence on me musically: he could do blues, rock, country – everything – and, for me, he took every song to a higher level than the original, in every way. Even though he could really rock, he was always incredibly classy and versatile. Actually, he was the classiest act I can think of, and I always hoped that a little of that would rub off on me.

Judy and I recorded several more of my original songs for the Dore label, including 'Why This Feeling' and 'Tell Me'. For contractual reasons, my mother, Regina Maus, was given credit for my songs, which is why her name appears on the recordings. Lou Bedel also got his name attached to one of my songs by changing a word or two and taking credit for some of the writing. It was at this time that I started to become aware of the various scams that publishers and record companies resorted to in order to avoid paying artist royalties.

I've been asked several times about having recorded two songs called 'Beautiful Brown Eyes' and 'Toastin' Marshmallows' with my sister and someone named Billy. Although I do have the original acetate of the John and Judy versions, I can say, absolutely, that Judy and I never recorded these songs, or anything else, with anyone named Billy.

I was always drawn to attractive and pretty girls – not always pretty in the classic sense – who were fashionable and could hold a decent conversation. Usually, they were stable, quiet, family-oriented girls; promiscuous girls who were loud and obnoxious never appealed to me. But, generally speaking, the girls I ended up with had to make the first move themselves, or through their girlfriends, as I was reserved and shy.

In my senior year at high school, I got involved with a girl named Gloria, a junior a year younger than I. She was very petite with blue eyes, and wore her hair in a beehive to look taller. She was always dressed in the latest fashions. We started dating and I eventually asked her to go steady with me, symbolised by the ring I gave her to wear on a chain around her neck. It meant that we were officially boyfriend and girlfriend.

Gloria had a girlfriend named Marianne, who – according to Gloria – was very sexually active, and we would talk about everything that Marianne told her. Naturally, this gave Gloria and me ideas, and one thing led to another, which was the first time I had any real sexual experiences, although still without intercourse.

I occasionally took Gloria to the college parties where I was playing but, unknown to me, she was giving her number out to

other guys. My guitar player, Kenny, pointed out what was happening and when I saw it too I broke up with her. We never spoke again. Having had no experience of this kind before, I was really pissed off, and that became lesson number two (the first being the measles episode). The whole thing upset me quite a bit because I had been totally trusting and had never once thought of taking advantage of my opportunities to cheat on Gloria, of which there were many.

After my break-up with Gloria, my life became busy with playing jobs and working on cars, and I didn't really look for another girlfriend for quite a while.

David Marks and the Wilson brothers had, meanwhile, formed a group, and, when they signed a recording contract with Candix, Carl came to the music store where I was working and expressed his concern about the name – The Beach Boys – that the record company had chosen for them. He didn't like it, thought it was embarrassing. I told Carl that in my opinion the name of the group was the last thing to worry about. Having a hit record was the important thing.

By November 1961, the guys were using my family's garage to introduce me to their new song, 'Surfin''. My father didn't like the song too much and didn't have a lot of hopes for The Beach Boys, but the record came out on Candix and was a big hit. That was the beginning of much success for The Beach Boys. Soon we would all be playing at Pandora's Box in Hollywood on a regular basis.

That year I bought my first Fender Stratocaster guitar. I was playing a lot of shows and working in the local music store. The owner said she could get the guitar for me at a discount, so I jumped at the chance. The Stratocaster was finished in cherry sunburst, with a white pick guard, a rosewood fretboard and a tremolo arm. I was so pleased to have that guitar. David Marks bought my Carvin, and I remember that his dad refinished it in a terrific electric blue. A few years later, Fender came out with a new guitar called a Jaguar, and I had to have one. I got a hold of the eighth Jaguar ever made; it was white with a tortoiseshell pick guard, a rosewood fretboard and a locking tremolo arm.

By now I had graduated from high school and enrolled as a full-time student taking access courses at El Camino Junior College in LA with the idea of continuing on to university, as I didn't know how long or successful my musical career would be. But then I found myself playing more and more, and the schedule became so gruelling that I finally left the college before finishing up the year.

In 1962 I signed with Mac McConkey, who ran the McConkey agency in Hollywood with his mother, Gail. He booked all my auditions and jobs for several years. When my sister and I were in our late teens and early 20s, dance crazes were sweeping the clubs and, at my urging, Judy became the first 'twist girl' in Hollywood. The idea really caught on and soon lots of bands were incorporating their own twist girls on stage.

As for myself, I didn't strive to present a particular image on or off stage, but I did prefer certain looks for myself and my bands. I can't say that I emulated any particular artist; I just wanted to play my guitar really well.

In 1959, I found a drummer, Jimmy Lendennie, through the local musicians' union. In 1961, I hired a guy called Freddie Patterson to play rhythm guitar and add vocals, and we started playing a lot of clubs around Hollywood, including Moulin Rouge and Come to the Party (later Whisky a Go Go). Now we were called John, Judy and the Newports, a name chosen by the McConkey Agency.

The four of us were playing the fraternity and sorority college circuit, and although the band's name changed from time to time, it always had 'John and Judy' in the title. We were performing mostly on the campuses at the fraternity and sorority houses of the University of California and the University of Southern California. We became the most sought-after band and always had lots of work. John, Judy and the Newports were asked to play for Jimmy Durante's first anniversary at his beautiful big house, which overlooked the Sunset Strip, right off La Cienega. Jimmy had become an icon in America with his television shows and recordings. He was extremely friendly and chatty, wanting to make sure that we were very comfortable.

That night, he sat in with us for a couple of songs, which he played on the piano and sang. When the dinner was served, he even insisted that we eat with the guests, which was completely unheard of. When the three-hour job was up, we asked him if he wanted us to stay longer, and he asked us to play until the party was over – it turned into a six-hour job. The only awkward part was that we

were a union band who played for union-scale wages, and I didn't know what the pay scale was for the extra hours. Jimmy asked me at the end of the night, 'How much do I owe you?' When I told him I didn't know what to charge him, he said, 'That's simple,' wrote out a cheque for double the amount of the contract, and also gave me a generous $25 bonus and suggested I treat the band to coffee on him. That $25 would have bought a week's worth of coffee back then. Jimmy was a really kind, gracious and generous man.

When I was 18 and had graduated from high school, I got called up for the army draft. Nobody in my family wanted me drafted to serve in the Vietnam War, but I went to take the physical, knowing that I wouldn't pass due to the knee injury. They also told me that some of my optic discs had dissolved from the pressure of the severe migraine headaches I had experienced frequently from the time I was around 14 years old. Anxiety seemed to bring the headaches on, and they would plague me for years, at the worst times, as happened when Scott and I were scheduled to perform for the first time on *Shindig*, the hottest rock'n'roll television show ever. The optic disc discovery led to my undergoing a battery of tests, which ultimately showed that neither my eyesight nor my general health was in any permanent danger; but, unfortunately, I continued to have migraines, which affected my vision. That aside, I was quite relieved that I wouldn't have to go to Vietnam, as I didn't believe we really belonged there.

One night, we had a job in Malibu at a club that served food, but the stage was in the bar area, off limits to yours truly because I was under age. Luckily that night I had an extra-long guitar lead, as I had to go outside to sing and play, sitting on a bar stool, peering through the window all night at the rest of the band. It sounds ridiculous now, but at the time we had a job commitment and went on with the show. People came in and out, staring at me curiously. The job lasted five hours!

Late in 1962 our band got a job at the Oasis nightclub in Honolulu, Hawaii. We played six nights a week, with two 40-minute shows each night. We had a record out called 'Yes, We're Moving', one that I wrote and really liked, and it proved to be quite popular in Hawaii. My parents accompanied us and we were given an apartment near the beach.

I thought that Hawaii was terrific. I went to Waikiki beach every day, where I slept, swam, bodysurfed and generally hung out. I was curious about some of the Japanese girls who were also appearing in the show. One was Mikimoto, 'the Pearl of Osaka', an exotic dancer dressed in a kimono, who eventually stripped down to just pasties and a G-string. She was the most titillating performer of the *Japanese Revue,* and we caught each other's attention, began flirting and became quite friendly. Mikimoto would seek me out at Waikiki Beach during the day.

I still hadn't slept with a woman at this point. Ken, the Japanese manager of the club, somehow found out that I was basically an inexperienced virgin (the Japanese called it being a 'cherry boy') and teased me a little bit, then finally decided to remedy the situation. One of the regular clubgoers, an attractive Japanese woman who was about ten years older than I was, had made it clear to several people that she wanted my body. Ken arranged for her and me to have a rendezvous, at which time she decided to have her way with me, and I let her. She decided to be my personal trainer in the art of making love.

Now worldly and fickle, I noticed a very pretty petite Japanese singer who had joined the show, and became attracted to her. Her name was Naoi, and she was very interested in me, too. Unfortunately, we never had much time together because I returned home shortly after we got involved. A lot of internal strife had broken out within my band and we had no option but to leave a great job that probably could have lasted at least another couple of months. The group immediately broke up after we returned to California. I had another job lined up, but didn't have a band. I advertised for one through the musicians' union, and very shortly afterwards The Stringalongs, who'd had an instrumental hit in the late 1950s called 'Wheels', arrived on my doorstep at Inglewood Avenue in a car filled with their instruments. We had a tryout rehearsal in the front room and it looked like things would work out well, all of us knowing the same repertoire. As soon as I hired them I found out that they were completely broke, and that one player's wife was pregnant. I think they were actually living in their car. I advanced them some money, which was not at all common.

They turned out to be perfect for one bizarre job in which I was asked to back a vaudeville-type singer named Jennie Jackson,

whose claim to fame was her 52-inch bust. Unfortunately, we didn't last too long as a band because we didn't have enough work to keep us all busy enough to make money. The poor girl married to the band member had a miscarriage at the hotel during one of our gigs, which resulted in my paying for doctor's expenses, as nobody else had any money. After that, The Stringalongs and I parted company, and I was back to searching for a new band.

CHAPTER 2

THE WALKER BROTHERS GET TOGETHER

THE LEADER OF THE BAND
JOHN WALKER

In 1962, Judy and I were booked every Friday and Saturday night as the house band at Pandora's Box, a very hip club on Sunset Strip. It was a coffee house with entertainment, no booze allowed. There were lots of guest artists such as Bob B Soxx and the Blue Jeans and The Beach Boys. It was here, around November 1962, that I met Kathy Young, who was to become my first wife. She played two nights as a guest artist, with us backing her. Most of the performers at Pandora's were seasoned professionals, but I did not get the impression that Kathy was. She seemed a little nervous, and shy about performing, but I felt that was due to the fact that she didn't have all the material for her set.

Kathy grew up in Long Beach, California, in a very typical middle-class family. She was a little different from the other girls I knew because she liked a lot of sports, and had a competitive streak. She told me that she had always wanted to be a singer and make records. She had had her first hit record, 'A Thousand Stars', at only 14 years old, in 1960, followed by 'Happy Birthday Blues' and 'All You Had To Do Was Tell Me', the latter with Chris Montez. Kathy had also appeared on Dick Clark's *American Bandstand* with 'A Thousand Stars' and starred in a lot of other popular TV shows.

Because Kathy didn't have music for all the songs she wanted to sing, quite a bit of rehearsal was necessary, and I had to spend more time than usual with her, learning her music. Fairly tall with brown hair and blue eyes, she struck me as being very pretty and rather shy, and I was soon interested in getting to know her. Our first 'date' was walking down the street during our break to a hotdog stand. I was becoming very fond of her and asked her for her telephone number. When she didn't hesitate to give it to me I figured she must have liked me too. We managed to date when neither of us was working and I soon felt that Kathy was the perfect girl for me. I was always completely infatuated with each of my girlfriends – head over heels every time – but I ended up feeling protective towards Kathy because she seemed young and naïve in the music business, and therefore vulnerable.

I had met Don Wayne, her manager, and Jim Lee, the owner of her record label, when they came to see her show one night. Don asked me if I would consider backing Kathy on future shows, and I agreed. It was arranged that Judy and I would do our set and then back Kathy for hers. As Kathy and I were thrown together more often, I became more and more involved with her.

After about three months of doing shows together and dating, Kathy became very emotional and clinging, and revealed that she had a problem that had to be dealt with, something that, in those times particularly, would have caused her and her family a lot of pain and embarrassment. I found myself showing her nothing but support, which surprised me because of my conservative upbringing. Then she had to go away for several months, during which time I wrote to her two or three times a week, called her as often as I could, and never even considered getting involved with anybody else. Our relationship resumed where it left off when she returned home.

One night, later in 1962, the guest group at Pandora's Box were The Routers, a surf band who had a hit called 'Let's Go'. The bass player was Scott Engel.

The next day Scott asked if he could join my band as a bass player. I wasn't happy with either my bass player or drummer at the time, so the deal was for Scott to find a good drummer, then they would both be hired. He found a guy named Spider Webb, a flamboyant drummer reminiscent of Gene Krupa, one of the best in LA at the time. We all rehearsed in my family's garage on Inglewood Avenue, and played as if we'd been together for 50 years. I had my strongest band to date, now that Scott and Spider had joined us.

Scott was not the kind of focused, serious musician I was used to playing with. As I got to know him, I discovered music was secondary to his art studies and that he avoided commitments that might interfere with them. He liked to stay close to home and school, and for a long time he turned down jobs that would take him away from Hollywood. I think that was one reason why he left The Routers and joined my band, so he didn't have to tour.

Scott was born on 9 January 1943. He lived in Hollywood with his mother, Betty, whom we all – including Scott – called Mimi. Mimi was tiny and feisty, and Scott absolutely adored her, phoning her often and buying her presents. She loved her Manhattan cocktail around lunchtime, and cooked great Mexican food, Scott's favourite at the time. Scott rarely spoke of his father; he told me that he lived back East and was high up in a big oil company, but they were not involved with each other. Mimi and her sister, Aunt Celia ('Aunt Seal'), doted on Scott, and he ruled the roost, coming and going as he pleased, and not really answering to anyone. He could do no wrong, but even Mimi referred to him as 'the brat'.

I heard from somebody else later that Scott had been Eddie Fisher's protégé, but that the whole thing had fizzled out when Fisher, who was married to 'America's Sweetheart' Debbie Reynolds, ran off with the scandalous woman Liz Taylor. America thought Fisher had treated Debbie Reynolds terribly. Certainly this brought Scott's career temporarily to an end, and it may have affected him deeply.

I didn't know when I met Scott that he had done any recording. One time at his house he asked me if I had heard the new Dalton Brothers record. I said I didn't know who they were, so he played a record featuring two guys doing a Spectorish-style song. He was anxious to know what I thought, never revealing that it was him singing with his friend, John Stewart. I told him it was OK, and no big deal, which it wasn't.

Scott never displayed any wild behaviour. He was a quiet, laid-back, normal guy with a good sense of humour. He didn't seek attention, or garner any extra attention either. He was good at art, but I never really saw much of his work until we were in the UK and he would draw portraits while we were touring. He didn't display his pictures around his house in Hollywood or take it out to show me. He liked foreign films, and listened to classical and jazz music. Aside from John Stewart, I never met or heard of any other friends he had. He was quite a private person.

Scott never got into discussing his personal relationships or girlfriends. I know there was a waitress at Gazzari's named Ann who fancied him, and that they became a quiet item. Aside from commenting about some attractive woman we'd all seen, he kept his thoughts about the ladies to himself.

As soon as Scott and Spider joined my band, I called Mac McConkey, and he got us a booking at the Kismet, a cool nightclub and a great place to play. We billed ourselves as Judy and the Gents. I was the lead singer, with Judy – our 'twist girl' – dancing and singing a solo from time to time, and Scott at first singing backing vocals with Judy and then harmony to me. Eventually, I got Scott to do a little lead singing, although he was stubbornly reluctant; he seemed to have a hang-up about singing. Our repertoire was strictly rock'n'roll with an occasional ballad, typical of the Hollywood dance club sets.

We were an immediate hit at the Kismet. The club was packed every night we played, and our reputation grew. Mac McConkey sent us to John Reed, the famous Hollywood photographer, to have publicity shots taken of the group; these included the famous one of me, Judy and Scott with a goatee beard. One night, the vice squad raided the Kismet to check out the players and ask for ID. Scott and I were both 20 – a year shy of the legal age to be in a club. He had a decent phoney draft card that passed the vice squad's scrutiny, but I had nothing. So Mac and I quickly arranged to drive down to Mexico to buy me a phoney ID card. We ended up in a whorehouse in Tijuana, drinking Cerveza while the guy was supposedly getting the card ready. We caught onto their game of making us wait for ever while showing porn on 8mm films and parading scantily clad women in front of us for several hours.

It was while hanging around in this place that I was first offered dope: 'Would you like a little dope, señor?' I decided against it.

Eventually, after several hours of waiting, we finally insisted on them producing the ID, which they did, and we left for California. As it turned out, the phoney ID would have never done me any good, as the card was of the wrong 'issue' year and could have landed me in a heap of trouble had I produced it, which, fortunately, I never had to.

I decided to get myself a proper phoney ID, which involved going to another county in California, applying for a driver's licence and making a name up for myself, which I decided should be John Paul Walker (I had been using the name John Walker professionally for four years because I didn't like the way people pronounced my real surname). I also had to state that I was 21 and actually take the driving test, being careful not to drive too well in front of the test instructor, as I was supposed to be a novice. Little did they know! But I ended up with a valid California licence showing my new name and age, which enabled me to play clubs again with no problem. What I had done was actually quite risky – I had committed a state offence, which could have landed me in jail had I been found out. Not surprisingly, I burned that ID when I turned 21.

I was friends with a singer called Donny Brooks, whose record 'Mission Bells' became a Top 3 hit in America in 1961. In the summer of 1963, Donny told Scott and me about a job that would pay big bucks. At the time there was a massive surf hit called 'Wipeout', by The Surfaris. In actuality, there was no real band called The Surfaris, only a guitar player and some session guys who had lucked out. Consequently, there were lots of fake Surfaris playing all over the place.

Scott and I, with two other guys, formed yet another Surfaris band, and took off for the Midwest – about 1,500 miles away from home – to play surf music in a cluster of little towns smack in the middle of America. Scott and I were driving a 1952 Plymouth and the other guys were in a 1959 Chevrolet. We made sure there were Surfaris signs all over the two cars.

About halfway through the tour, we got pulled over by the police, who asked if we were really The Surfaris. Scott and I said yes, and the police informed us that the car belonging to our other two band members had just rolled down a hillside and they were now in hospital. We had a show scheduled for that night. The

drummer had suffered the worse injury – bruised ribs – but the doctor taped him up and we played that night without a hitch.

Our car now started to act up and, with the other one totalled, we had no transportation. Fortunately, a local mechanic came up with a seemingly perfect solution, and we ended up purchasing a 1938 Packard hearse, which held all four of us plus our gear. We left late that night to head back to California, but about five miles out of town we noticed quite a bit of steam coming out of the bonnet. The engine was overheating, so we had no choice but to begin walking back to town. On the way, yours truly saw a shortcut through some fields that would cut about four miles off our trip back. We took it but about halfway into the field we noticed a large black shadow in the distance. When the shadow started moving and snorting, we turned and ran like hell to the fence. We had walked into a bull's pasture. We then took the longer, safer route back to town and got to the hotel exhausted.

The next day, we asked the mechanic what he could do, but he just towed the hearse back to town with all our gear inside. At that point, we decided to fly home, but the only plane leaving the area was an old DC3 – a popular plane during World War II. We took that plane to Denver, and got a more up-to-date one home. That was the end of the infamous, disastrous 'Surfaris' tour through the Midwest.

When I got home, very discouraged from all the nightmares we had encountered on the road, I called Kathy and told her about everything. I was completely shocked to find that, instead of understanding the difficulties I had dealt with while on tour in the remote, isolated states of the Midwest, she told me in no uncertain terms that she was breaking up with me because I hadn't called her enough while I was on the tour. She didn't want to understand that public phones were a rarity in that region. I thought this was very mean, selfish behaviour on her part, and it really hurt me badly, after I had been so protective and supportive towards her.

After we broke up, I did what I always do when something upsets me: I immersed myself in my music, just playing and playing, to drown the negative emotional impact. That was lesson three for me, to which I did not pay attention.

On the heels of the Surfaris tour, Judy and I were hired for a job in Sacramento at the Trophy Room, but Scott was in college and didn't want to leave LA. I had met a bass player named Joey Paige, who had just come back from England and had the Beatle haircut and wore 'Beatle' boots with Cuban heels from Anello & Davide – which I really wanted – and he ended up playing bass for me in Sacramento. He had seen The Beatles in the UK and introduced me to their music. The Beatles were not yet famous in California, but the audience loved the songs from their first album, and so did I.

During my time at the Trophy Room in Sacramento, I got involved with a girl who was a regular clubgoer, otherwise known as a groupie. For the three weeks that I was there, we spent a lot of time together at her house, mostly after the shows, and then I would go back to my hotel. We never really got very serious – it was all fun stuff – and so we never kept in touch after I got home.

During a return engagement at the Trophy Room about six months later, the last thing on my mind was the girl I had met several months back, and I was surprised when her girlfriend came into the club and informed me that her friend was pregnant and I was the father. She warned me that the young lady was going to serve me with a paternity suit if I didn't marry her. I knew that there was no possible way that I was responsible, and I can even remember the exact words I said to the friend: 'There's no way I am the father. Christ, we never even had sex!' Perhaps because I remained calm and confident, I never heard from either of the girls again.

I realised that I had got involved with an emotionally insecure person, an experience that changed the way I felt about my audience from that moment on: I began to look out over the crowds each night, and to me most of them looked lonesome, as if they were sad and searching for something. It was like watching a big singles pickup scene night after night, with the same scenario playing out over and over again. Audiences don't realise that they are not the only ones watching a show.

After that I thought twice before getting involved with any club clientele. Later, in the mid-sixties, my attitude to audiences would change a lot because the actual audiences changed: I started to see people who were genuinely enjoying themselves and the music. They wanted to have a good time – and it made me feel good to be a part of that.

When we returned to LA Joey had other commitments, and I lost my drummer. I didn't know what Scott was up to at that time, so Judy and I were back to having no band.

I was attending the LA Trade Technical College studying technical illustration for six hours a day, and playing six nights a week into the wee hours of the morning, burning the candle at both ends. Eventually, I started to feel unwell, and my doctor told me that the fluid between my lungs and chest cavity had drained out and that my lungs were sticking to the chest cavity. The pain became increasingly unbearable every time I took a deep breath and tried to sing, so the doctor gave me a painkiller with morphine in it, warning me that I might feel a little light-headed when I took it. I went back to the club that night – pain-free – and then all of a sudden it felt as though somebody had stabbed me in the chest with a knife. I almost collapsed on stage. During the break I took another pill and somehow finished the next set without being able to feel the strings on my guitar – I was as high as a kite, but pain-free. I managed to drive home and sleep it off, and felt better after a week or so.

We got a job playing at another Hollywood dinner club on the Sunset Strip called Come to the Party, which later became Whisky a Go Go. A friend of Scott's would come to see us play there. He called himself Jet Powers and was another Hollywood 'face' trying to find singing jobs and showing up everywhere; later the world would know him as PJ Proby. Whenever Jet showed up, the three of us would inevitably go out for some heavy drinking after the show. I drank Vodka and 7-Up, Scott drank 151 rum with Coke, and PJ drank everything he could find.

During 1963–64, I was using a lot of different players in my band. Scott and I had lost touch for about a year – he was still in school and Judy and I were playing jobs all over the place. The twist-girl phase was dying out in Hollywood, and trios were the new fad. Judy got a job dancing and singing with a rock'n'roll band that had some work in Las Vegas, one of many that tried to make it big there. It was around this time that I cut my first solo record, 'What a Thrill'. I had met Don Drowty, the lead singer of Dante and the Evergreens, a doo-wop group from the late fifties. Don had worked with Lou Adler and Herb Alpert, who at the time had the Almo label and were looking for recording artists. I wrote the song, which featured The Blossoms as the background singers. Dante wrote the B-side, 'Beginning of the End'.

Towards Christmas 1963, about six months after we had split up, Kathy and I got back together again. I was playing with Judy, Scott and a local drummer at Come to the Party when Kathy came into the club and said she wanted to talk to me. She told me that she had been wrong, that she still cared for me, and that she thought she had made a mistake. She said she would like to go out with me again, and wanted to know if I still had any feelings for her. But even though I wasn't involved with anybody, I was gun-shy after what she had done to me not that long back, and gave her a noncommittal answer, suggesting that we start dating and see what happened. Happily, things worked out fine after that and all the old feelings came back.

In early 1964, I got a call from Donny Brooks, who asked me to play guitar for him at an audition at a hotel on the Strip. I asked him about the line-up and he told me that Scott Engel was on bass. Scott and I were pleased to be working together again because we both had definite ideas about how music should be performed, and professionally we got along very well.

I came to realise that in the last year or so both Scott and I had changed in our whole approach to music, becoming much more serious: he had played bass in a surf music style and been very attached to his big Fender Bassman amplifier. I had been the typical supper-club performer with lots of gadgets and effects on my amplifier. Now Scott bought an Ampeg B15 (the preferred amplifier of serious bass players) while I switched to a Fender Telecaster guitar and had a classic 1959 Fender Twin amp – no effects, just great tone. That first night, our rehearsal consisted of talking about the show, making a list of the songs we were going to play, and going out on the stage and playing as if we'd been playing together for several years.

Donny was hired permanently for the gig – he was the headliner and we were his backing group. We also played our own sets, six nights a week for two weeks, with Al 'Tiny' Schneider as our new drummer. I hired Tiny because he was an extremely powerful drummer who could give me the strong bottom end that I wanted in my band. He was perfect for the job. We've maintained a friendship over the years, despite losing touch for long stretches. In the early days he was very laid back, but over the years has become much bolder and more outspoken in what he has to say. He still plays drums for blues bands in Southern California. He can be very reflective, philosophical and dependable, which are the things I like best about him. Tiny was very encouraging and helpful when, in 2004, I decided to perform again after not having done any live shows for several years.

The band didn't have a name, so I suggested we call ourselves The Walker Brothers Trio. We wore dark jeans, black polo-neck sweaters, black blazers and black boots. Our hair was long, although not in a Beatle style. Scott and I had our hair cut at the hair salon owned by Jay Sebring. We looked pretty cool.

Music was generally divided into four basic categories in the late fifties and early sixties: surf music, jazz/blues, country and rock. When I formed The Walker Brothers Trio, I wanted to play our own variations of all four genres, and that must have contributed to our success. We hired a new agent named Chuck Granger, and auditioned for every club in town, including the Troubador, the Whisky a Go Go and Sister George's – but after a few months, with no success in sight, we decided it might be time to split up.

We had just one more audition on the Sunset Strip. The owner hired us, not for a club on the Strip but for one of his clubs in the Irish sector of LA. It was called the Beverly Cavern, a big place with a dance floor, but virtually no clientele. We played six nights a week, five hours a night, and our only regular fan was a supermarket employee who worked a block away at Ralph's. We literally played to the tables and chairs for three weeks. My father even came in to check us out, and when I got home hours later he was waiting for me with a bottle of wine on the table. That was a bad sign. The Beverly Cavern was our last straw and we decided that was it – we would definitely be splitting up.

But then Donny Brooks called to ask if he could bring in some club owners so he could audition for them, using us as his backup band. It was lucky for us that one of the club owners was Bill Gazzari. Bill stayed on after the others had left, handed me his card and told me to call the next morning at 11. So I did, and he told me that when our time was up at the Beverly Cavern. He wanted to hire us to play alternate sets with his other full-time band, The Sinners, at Gazzari's, his popular and successful club on La

Cienega Boulevard, right in the heart of restaurant row.

Along with Whisky a Go Go and the Troubador, Gazzari's was one of the top clubs in Hollywood. It was actually a bar, dance floor and restaurant. Bill's mother was the chef, and his sister, Rose, was a hostess. The club looked like an Italian restaurant with red-and-white gingham tablecloths on the tables, little white lights and decorations. The bar sat about ten people, and the dance floor was always jam-packed with people dancing the Jerk and the Twist. We decided to change our look for our new job and began wearing dark trousers, white button-down shirts, skinny black ties, light-blue jackets and black boots. We kept our hair long, but we were still brushing it back.

Bill Gazzari was to end up helping us tremendously with recordings and contracts. He was a very supportive guy, a real crusty 'Mafioso' type, who had a deep, gruff voice with an Italian accent. We found we could trust him completely to take care of business. I felt Bill sincerely had our best interests at heart, and so it turned out. His mother decided that Scott and I were too skinny, and always made Italian dishes to feed us up.

Within a very short time it became clear that The Walker Brothers Trio had become the main draw at Gazzari's, so Bill let The Sinners go when their contract expired. Scott, Tiny and I would then meet at the club for a few afternoons each week to rehearse new material, which significantly contributed to our popularity.

Then things started to happen. Every night the queues to get into the club wrapped around the block. One night, outside on a break, I saw the family car drive up with my parents inside. I went to get Bill and said, 'My mom and dad are here – can we get them a table?' My parents just walked past everybody in line and, as I ushered them inside the door, Bill was hustling some clients away from their table in his gruff Mafia-type voice to make room for them. My dad later told me that he thought the queue outside was for the restaurant next door – he couldn't believe that all those folks were actually waiting to see us.

We were having a great time and were very enthusiastic and punctual when it came to rehearsals and shows. Contrary to what has been stated in *A Deep Shade of Blue* and elsewhere, Scott never expressed any fears of performing – ever. However, Tiny and I began encountering one frustrating problem with him. The band

took a 15-minute break after every 45-minute set, but at the end of almost every break, every single night, one or both of us had to go and hunt for Scott and pull him away from a conversation or a drink he had just ordered; he always lost track of time during the breaks. Finally, Tiny and I just went out on the stage without him and began playing. Invariably, within several minutes, Scott would join us. Tiny used to get pretty irritated with that, but it didn't bother me then.

I've been referred to as the toughest member of the band to deal with – which was absolutely true. I pushed the agents to keep lining up auditions with the clubs and, as the leader of the band, I insisted that the clubs have the correct stage and sound setup for us, never leaving anything to chance if at all possible. Back then, the clubs provided the PA systems, often with no technician, so I had to make sure the levels were the best they could be for our show each night. It was the same with the lights. Years later, I discovered that things worked a little differently in the UK, and there were times I would have to come on a lot stronger when dealing with certain British club managers or owners, as the UK Musicians' Union had different policies from those in America.

Later in 1964, Nick Venet came to see us at Gazzari's. Nick was an A&R man at Mercury Records; he had a lot of clout and expressed an interest in signing Scott and me. Nick was a great-looking Greek guy with dark, curly hair. He wasn't very tall but made up for it with a lot of 'star' presence and was a very sharp dresser with tons of pizzazz – which made us suspicious. At the time, there were so many phoneys coming into the clubs each night, and they were always offering us deals, so we disregarded his advances and didn't take him seriously.

Nick talked to Bill Gazzari and told him that he was quite serious about giving us a contract with Mercury. Bill checked him out, learned that he was OK, and told us to sign the deal. Soon, Scott and I found ourselves in the Mercury offices in the Hollywood Bank Building on Sunset Boulevard, being signed on strictly as vocalists, not as instrumentalists, which was fine with us at the time because we both considered ourselves singers who played instruments, and not the other way around. Tiny seemed pleased for both of us, and we all knew it was better for the group to be signed to a major label.

Mercury soon began to call Scott and me The Walker Brothers, a promotional idea that was supposed somehow to connect us with other famous historical brothers such as the Wright Brothers (aeronautics) and Warner Brothers (movie studios). Right away, Mercury set up publicity photo sessions for Scott and me; one photo became particularly well known in the UK: it showed the two of us looking very blond with our hair blown back, down on one knee on a white-striped pavement.

The record company was moving forward very quickly with our first single, 'Pretty Girls Everywhere'. Nick Venet chose the song; it was a standard blues song that Scott and I had known for years. Eugene Church had recorded it back in 1958. I sang lead and Scott sang harmony. Nobody had any ideas for the B-side, but at the time a dance called the Jerk was very popular, so Nick asked someone to write a dance song called 'The Jerk'. Scott had already been working on something, and within a day had quickly changed it; his song, 'Doin' the Jerk', became the B-side. That same year, 1964, it was featured in a movie called *Beach Ball*, with Scott, Tiny and me performing it on stage.

For the 'Pretty Girls Everywhere' session, we worked with Shorty Rogers and his band. Shorty was quite well known as an arranger, and as a brass-band leader in particular. We recorded at a great studio, RCA in Hollywood, and had just a few hours to complete both songs. Nick Venet was the producer, which in those times somehow mysteriously automatically 'entitled' him to all publishing rights of the B-side, even though Scott had written the song. We didn't question things like that back then, because it was common practice for artists to just sign almost everything away to managers, producers, whoever.

One evening, a fellow named Jack Good walked into Gazzari's. Again, nobody took him seriously. He was British, and said he produced rock'n'roll television shows in England such as *Oh Boy!*. I had actually seen some bits of this show in America when I was 15 or 16, but that didn't persuade me to believe that this Jack Good was really involved. He told us that he was producing a new show called *Shindig* in America, and wanted us to be guests on it. We just shined him on and didn't believe him, so once again it was

Bill Gazzari who came to the rescue. Bill convinced us, in his rough, crusty Italian way, that the guy was for real and we were going to do the show.

We appeared on the third *Shindig* show and performed 'Doo Wah Diddy Diddy' – a Manfred Mann song – and another, 'Slow Down', recently been recorded by The Beatles. The pace of the show was very fast, featuring one artist or group after another, with lots of dancers and different sets. I had a terrible migraine for the entire day of the performance. It didn't help that neither Scott nor I knew the songs very well. I had such mind-numbing pain that I have very little recollection of actually performing on the show.

Shindig was an instant success. It was such a phenomenon that *Newsweek* magazine featured an article about the show, which happened to include a photo of Scott and me on the *Shindig* set. To make it to *Newsweek* – a very popular weekly national magazine – was a very big deal for us. I remember when Scott walked into Gazzari's around nine o'clock one night, with the magazine rolled up in his hand, asking me if I had seen the latest *Newsweek*, to which I said no, and he proudly showed me the photo. We, Bill and everyone else were just thrilled and taken aback with our good fortune, and my father had another bottle of wine on the table when I got home in the wee hours of that morning. Someone at his work had also spotted the picture.

The Walker Brothers were now more and more in the public eye, and becoming nationally known. Business was booming at Gazzari's, and soon we were seeing some famous actors, actresses and rock'n'roll personalities – including The Rolling Stones and The Byrds – in the audience watching our show. The Brits had a completely different look from the LA musicians. With few exceptions, they had European-tailored clothes that gave them a sharp, customised look. They also had long hair that became their trademark. Although our look was great in Hollywood, Scott and I realised that we had a very conservative image compared with the Brits, so we decided to lose the Sebring haircut. Scott went to a stylist regularly to imitate the early Beatles style, while I let my hair grow and styled it that way myself. For both of us, this required a great deal of practice blow-drying and shaping our hair, and using lots of styling products. It wasn't until I got to the UK that I went for an all-out proper cut at Vidal Sassoon.

Keep in mind that the average American was still shocked to see guys with hair that was two, three, four, five or more inches long. When we made our nightly trip across the street to Thrifty's drug store to buy wine, the patrons actually stopped and stared as we walked in, as if we were from another planet. Guys would whistle at us, and folks very likely questioned our sexual orientation. We just blew it off, but I guess we were each a little too chicken to face the stares and flak alone, so we always went in together for moral support. I remember watching a guy at the bar one night with a drink in his hand, staring back and forth between Brian Jones and Bill Wyman with their long hair, and then at us with our long hair, and looking so confused that he actually missed his mouth and poured his drink slowly down the front of his shirt.

One night, at the club, we met yet another television producer, this time from the local KHJ television studios. He wanted to put together a rock'n'roll show for television. This time we wisely decided immediately to send him off to Bill to talk about deals, and the final outcome was a television show called *Hollywood A Go-Go* featuring The Walker Brothers and the Gazzari Dancers. KHJ happily bought the idea, Bill made sure we were taken on, and we started with a 13-week series. We prerecorded three tracks for each programme, and were featured alongside guest artists such as Sonny and Cher, Dick and Dee Dee and Lou Christie.

One night, the vice squad came into Gazzari's to check our IDs. Fortunately, mine was now 'valid', and Scott had an old beat-up draft card for his. They wanted to see his driver's licence, but he told them he didn't drive, which resulted in his having to leave his mother's car in the parking lot for about ten days, just to be on the safe side. After the vice squad had left, Bill came over and mockingly said, with a twinkle in his eyes, 'It's a good thing youse guys are over 21,' knowing full well we weren't.

My attitude towards my guitar playing changed dramatically one night. A guy named Eddie Kaplan, known around Hollywood as Count Eddie, used to go around the clubs as a 'sit-in' guitarist. He asked us if he could sit in with us, replacing me. The first thing he did on stage was go over to my amp and completely readjust everything. Then he played. Not only was he an extremely good player, but his presence and authority on stage blew me away. It was then that I realised that, even though I was

a good player, I was sorely lacking in authority. Eddie unwittingly gave me a great lesson in something that had never occurred to me before, and when I went back up on stage, I left the controls exactly as he had them set, which immediately gave me this big heavy guitar sound. It signalled the beginning of my taking more control of my audience.

Eddie and I ended up being fairly good friends. Over time he gave me many tips about my technique, telling me that I needed to be a lot more aggressive so that people would listen to my guitar playing, not just my vocals. Up to that point, I had considered my guitar playing as background, but Eddie taught me how to capture the audience with it. He also introduced me to the great blues guitarist BB King, giving me some records and ordering me to learn the songs. One of Eddie's best tips was, 'When I play, *you* listen.'

Around the end of 1964 Gary Leeds started coming into Gazzari's frequently. Scott and I knew Gary from the Hollywood club circuit, although neither of us had ever worked or socialised with him. He had a good reputation as a drummer with The Standells, but then he dropped out of sight for a while. Scott and I were surprised to see him in the club, and went over to visit him during our breaks. We both noticed that his entire look had changed, and that he looked really cool with his Beatle haircut, English clothes and boots – very hip.

Gary has always had a unique, dry sense of humour, quick and sharp-witted. He is the master of offhand, ironic statements, and can turn any event into a comedy. Gary always loved to mimic people – like Bongo Wolf, a drummer he knew through the McConkey agency, who was a pear-shaped guy with a tiny head and a terrible, nasally voice. Gary vividly recounted the famous story about the night Bongo was set up with a prostitute by Mac McConkey. Bongo was 39 years old and still a virgin; but he scared off the woman by putting on his vampire teeth and playing his bongos, not figuring out that she was there for other reasons. There was even a rumour, which was probably true, that Gary used to dress up like a werewolf and run around scaring people in the Hollywood Hills. He was even shot at. People took this seriously, as werewolf movies were all the rage back then.

Much as Gary joked around, I always thought of him as being

quite shrewd about people and business. He's also very diplomatic, and found ways to smooth things out between us and our management on many occasions. Gary is sociable, and he handled the press brilliantly at all times. Unlike Scott and I, Gary was out and about on the town a lot.

Gary liked to cook, but it was never spontaneous. Everything was planned out, and he was very thorough in his methods. He even had a meat thermometer. Gary checked his watch for everything, for counting down the time for the food to cook, for taking sleeping pills, whatever – Gary and his watch were inseparable. He always had to have a window seat on flights, and he got into the habit of counting aloud the number of runway lights that we had passed on take-off, and would panic if we got past a certain number of lights and the plane wasn't off the ground yet. He'd yell, 'We should be in the air by now! Only ten more lights to the fence!' Scott would cringe and get nervous – he hated Gary's countdowns.

Gary had recently toured the UK as PJ Proby's drummer, and told us about his adventures there. He said that London was really hip, and that there was a great music scene there. Scott and I lapped up every detail as we had been considering going to Britain to check out English groups such as The Beatles, The Rolling Stones, The Animals, Peter and Gordon and Herman's Hermits that were becoming popular in California.

British music was completely different from what we were used to hearing on the LA radio stations and in the US Top 40 – the musical content, the arrangements, the accents, the voices and, most importantly, the sound of the recordings, which were apparently recorded live in the studios. That made a real difference, as America was into overdubbing. Also, when there were two guitar players in British bands, one played lead and the other played rhythm; American bands often only had one guitar player and someone on keyboard. Scott and I thought British music was very cool, and started using the top UK songs in our sets. The audiences loved them too, regularly requesting Rolling Stones and Beatles hits.

One night, Gary came into the club and told us that we really would make it big-time if we did decide to go over and play in England. We didn't take him seriously, but it was fun to hear about it. He was relentless, however, and soon came into Gazzari's with the man who would become known as 'the mysterious backer', whom we later found out was Gary's father. This man watched our show and apparently liked what he saw. The next night, Gary came in again and said that the gentleman wanted to back us for a UK trip. He was offering to pay for Scott, Gary and me to fly over, and help us out with living expenses for an indefinite time. Yet Scott and I still didn't take Gary's plan seriously. We thought it was just another Hollywood story. We were on our way in America, we were in a weekly TV show, we were working pretty hard and had a thriving career where we were, so we didn't jump at every offer that came along.

But Gary came in again, encouraging us to take some time off from Gazzari's and go to the UK, promising that everything would be arranged for us: we just had to name the date. He told us, 'You guys are nuts if you don't go there.'

Gary was the catalyst. Scott and I talked it over and at last decided we would take the offer and go. I told Bill Gazzari the whole story, and he encouraged us to go, with his best wishes. He still wanted us back in his club on our return to California; he was in the process of building a new club right on Sunset Strip and wanted us to be his featured band, but we ended up going to the UK before this ever came to fruition, and even though we'd got his blessing on the new venture, I feel bad that we never played there, and that we never really repaid our debt of gratitude to him.

Contrary to what has been reported, there was never any problem arising from our breaking our Gazzari's contract. I always visited Bill when I returned to California over the years, and he was really happy to hear of The Walker Brothers' success. He would invariably ask about Scott, and I think it hurt him that Scott never bothered to keep in touch with him. I regarded Bill as my first 'godfather' in the business, and he turned out to be one of the most trustworthy in the cutthroat music industry of the day.

By January 1965 things were very serious between Kathy and me, and I had asked her to marry me. We got engaged that month. It was the first time I had ever considered getting married to anyone. I actually imagined a perfect fairytale marriage in which everything fell into place, and that we would always be in love and live happily ever after. Looking back, I realise that I was still pretty clueless around women, actually rather naïve, and that Kathy was probably a lot more experienced.

At the time I was happy with the way things were shaping up professionally. Scott, Tiny and I finally had a great club to play in, The Walker Brothers were fast becoming a success in Hollywood and, to top things off, we were going to London.

Scott and I had discussed what to do about Tiny, as the backer hadn't included him in the offer. We both felt awkward about leaving him behind, and yet didn't want to turn down the opportunity; most importantly, we anticipated that the three of us would be back playing in Gazzari's again in a few months. So I was upfront with Tiny and told him we'd be leaving in about a month. Tiny said, 'You have to do what you have to do,' and wished us a lot of luck.

At first there were absolutely no plans for us to do anything in the UK. We didn't have a British agent or manager; we had no music contacts, no UK recording contracts, no work permits, and no firm prospects of a music career in the UK. Scott and I considered the trip to be purely exploratory, and left it to Gary to make all the arrangements. Right up until we left, Scott and I were both busy with playing at Gazzari's, recording, and our private lives, and I waited right up to the last minute to pack, giving very little thought to the journey – an 11-hour Pan Am flight – and what would follow.

On 16 February 1965, the day before we left for England, we finished up recording our second single, 'Love Her', at RCA studios; it was backed with 'Theme from the Seventh Dawn'. Again it was Nick Venet who chose the songs. 'The Seventh Dawn' was originally meant to be the A-side, but 'Love Her' was chosen because Nick decided it was the more commercial of the two. Nick had got Jack Nitzsche to do the arrangements, which was a real departure. Jack was a famous arranger who had gained his reputation through his association with Phil Spector, having arranged all Phil's recordings. His wife Gracia was in a very popular group called The Blossoms, who backed almost every Phil Spector hit record, and had backed me on my solo single the year before. Billy Strange played guitar – he was the ace player in

Hollywood and did a lot of work with Phil Spector – along with other great professional session players.

It was at this session that The Walker Brothers' classic style evolved – almost by accident. We were a straight-out rock'n'roll band, and damned good at it too. Until then I had been the lead singer with Scott singing harmony, but Scott had the deeper voice and that was what Nick Venet wanted for the song. He decided that Scott should sing a verse with only the bass as accompaniment (which nobody had done up to that point), and then, during the hook, the band would join in with a great swell and me singing harmony. This arrangement was a departure for us, as well as being a bit daring at the time.

When Nick said, 'I'll have Scott sing solo with the bass,' Scott was terrified – I know his facial expressions pretty well. He was looking at me as if to say, 'Don't make me do this, it's not working. Don't leave me out here.' It was a tense moment because, when you record something, it's there to stay. But I knew it was working. I didn't care that Scott was going to be the lead. My whole point, then and since, was to make the best music I could. So I started singing harmony lines. I don't do standard harmony lines; I hear something, and I hear a way of enhancing it, even if it might be musically incorrect. The point is, what does it sound like? What does it create? With 'Love Her', the whole thing went ten feet off the floor.

We were still only working with a rhythm section and vocals. The band comprised piano, brass, rhythm and bass guitars and percussion. We didn't have a full orchestra. At the end of the session, Nick told Jack that he wanted to add strings, even though it meant going way over the recording budget, which was taking a huge chance on two new artists. Nick decided to dig deeper in his pocket and get the strings, and with that The Walker Brothers' sound was born.

On the same night (16 February) in the same studio, The Rolling Stones had just finished recording 'The Last Time'. As they went out, we went in and added the strings. (Coincidentally, several months later we were being interviewed on the UK television show *Ready Steady Go!* by Cathy McGowan, who asked me to introduce The Rolling Stones with their new record, 'The Last Time'.)

During these sessions, we recorded only 'Love Her' and 'Theme from the Seventh Dawn'. I don't remember ever having recorded 'Don't Fight It', which appears on The Walker Brothers' second US album on the Smash label, but was never released in the UK. I can only surmise that someone recorded it during a live show.

The next day, 17 February 1965, we flew to Britain. It was a warm, sunny day in California, and when we all met at LAX we were excited. Judy alone saw me off that afternoon. My parents and Kathy were so upset about my going that they didn't go to the airport, but I had no second thoughts about the trip, regardless of the fact that I was newly engaged and my family didn't want me to leave America. Scott was also leaving behind his girlfriend, Ann, the waitress at Gazzari's, but was excited about seeing the art galleries, museums, and historical sites we had read about in books.

Gary's father had arranged for someone to look after us in the UK. His name was Claude Powell, and he was also in charge of the money. He came over on the plane with us; we all met up at the airport on the morning that we left. Claude was a quiet, unassuming guy – probably in his mid-thirties at the time – who seemed miscast for his role in looking after three young rock musicians.

During the flight we were quiet, sleeping or looking out of the window, keeping our thoughts to ourselves. I remember being impressed with the first-rate food and service on the plane, and thinking about what was in store for me, and feeling quite matter-of-fact about it.

SWINGING LONDON – AND HOLLYWOOD!
GARY WALKER

How did we meet each other? There was a rumour that we crashed our cars in the mountains of Griffith Park in Hollywood, but that was just a publicity story. I think we actually met in May 1962 when, on my nights off from playing with The Standells, I went to see Scott and John playing in Gazzari's. They did their regular set, just as we did, throwing in a few new things that they preferred to play. They were both very tall, and being up on a stage gave them

even more height. I would sit at the table at the back of the club and have a Coke. I didn't drink alcohol because I was under-age and feared that the police would put the heavies on me, as it was (and still is) illegal to drink alcohol in California until you're 21.

The first few times I met Scott and John, we would just say hello, and that was about it, and the very first time I don't think we even got that far. But gradually I became friends with both of them, particularly with Scott, and we'd hang out together. I'd often stay overnight at his house in Hollywood, and sometimes I would go to John's house in Inglewood.

Occasionally groups in the Hollywood clubs would ask visiting musicians if they wanted to 'sit in'; this happened a lot, with John inviting me to join him because Scott would always go missing in the break.

John was a New Yorker. Scott and I, being the only children of divorced mothers, were spoiled – although not to the point that we turned out badly – whereas John, having a sister, had had to make compromises and learn to share. This gave John an edge in that it made him see both sides of a coin a little better than we did. It helped him in his role as leader of the group, and in life generally. He had to make less of an adjustment than Scott and I would in certain situations, and could see the overall picture better. John's different slant on a problem could be an advantage.

I didn't know until later that, when John was younger, he'd wanted to be an actor, but looking at some of the videos of The Walker Brothers you can see his acting ability in his stage performance. This came quite naturally to him. When John had to do auditions for the different parts that came up, a guy called Dickie Dodd would always show up, and this got to be a thing with John – and no doubt also with Dickie. Dickie Dodd was also the drummer who replaced me in The Standells when I left to go to England. I didn't know about these coincidences, and neither did John, until we started to put things together for this book.

John was – and is – a very good guitarist, and helped Carl Wilson and Dave Marks, who were original members of The Beach Boys, to play better. They would come round to John's house and drive his parents mad. John and I went to see them perform a few times at high school dances around the LA and Hollywood area. At that time they didn't know many songs, and looked very uncomfortable on stage, just as we had in the beginning, and Carl was a little nervous because John was watching him. He'd ask John what he thought of their act, and John would suggest that the guitar was too loud or that the vocals could be louder. Carl, who wanted The Beach Boys to be the best they could be, always respected what John said.

When John, Judy and Scott were playing together, John did all the negotiating with the different agents, and mostly had the final say in the matter. He was the leader, and the moves he decided upon were usually the right ones for the group, but if he felt that the others needed to be consulted he courteously included them in the discussions. John had been brought up to have excellent manners and would put you at your ease right away, but when the chips were down he could also be very forceful and take no prisoners. A lot of the time, when things didn't go as planned for The Walker Brothers, John would sort it out rather than me or Scott.

Of course John was very good-looking and kept himself in good shape. He'd been a very fast runner at school, which would be an asset later when the fans chased us, and he had played a lot of sports and enjoyed baseball. When we played the clubs in the early sixties, our act was so physically demanding that we could easily sweat off four to six pounds a night. When we'd finished playing, we were so starved that we would eat huge dinners at two or three in the morning – fortunately, with no repercussions to our health.

The Walker Brothers' shows that came later were heavy workouts, and we did lose a lot more weight than in the earlier part of our career. Scott and John were no longer playing their instruments and were required to dance and perform, which might have taken a toll on us, but luckily we were young enough to take it.

Out of the three of us, John had the movie-star look. Scott and I would always say how much he resembled Charlton Heston, the famous actor. John was, and still is, a great cook. He was also very good at woodworking, and could build almost anything from bedroom furniture to tables and chairs; it just came easily to him.

John has always been a conservative dresser compared with Scott and myself – we were always in jeans and sweatshirts. But John was Mr Chic, adopting a very fancy style with great presentation. He always knew the right suit and shirt makers in London. When we went to important meetings, he would say to me, 'Leeds, look at their shoes. You can always tell by their shoes where they're at.' Scott and I were more casual, usually wearing jeans; I liked to dress that way because it was comfortable and I felt good, while Scott perhaps felt that dressing down would help him maintain a low profile. That's not to say that John didn't wear jeans at all – but they had to be tailor-made and, of course, very tight.

John once bought a Bentley R-type, the older one from the 1951–55 series, and we would go out in the country for a spin with a picnic lunch and some nice red wine he had picked out. To Scott and me, John was a country gentleman at heart, liking the finer things in life. But John watched the money a lot more than Scott and I did, and always wanted to know where it was going – not that we could ever find out where any of the money we earned went to. Scott never wanted to hear the M-word; it was not in his creative plan, as no true artist ever did anything for money.

John wanted to get married to the right girl and start a family. It was the thing to do, and we all ended up doing it at some stage. When John met Kathy and decided that she was the right girl for him, he told us how great she was and became very dedicated to her. He wanted them to have a nice house and some dogs, and definitely a great car – in essence, the American lifestyle; it was all to do with that. And I think that John did like being married.

Scott Engel was about six feet in height and had the kind of blond hair that was associated with the Californian sun, sea and surf lifestyle, but I did suspect a bit of sunshine from the bottle. When I first met Scott, he seemed a little nervous and shy – he's no different now from the way he always was. Even in those days, he was straight out the back door after a show, and nobody could ever find him. Maybe he wanted to escape the crowds, or maybe it was because he was so dependent on his mother, or afraid of being let down. I was the opposite, Mr Comedian, full forward, go straight ahead, and I just started talking to him. We just got along really well, and my being like that helped because it brought out his sense of humour. Scott can be one of the very funniest people I know, but no one ever sees that side of him.

Scott lived with his mother, Betty, in a house that looked like a mock castle on Scenic Drive in Hollywood. It was very big and contained about 12 apartments. The 'chateau' was painted a light grey and had a dark-grey roof, trimmed in white. Most of the flats had turrets, which is something you don't normally see in LA, except in the movies, so the building had a bit of Hollywood magic. You could see the big white Hollywood sign up in the hills from Scott's bedroom window. Later, Scott, John and I would find that London was to be just as exciting and glamorous as Hollywood, if not more so, especially when it was new to us and the Swinging Sixties were at their height.

Scott was once thrown out of Hollywood High School for blowing up a toilet. He had gone with a friend of his to Tijuana, where you could buy big fireworks called cherry bombs; the effect would be kind of like what happens when the Navy drops depth charges. A few days later, back at high school, Scott and his friend lit a cherry bomb and flushed it down the toilet, and of course the explosion completely destroyed it. Some teachers just happened to be nearby and caught the unfortunate culprits. I think Scott got away with a suspension for three or four weeks, as they couldn't actually prove it had been him, only that there had been no other students in the area.

Scott and I got to know each other after finding out that we had a lot in common. We both had mothers who were obsessed with us; we were very lucky to have them care for us so much but it was also stifling, and this shared experience brought Scott and me closer together. I remember going to the movies with Scott around 1962, to see *Long Day's Journey Into Night* in Hollywood. Based on Eugene O'Neill's play, it starred Katharine Hepburn and Ralph Richardson, and portrayed one fraught day in the life of a dysfunctional family. Afterwards, we were both struck by how it mirrored our own lives. Conversations with my parents would start out nicely, but for some reason they would deteriorate into arguments, and things would get worse as it got later into the night. This wasn't fuelled by alcohol, as in the film, but my mother and I would engage in verbal battle for hours, each of us refusing to back off. These scenes were just like the ones in that movie – it could have been Scott or me up there.

Scott and I found that we shared a love of movies and music;

they offered escapism and could transport us to happier and more exciting places, and fire ambitions in us. We went to a lot of films together, and later used all the inspiration we had gained from movies to influence our work and shape The Walker Brothers. All Scott ever wanted to do was to make music. The last thing that was on our minds was the money, or the fame that would come in time.

Around 1961, Eddie Fisher had heard Scott singing and could hear the potential. He wanted to take him under his wing and make him famous; he was even going to form a record label of his own, but along came Elizabeth Taylor, so that didn't happen. Later, when Scott was singing with The Walker Brothers, Andy Williams wanted to give him a million dollars to make him a big star worldwide in return for a percentage of the whole package, including songwriting and recording deals. Scott turned it down. He didn't want that kind of stardom.

Scott did drink, and I thought that was a bit nervy of him, considering what could happen if you got caught drinking underage. It wasn't anything heavy, though. A few years down the line, we would all get drunk together and have a good time, and, because we were young, it didn't stop us from doing our job the next day.

Scott didn't smoke because he wanted to preserve his voice, and found it very hard to understand why people took up the habit. I had to agree. I didn't start smoking until I was around 22, and wouldn't have done so then except for wanting to ape The Beatles. If it was good enough for them, it was good enough for me.

The only reason why most people can't get to know Scott is because he doesn't want them to. But he and I were friends. We probably wouldn't have become such close friends if we hadn't been forced to spend so much time together in Britain when the fan hysteria stopped us from going anywhere. We had to depend on each other because there was nobody else.

Scott has always been quiet, and that makes it hard to know what he is thinking; but he is also excellent company. He has a great sense of humour, and can be very funny, sometimes unintentionally. I never really believed that Scott was colour-blind until he bought a lurid orange Volkswagen Beetle. It was incredible to me that anybody who saw the colour of that car would have bought it, least of all someone like Scott, who was so paranoid about not being noticed.

Scott has a presence that's hard to define. I also experienced this with Orson Welles. One suspects that history will show them to have been exceptional people. Yet Scott also has his human frailties, as we all do. One of his biggest fears is of being disfigured or contracting some disease that would cause a slow death. Whenever we did shows and the promoters asked us to meet some disabled fans or children in wheelchairs, I mostly would go, and sometimes John did; I'd chat to these kids and perhaps give them a pair of drumsticks. Scott was the only one who would refuse; he just couldn't cope with it. I don't know why, it just got to him.

On the other hand, there was one occasion when we heard a screeching of brakes outside our flat in South Kensington, and Scott was the first to run out of the door. A car had hit an old Indian gentleman and driven on without stopping. The man was lying in the road with blood on his arm, and his eyes had a glazed look. Scott was holding the man's head, rubbing it and reassuring him that he was going to be alright. There were quite a few people on the scene, but no one else wanted to help, just Scott. I called the ambulance and Scott wouldn't move until it came, kneeling there and talking all the time to the man and trying to help. I told Scott, 'That was a very impressive thing you did.' He said nothing.

Scott never discussed his private life with me. I think he had one or two girlfriends, but I can't remember their names. One was also going with a singer called Donny Brooks; I think she was cheating on him with Scott. Scott is definitely not gay, as has sometimes been rumoured.

Scott spent most of his time drawing. I think that was what he was planning to do professionally, because he was an exceptional artist. He went to the Juilliard School of Art, and had a natural ability to draw what he saw; he did portraits of Ray Charles and other famous people that looked just like photographs, but he was never satisfied and would always change them or throw them in the trash. All three of us were very good at drawing; it had been one of our favourite subjects at school. I mostly would draw fire trucks in a corner of the paper and maybe a dog somewhere else and two people walking, all very surrealistic. Sometimes I would sketch a face, but Scott was the one who could do those really well, and sometimes he did landscapes. John drew monsters with tentacles and suckers, which Scott and I liked the best, because they looked just like the old movie posters of monsters and flying saucers.

We had a lot of fun at Château Engel. Betty was always cooking us food; she looked after me like a second mother, and spoilt Scott a lot, just as my mother spoilt me. Then I would go off with The Standells, and Scott would go off with The Walker Brothers, or whatever band he was playing with. We often played six days a week from nine in the evening until two in the morning, with only 15-minute breaks. It was like training for running the mile or something and we were in really good shape. Because of the time we'd spent on stage in the American clubs, when we played in the UK, we had what it took to succeed.

Scott and I went to clubs to listen to Jack Jones because he had a sophisticated voice and sang standards rather than rock or blues. We often frequented jazz clubs in Hollywood, where we could listen to excellent players such as Les McCann, Bill Evans and Ray Brown, who was probably the best bass player in the world. We used to listen to BB King and the great blues guitarists and their drummers, who did a thing called the 'shuffle', which I learned how to play. People came to the clubs just to hear this shuffle beat, and my ability to play it got me gigs with different musicians in Hollywood. It also helped to give The Standells more credibility with other professionals.

Hollywood has always been famous for its studios and actors, but at that time exciting new clubs were opening up everywhere, and the nights were vibrant with bright lights, loud music and warm winds. Hollywood was the place to be, and we were packing them in every night, while on weekends it went crazy. Each week we had to learn the current Number 1 song and some new tunes to keep the show up to date, which is what kept the people coming back. When I was with The Standells, I would have a drum solo at midnight, which became quite famous. It was hard work, and I was kind of tired by that time, and because it was so hot you would end up really sweaty. We finished around two in the morning when the clubs shut, and would then go out to eat. We were always so wound up after playing in the club that it took us a while to calm down, and of course we would be starved and needed to replace the energy we used. We'd eventually get to sleep around four or five in the morning, get up about four in the afternoon, then start all over again the next night. When it was really hot in the summer, we'd go and crash out at the beach, which wasn't far away, and sleep there.

In 1964, all people talked about in the clubs of California was The Beatles. All you ever heard on the radio was their records, and everyone was excited about 'Swinging London'. You could go into department stores in LA and buy Beatle wigs, Beatle dolls and everything connected with Britain. There were television shows about Carnaby Street, clothes designer Mary Quant and new British pop groups we'd never heard of. We began to realise how important the UK scene was.

I remember waiting for The Beatles to appear on *The Ed Sullivan Show*, the number one show in America for media exposure. Eventually, The Rolling Stones and many other British groups appeared on the show, which was the only way you could get to see them. Then The Beatles toured America and played at all the big stadiums, which nobody had ever done before. I remember the pictures and the TV interviews, and noticing a slightly chubby guy with a receding hairline and glasses, who was looking after The Beatles on their American tour. I never realised then that eventually he would be working with us. His name was Brian Sommerville. Brian Epstein, The Beatles' manager, had hired him to do the publicity work and arrange all the media coverage in America for them.

It was around that time that we started growing our hair longer. Along with many other musicians and actors we used to have it cut by Jay Sebring, whose shop was in West Hollywood. He took 45 minutes to cut your hair and then he used a hairdryer, something unheard of at the time in men's hairdressing. You could always tell if people were musicians or actors because they had this hairstyle. If you look at the old publicity photos of The Standells and The Walker Brothers, you will see that our hair was one of the most important aspects of our image.

None of us ever could have anticipated what would happen to Sebring in 1968. I remember Dennis Wilson of The Beach boys telling me about a guy he met called Charles Manson. Dennis had picked up two girl hitchhikers who were part of what Manson called his 'family', who introduced him to Manson. He was a writer and musician, and when Dennis heard some of his music he liked it. I believe he even recorded a couple of Manson's tunes with The Beach Boys. Later Manson met Terry Melcher, Doris Day's son, who was then staying at a house on Cieolo Drive with Candice Bergen, his girlfriend. Manson wanted Terry, a record producer, to sign him up for a record deal, but Dennis and Terry eventually decided to have nothing more to do with Manson.

Some time after Terry and Candice moved out of that house on Cieolo Drive, Roman Polanski leased it for himself and his wife, the actress Sharon Tate. Manson turned up there from time to time, trying to get in touch with Terry or Dennis, but was repeatedly told that Terry had moved out. The house was the site of the brutal murders of Sharon Tate and others, including Jay Sebring, who were slaughtered by members of Manson's 'family'. I remember how scared everyone in Hollywood was, and that famous people were hiring bodyguards because nobody knew who was responsible for the killings or why they'd happened. Scott and I couldn't believe that Sebring, our hairdresser and friend, had been killed. I guess we were quite lucky: we had once moved in that circle, and could easily have been in the wrong place at the wrong time.

I first came to England with PJ Proby in 1964. Earlier in the year The Beatles had invited PJ to Britain to record a television show called *Around the Beatles*. More likely, Jack Good had talked them into the idea. It was produced and directed by Jack, who would soon invite The Walker Brothers to appear on *Shindig*. PJ was immensely successful on that show, and it really launched his career in England.

When PJ returned to California, he came to see me and asked if I'd like to go to Britain as his drummer. Of course I said yes, but we had to convince my parents. They were fine about it, but they could not have foreseen that this trip would lead to our lives changing for ever.

The bad side of it was that I had to leave The Standells. We had become very good friends I found it hard to leave them, but I knew I might never have a chance like this again. I always hoped that they forgave me, and I was reassured by knowing that Dickie Dodd, who replaced me, was a lot better for the group.

I arrived in London with PJ in the summer of 1964. His management put us up in a hotel in Earl's Court. I remember PJ having an argument with the manager, after which PJ said, 'Leeds, I am going over there to piss in the corner,' which he did. Happily, the manager never found out.

We went out at night to the clubs. We met The Pretty Things, and PJ got friendly with the lead singer, Phil May, who invited us to go to his flat in Chelsea the next day. There, we sat around a huge table with Brian Jones of The Rolling Stones, also a friend of Phil's. Brian didn't remember me, but we had met for the first time at Gazzari's the year before when I went to see The Walker Brothers. We'd sat at the same table on that occasion, and he'd asked me for a fag, and of course I was totally shocked because a 'fag' in Hollywood was a gay man; I was quite relieved when I realised he was asking me for a cigarette! Brian was also in town early in 1965 when the Stones were recording 'The Last Time' at RCA Studios with producer Jack Nitzsche; The Walker Brothers followed them in later that night to record 'Love Her' with Jack and Nick Venet.

Carl Perkins was another guest on one show I did with PJ, possibly *Ready Steady Go!*. He couldn't believe that The Beatles knew of him and loved his records. He was a true gentleman and so easy to talk to, and it seemed he didn't know how much he had contributed to the music scene. I said, 'Carl, you should be quite proud of the foundation that you laid down for all of us.' And he replied, 'That's All Right Mamma', and went out to do his spot on the show.

The first time I was ever mobbed was at a PJ Proby concert. I went to meet him at the stage door. There were about 20 fans waiting, and they must have thought I was a fan too. I started talking to one of the girls and told her I played the drums for PJ – and they were all over me like bees to a honey pot. Just in the nick of time, the stage door opened and I was dragged to safety. Later, I realised that one of them had taken my watch, which had been given to me by my parents and meant a great deal to me. But that was nothing compared with what came later.

After staying in Earl's Court for a few weeks, PJ and I moved into a mews house owned by Shirley Bassey, a stone's throw from the Royal Albert Hall. PJ threw a few parties at this house, and they would sometimes last all night long. When I came downstairs in the morning, I would not be surprised to find a couple of girls passed out on the floor with hardly any clothes on, empty beer bottles everywhere, cigarettes, panties and bras strewn all over the floor. Before PJ had a chance to insist that I splash out on more cases of beer, I would hurry out and get some food supplies in. The poor au pair would be left to clean everything up and throw the girls out.

Diana Dors, the famous movie star, would also come around. PJ told me that she and her husband had a two-way mirror on their ceiling, through which they could spy on people shagging down below. Diana liked PJ, and we were both struck by how like Jayne Mansfield or Marilyn Monroe she was. We couldn't believe the presence she had: she seemed to fill the room. She was a really upbeat person, and very approachable. PJ and I couldn't get over her real name being Diana Fluck, which, after a lot of drinks, could get tricky.

I first met The Beatles during this trip. One night, PJ took me to the Ad Lib club. It's gone now, but it used to be in Leicester Square. John Lennon and Paul McCartney were there, and perhaps Ringo Starr. They invited us to sit at their table. PJ got along with them very well, but I didn't say much because I felt I was really a nobody. I was nervous and couldn't talk normally to these guys, although they got quite talkative with me because I was a musician like themselves.

As the evening went on, and everybody was getting a little more tipsy, my attention was drawn to one corner, where a lady was dancing on the table. John Lennon said to me, 'She always does that table dancing.' Then he told me, to my horror, that she was the daughter of a famous politician. I noticed that she wasn't wearing any underwear. John said, 'Yes, that's normal too.' It was also normal that she got really drunk, and normal that she got thrown out. That was my first run in with The Beatles.

On another occasion I got talking to Ringo Starr about the time they'd played Las Vegas on their US tour. I asked him if he had slept with any of the showgirls, because that's what we really wanted to know, as The Beatles could have had any girl in

America. Scott, John and I thought we wouldn't have minded that either. When I had played Las Vegas with The Standells, none of us ever even met a showgirl! But, no matter what I said or did to persuade him, Ringo would not tell me.

It got increasingly harder to obtain work permits from the British Home Office, which meant I wasn't able to play on stage with PJ, who had to use British musicians instead. On top of this, his drinking was getting increasingly out of control, and we weren't eating anything because all the money went on his booze and partying, so in late 1964 I left England and went back to California.

Having checked out the London scene I had a strong feeling that Scott, John and I could make it big in the UK, and when I returned to the States I broached the idea with my stepfather Jack first, saying I wanted to talk to Scott and John about trying our luck in England as a group, with me as the drummer. It was Jack who made it possible for us to go; he was 'the mysterious backer' of whom the press made so much. He said he was prepared to put up $5,000, which he was to top up when we needed it. He saw this as an investment opportunity as well as giving me – all of us – a chance to have a shot at the big time. Well, he wasn't wrong, and we became very successful.

I approached Scott and John, laid out the deal, and left it with them. Scott really did want to take up the offer, because he loved Europe, its films, its culture and everything about it, and of course this was at the height of the sixties when everything was happening in Britain. I think John wanted to go just to see Europe and England and be where it was all happening. I was convinced that the three of us could really do some damage here, and I was proved right.

I had many talks with the boys, trying to get them to agree to go for it. There were also a lot of meetings with all the parents. When we finally made up our minds to go to England, Scott's mother, Betty, wasn't too happy and neither were my parents, or my girlfriend Janet, who feared that the separation would pull us apart. But I believe they were all happy at the prospect of our perhaps enjoying some success there and then coming home, which was the original plan.

Janet and I had been together for about two years, and I probably would have ended up marrying her. I knew she was basically OK with our going: she told me so. Like a lot of Americans, she was mad about England and The Beatles, and said she would be visiting as much as she could.

There was just one problem. The Walker Brothers already had a drummer, Tiny. Tiny was a very good drummer and, when Scott and John decided that they were going to Britain, it was hard on Tiny, who was good friends with John. We knew he would not have to worry about getting work because he was such a great drummer, while John and Scott thought they wouldn't be gone long anyway, and would be back in the States again shortly.

Contrary to what has often been reported, Jack did not put up the money on condition that I replace Tiny in the group. That was all my idea. The rest is history.

Because I was drumming with The Standells I didn't have much time to see John and Scott in the first weeks of 1965, but I did catch up with them at RCA studios. Scott invited me to come to the studio when they recorded 'Love Her'. I'd told Scott that RCA was a bit of a square studio and that the only people who recorded there were older artists such as Frank Sinatra. Scott asked me if I knew that this was also where Elvis recorded; I was very impressed. He also said we were following The Rolling Stones in; they were recording there with Jack also, so I was very impressed for the second time.

When we arrived for the session, the Stones had finished their recording. Nick Venet came with his girlfriend, the actress Tuesday Weld. She was very big with the younger crowd and made a lot of teenage films. I was trebly impressed now!

Both Nick and Jack said they thought Scott's voice would be better for 'Love Her' than John's, which turned out to be the right decision. Scott had a voice more in the vein of Frank Sinatra or Tony Bennett, smooth and mellow and deep. John's was a little higher, gravelly, and ideally suited to rock'n'roll.

In the studio, John and Scott were having a little trouble getting into the song, so I asked Nick if I could go out and lead them. That sounds funny now, and I don't know what made me do it, but it seemed to work, and I got quite carried away, directing them, waving my arms and mouthing the words, which seemed to get John and Scott really into it. I think they did only two or three takes before they finished the song. When they added the full orchestra, everybody loved it. Jack was happy; Nick thought it was a hit, and he said it must have been Leeds and his directions that had inspired such a good performance. I like to think so! I was even more impressed.

That was on 16 February 1965, the night before we left for Britain. We packed our cases, and, along with the families and Janet, off we all went to Los Angeles International Airport. My mother and Janet were very sad at the prospect of saying goodbye.

At the airport, it was just a normal, busy day. We were really up for this, and the more excited we got, the more we started to make fools of ourselves. We were a bit too loud, like a load of schoolkids. We attracted a lot of funny looks because of our long hair, which had not yet become acceptable in the States, but we seemed to get extra-special treatment on the plane because the crew obviously thought we were famous, even though they weren't sure who we were. I remember that Scott didn't seem at all scared of flying on the trip over. All we did was talk about England. The plane seemed to take forever to arrive, and we couldn't sleep, as we were too excited. Scott said he couldn't wait to go to the museums and the art galleries. I wanted to see where Jack the Ripper had killed those women, visit Loch Ness to see the monster, and meet The Beatles again – and the British girls!

CHAPTER 3

WALKERMANIA!

THREE GOOD-LOOKING GUYS
WITH VOICES LIKE ANGELS
GARY WALKER

I remember arriving in England. As we came out of the clouds and were coming in to land, we noticed white stuff on the ground. Scott said, 'Is that snow?' I said, 'I think it is!' This was quite a treat, because in California all we ever saw were pictures of snow.

Claude Powell had come along with us as temporary manager. He'd been a good friend of mine since I was in high school; I'd worked in the gas station he ran. He also put up some money for the venture. He did the best he could for us, but unfortunately Nick Venet came to England, and took over the show because Claude was unfamiliar with the music business. I was very upset about this, Claude being a very close friend, and I almost quit the group; however, I stayed because I knew deep down that we had a good chance of success and that I could then reimburse him.

We landed at Heathrow around six in the morning. When we got outside, we almost froze on the spot because we were wearing just T-shirts and jeans. We were really cold. As we drove into London, John said to me, 'Leeds, where's the beach?' I said, 'I don't know, John, it can't be far, we'll find it!' and calmed him down.

For the first week or so, we stayed in lodgings in Courtfield Gardens at Earl's Court, then we took a flat nearby at 1 Onslow Gardens. This was a gigantic four- or five-storey house with a basement, where the landlady lived with her daughter. The first floor had two flats with balconies; ours was the one on the right, which had three beds. The first thing that struck us was how tall the ceiling was – you needed binoculars to see the light fixture. The room was very spacious with a nice view from the balcony window across the street, where there was a big green square with flowers, bushes and large trees. It seemed perfect for our needs, because we had space for all our instruments and belongings. There was a gas fire to one side of the room, but because we were from California we felt very chilly. I remember the three of us pushing the beds near the heater and huddling as closely around the fire as we could get without setting light to ourselves. At night, I had so many heavy blankets on me that I woke up in the same position in the morning as I had gone to sleep in, because I couldn't move.

My father and mother had given me $100 for emergencies. One night, though, we all got drunk and, being inebriated, I thought I should hide this $100 somewhere, found a place and where I was confident no one would find it. Then I went to sleep. About two days later, I thought I'd better check on it, but I'd hidden it so well that I couldn't find it anywhere. I never did find it, and it's probably still there.

By a strange coincidence, when Walt Disney came to stay in England, he stayed in Onslow Gardens – I think it was at Number 6. We were living there at different times, and I was only aware he'd been there after reading about it later in a book, but it was uncanny to think that once again our paths had crossed.

When we arrived in England, we were just like any tourists visiting a country for the first time, and couldn't wait to see all the famous sites: Big Ben, the Tower of London, all the art galleries – Scott particularly wanted to visit the art galleries. The first place we visited was the Victoria and Albert Museum. We never got too homesick to start with because of all the new things that we were seeing. Britain was just as we had imagined it, with its little houses and famous buildings. The three of us would walk around South Kensington and get lost after ten minutes because all the houses

and streets looked the same. We thought that we would never learn our way around London. If we missed anything about California, it was being able to shop and get food late at night, and watching TV well into the small hours – and the sun, which mainly John missed. We liked to shop at a store called Europa, where they sold very unusual food that you could get only in the States. There was a phone box near our flat, and we would call our families to let them know that we were OK. We also sent them some very English gifts. I remember they all wanted the Harrods plastic bag with the shop's logo on it.

Slowly London lost its shine, though, as we started to miss our families. I hadn't anticipated that I would be that affected, and the first Christmas we spent in England I cried for a while. It made me realise that the only thing that counts is your family, and how important it was – and still is – to me. The separation had also taken its toll on Janet. When she eventually did come over to see me, we weren't as close as we had been. It wasn't meant to be, and she ended up marrying one of the members of Arthur Lee's group Love.

Scott and John were already under contract to Mercury Records in the States, which meant that they were also contracted to Philips in England, but only for a low percentage, like most groups starting out. It would be later on, when hopefully you re-signed, that you'd start to make some money. The companies made you pay for the recordings and the orchestra and anything else they thought was needed, which meant that when everything was recouped from the money outlaid on the sessions, you got what was left. This was very good for me because, although I was on The Walker Brothers' records, I was not bound by their contract (*con* being the key). When I was eventually offered a record deal, it seemed to be about the best you could get at that time. But – surprise, surprise! – I never got anything either. That's showbiz.

We got looked at a lot in those early days. I like to think it could have been our good looks, especially mine! Our first photoshoot was in March 1965 at Marble Arch in London, and we got a bit fed up because the strong wind was messing up our hair, which was all we cared about. To make things worse, two disc jockeys who had befriended us, Dave Cash and Kenny Everett, were hidden around the back of the Marble Arch uttering obscenities. They used to do their radio show near there, and we had become friends with them through the music biz. If it hadn't been for them and their conviction that we had the potential to make it big, we might not have had such big hits.

We even agreed to sing a jingle for Dave and Kenny's show. Much later, when Dave reminded me that we had done it, I could not believe it because that was something we just didn't do normally. Worse yet, it is still in existence on a tape somewhere. Dave and I are on the case, in search of this gem from our musical history.

During our early weeks in England, I often went into Philips Records and tried to convince them that they had three good-looking guys (I was pretty modest) with voices like angels. 'There must be something you can do,' I told them. To me it seemed that we were a highly commercial proposition: we had long hair in an era when no Americans had long hair and we sang big strong ballads that made you cry while everybody else was doing rock'n'roll. What more could a record company have asked for? It must have been at least three or four months before the penny dropped and things started to fall in to place. Philips had only the recording of 'Pretty Girls Everywhere', so they released that, hoping that someone would pick up on it, because we were here and available to promote the record, but it made a very minor impact. If it had been successful, the whole Walker Brothers style would probably have been totally different.

We made our first UK TV appearance on a show called *Juke Box Jury*, hosted by David Jacobs, in which celebrities sat on a panel, listened to records and voted them either a 'hit' or a 'miss'. After our record was played and they'd voted it a hit – thank heavens – we walked out from backstage as surprise guests. However, because we were all so tall the viewers could see our bodies only from the neck down until the cameras finally got our faces into the shot.

On 26 March, we performed for the first time on UK TV, on *Ready Steady Go!* singing 'Pretty Girls Everywhere'. I remember the show well. When we were living at Onslow Gardens we'd watch it on the telly with the landlady; The Beatles or the Stones

were frequent guest stars. Little did we know that we would appear on it only weeks later!

Philips showed little interest in us until they heard 'Love Her', released in April 1965 and our first single to chart in Britain, entering the Top 50 on 8 May and reaching Number 18 in June. In fact, it stayed in the Top 50 for three months. We had arrived!

Scott never wanted to go home. He liked it in Europe, as did I. John found it a little hard being here because of the lack of sun and the cold climate. Nevertheless, after 'Love Her' made the charts we decided to stay.

It was when we started to work that the logistical nightmares began. We were allowed to stay in England initially for three months, then we had to go leave the country for 24 hours – we chose to go to France – to get our visas stamped for another three months in the UK. Later on, our management applied to the Home Office for the work permits. There were strong actors' and musicians' unions at the time, and you were required to be members before you could perform on radio and TV. In the beginning, I was unable to appear because I was a musician and not one of the vocalists, which also led to problems with live stage shows. The union said that, because I was playing the drums, I was putting a British drummer out of work. So we added a drummer and a band, which put a lot of British people *in* work. We were the first group to have two drummers on stage at the same time, which gave us a bigger and better sound than anyone else.

Because of the high cost of producing The Walker Brothers' records, which required a very big orchestra, musicians had to be hired for the minimum time possible: the quicker a record was made, the less it cost. An artist doesn't care how much it costs so long as they get it right, but the record company does because it's paying for it, recouping the money from the royalties later. Therefore, the imperative was always to keep the cost down. None of us read music, and the arrangements were big and complicated, so with the union carping on about our not being British, it was agreed that I wouldn't play on some of the records. But it's never been revealed that, when the orchestra left, all three of us added an instrument here and a voice there.

We would practise at the flat or hire out a cheap room in the

area for rehearsals. It took us a while to get used to the acoustics in large UK theatres, as we had only ever played in small clubs. Our main gripe was that the equipment was underpowered for the size of the venues, undermining the sound and giving a bad impression of our performing abilities. This was the big topic of conversion among all the groups from The Beatles downwards, and eventually the complaints led to the development of the power stacks that could really push it out – but only if you were in the big league and could afford it. Because of the high cost of these systems at that time, and the fact that we had not yet made it big, we could not afford to use them. Even if we had had a system like that, more than likely we wouldn't have been heard anyway because of the fans screaming so loudly.

Success – and what Scott much later called his personal nightmare, although earlier on we had so much fun – really began the first time we appeared on the TV show *Thank Your Lucky Stars*, when we were mobbed. Within a very short time, and with interest being increasingly driven by the popular Radio London pirate station, The Walker Brothers had become an essential part of the London scene.

On 25 May we did our first live show, filling in for The Kinks, and chaos erupted. That was the beginning of the fan mania. I suppose we attracted it because we were three tall, thin, good-looking guys with American accents, long hair and – dare I say it – sex appeal, singing tear-jerkingly beautiful songs.

As we became increasingly famous, we thought about getting a manager, but had no idea whom to ask. A close friend of mine, Allan McDougall, introduced me to Brian Sommerville. Brian worked for Brian Epstein; he was the head publicist for The Beatles and had overseen their big break in America, which led him to form his own public-relations company. Brian was very well mannered and intelligent, and later became a solicitor in London, which was what he had wanted to do all along.

I first met Brian at his office in London's Denmark Street, which is where we would go to do press and interviews that he had set up. Denmark Street was – and still is – known as 'Tin Pan Alley', and was famous for all things to do with music. John and Scott bought their guitars there at Rose Morris, the oldest and most

A collage of John Walker. Clockwise from *top left* – John Walker, Sacramento, California, 1963; John and Judy at a record hop in 1959; Ritchie Valens at Gail Smith's garage party in the San Fernando Valley playing John's guitar in 1958; John and Judy at Redondo Union High School auditorium in 1959; John and Judy at a television show at Pacific Ocean Park, California, 1960; Judy And The Gents at The Trophy Room, Sacramento, California 1963; John's sister – Judy – in Hollywood, 1970; *top centre* Judy and The Gents (Vince and Chuck) at The Trophy Room in 1963 and *below centre* Ritchie Valens, John and Judy, at the garage party, San Fernando Valley, California, 1958.

Top left: First communion. John and Judy, 1951, at St James Catholic Church, Redondo Beach, California.

Top right: Mom, Dad, Judy and John on the beach in Venice, California, 1947.

Bottom: John's maternal grandparents – the Prohaskas – vacationing with the family in Knott's Berry Farm, California in the early 1950s. *Private family archive collec*

ove: John and Judy with Regina and John Maus and neighbour outside their first lifornian home, Carnegie Lane, Redondo Beach, 1947.

low: John in stage play *Dark of the Moon* at the Ivar Theatre, Hollywood, lifornia in 1955.

Private family archive collection

Top left: Publicity photo of John for television and stage promotion, 1953.

Top right: Chef Milani, television talent show host, presenting John with first prize award, 1955.

Bottom left: John's first band: John, Judy, and Jimmy Lendenny at Redondo Union High School, California, 1959.

Bottom right: Publicity photo for release of 'Annabella' in 1967.

Inset: Contract between John's band and Jimmy Durante to play his wedding anniversary, 1962.

AMENDMENT TO AGREEMENT

It is hereby agreed by and between the parties hereto that
exclusive recording agreement heretofore entered into by and
on said parties on September 10, 1964 and as amended on
ember 14, 1965 be further amended as follows:

1. By deleting the first sentence in Paragraph 14 and
rting the following in lieu thereof:

    "MELODY is hereby granted five (5) several options
    of extending this agreement for five (5) separate
    terms of one (1) year each."

2. By changing the royalty rates set forth in Paragraph 2
Paragraph 24 to 51 of 90%, effective as of September 10,
, and by changing the royalty rate set forth in Paragraph 2
records sold outside of the United states to 64% of 90%
ctive as of September 10, 1965.

In all other respects, said agreement shall remain in full
ce and effect, except as amended on September 14, 1965 and as
ded herein.

IN WITNESS WHEREOF, the parties hereto do hereby set
ir hands and seals this 10th day of December 1965.

                    MELODY RECORD PRODUCTIONS, INC.

                    SCOTT ENGEL

                    JOHN WALKER
                    (John Maus)

                    a/k/a The WALKER Brothers.

o: John and Scott in a 1963–1964
*b*licity photo.

ght: John in 1967.

et: Amendment to the original Walker
*b*thers Mercury Recording contract
*b*4.

John Reid, Hollywood; private
family archive collection

Top: John on tour in Japan in 1968.

Right: John getting into his Marcos outside Capable Management Offices, in Bickenhall Mansions off Baker Street.

Inset: John as captured with his Michael John haircut by Harry Goodwin in 1967.

ove: John's grandchildren, Kelsi and Jaden, 2009 (parents: Jamie and Alisha).

Photo courtesy of Jamie Andersen

et: Cynthia's grandson, Stanly, 2008 (parents: Adam and Heather).

Photo courtesy Heather Stewart

ow left: Joy Ryan, President of John's fan club.

ow right: John's personal representative, Ann Gwilliam.

John and Cynthia in June 2009.

famous guitar shop in the street. David Bowie – or Davy Jones, as he was known then – lived in his van on the street for a time. One day, when I was leaving Brian's office, Davy Jones asked me if I could loan him some money, so I gave him £20, as we have all been in poor street at some time or other, and he thanked me. Years later, when we lived on the King's Road in Chelsea in the mid-seventies, T.Rex's Marc Bolan lived around the corner (on Holmead Road). I told Marc the story about David and the £20, and how he'd never paid me back. 'If you think that's bad,' he replied, 'I lent him £2,000 and never got it back!'

One of Brian's clients was Philips, our recording company; another was a company called Capable Management. They represented Shirley Bassey, The Rockin' Berries and an Irish group called Them, whose lead singer was Van Morrison. There were two people running the company, Maurice King and Barry Clayman. Brian suggested we approach them, and I went to see them with Allan McDougall at 185 Bickenhall Mansions, opposite Madame Tussaud's in London. That was when we signed with Capable Management.

Maurice and Barry, apart from handling a few big names, were also booking agents for shows around the country. Maurice liked things that had a lot of class. We went out for a lot of nice meals, and we did have some very good times together. He had a club off Oxford Street in the West End of London, where we would occasionally practise in the daytime. We suspected that people traded in illegal goods there, which we found quite romantic, but we never knew for certain. The Kray twins came down there a few times, as well as George Raft, who played gangsters in the old black-and-white movies, but we never got to see any of them, and, when we asked to meet the Krays, we weren't allowed to. Unsurprisingly, we suspected that Maurice had some connections in the underworld: Scott would push him on it, and Maurice would tell Scott to shut up, as he didn't know what he was taking about. That's as far as it went with us; we felt that what Maurice did was his own business.

Maurice asked me one day if I knew how Van Morrison got his name. I said I thought it *was* his name, but Maurice told me he'd acquired it because he slept in the van that he toured in with his group. I told Maurice that we thought Van was really good, that he had a marvellous songwriting talent and was going to be immense, but it seemed to go over Maurice's head. We would later discover that, while Maurice had an ear for Sinatra's voice and had some major plans for Scott, he couldn't ever see the talent that Van Morrison had.

Barry Clayman was the manager I liked better: he was a lot nicer and easier to get along with than Maurice. We could have a lot of fun with Barry, and when he had something to say, we would listen to him. I don't think Barry was in on any shifty moves. He went on to become one of the biggest promoters in the world, handling acts from Tom Jones to Michael Jackson, and he also got a CBE from the Queen.

Initially we all got on well, but neither Maurice nor Barry had any idea of how big it was all going to be. I did.

I had decided that it was better to wait it out and not play one-night stands for five or six months, because the ultimate plan was to be one of the biggest groups in the world, and I felt that performing one-night stands would not benefit the group, even though the new management wanted us to do that because they wanted the money we could make.

Scott, John and I agreed that we wouldn't do the one-nighters at the clubs. The club scene was the virtual backbone of sixties music in England as in America. The Beatles and the Stones were constant visitors to the clubs; we'd all go to relax and listen to the groups playing there. We could have sat in at any time with the bands, but because we were now big stars, we did not. People like Long John Baldry and Eric Burdon performed in the nightclubs a lot, and because the in-crowd was used to seeing them, they were possibly a bit overexposed; so when we did eventually play some clubs, it was a little special because it wasn't an everyday thing.

Once, while we were at Maurice's club working on some tunes for a show, I ran into Jeff Beck, then guitarist with The Yardbirds. I admired him a lot and asked if he would like to come down and play some music with us. He did, and we played for least 45 minutes, and because he was into blues and R&B we got on really well. He told me later that he was surprised at how good we were, as he had thought that Scott and John didn't play any instruments. He also loved the shuffle beat that I played, as English drummers seemed to have trouble with it. Later, Jeff asked if I would play

some dates with him around the UK, and I would really have liked to accept, but The Walker Brothers had conflicting commitments.

Arthur Howes became our agent because he did a lot of the bookings for The Beatles, and if he was good enough for them, that was fine with us. Of all the people around us, Arthur was the one with whom we had the most fun. He had an American army crew cut, his smile was like the keys on Liberace's piano, and he held his ciggy flared out to the right in a camp manner, with the left hand posed on his left hip. I know we were all in it to make money, but I feel that he did like us. The liking was mutual, and we had some special times together. Arthur had a red E-Type Jaguar, in which he would zip around, so we nicknamed him 'all-the-way Arthur'. His office was at Piccadilly Circus, just across the street from Lillywhites, the sports shop. You could look across the street from the window of his offices and watch girls strip off as they tried on clothes in the shop. No, we didn't buy telescopes, that was a rumour – it was just binoculars!

My much-publicised reputation with the ladies was an urban legend started by John and Scott, who nicknamed me 'Casanova', and the more it got around, the worse it got. OK, I did go out with a lot of girls, but Scott did too if he met someone who had a certain look that appealed to him. I know he liked Françoise Hardy, the French singer, but he never got to meet her. He seemed to be attracted to girls with short hair, who had something to say about life. That was a bit heavy for me at that young age. Having fun was on the top of my list.

After moving out of Onslow Gardens, Scott and I shared a fourth-floor flat in Paultons Square, at the Fulham end of the King's Road. The décor was very bizarre: the front room was done all in blue, but the highlight was a bedroom with the walls and ceiling covered in red velvet, and mirrors all along one wall. I thought there was going to be an argument over who was to have it, but to my surprise Scott said, 'You take it, Casa, it's more you than me.' That was how it all started. Our faces were becoming known and some girls in the neighbourhood found out we lived there, and would come around and talk to us, promising to keep it very quiet. Sometimes we would invite them in for tea. These were the first girls we met, and we were too shy to chat any of them up. But that would soon change.

Scott and I went to the Marquee Club to see The Who, Manfred Mann and Davy Jones (later Bowie). Here we met two girls; they thought we were cute, and loved our accents. Being shy, we just talked to them nicely and tried to be polite. When the club closed, the girls asked us if they could come back with us. Scott and I thought this was great, and that maybe all the girls were like this in England. We took them back to the flat, and ended up having a pillow fight with hardly any clothes on. That was a one-off! But as our popularity increased, ever-increasing numbers of girls would follow us around.

My first British girlfriend was Susan Alchin. She had straight blonde hair and a face like Disney's Peter Pan, with a little pug nose and fairy eyes. When you see posters or models from the sixties, they all look like Susan. In 1965, when we were becoming popular, pop stars were supposed to be single, and getting married could spell disaster for your career. Even though John Lennon was married and it hadn't done him much harm, managers and record companies insisted it was important to maintain the fans' hopes of snaring you for themselves. Also, it was well known that most showbiz marriages ended in divorce, with all its adverse publicity. So Susan and I had to sneak around and not be seen together all the time.

In June 1965, John went home and secretly married his American girlfriend, the singer Kathy Young, and for a time no one was any the wiser. But there was one reporter, Chris Hutchins, who was hounding us and asking intrusive questions. Were we married? Who were our girlfriends? Was Scott gay? This guy would dig and dig. He'd waylay Susan when she left my place, and ask her where she had been, and did she know us? Susan knew the tricks, and told him she was seeing her aunt. Hutchins would even talk to the fans outside to see if he could get any info from them. When they asked me who that creep with the red hair was, the one who was always asking questions, we told them to forget about him, and to tell us if they knew anything that we should know.

Hutchins now began to suspect that John was married; he became obsessed with the idea and was determined to get to the bottom of it. He talked his newspaper into flying him to California, where he gained access to John's marriage certificate. That's how he found out the truth, and soon it was all over the

papers in England. It damaged John's image, and it took a while before the fuss calmed down.

In the summer of 1965, Arthur Howes booked us a series of summer concerts. We played several seaside towns, sometimes at end-of-the-pier theatres. There was briefly a fourth Walker Brother, Jimmy O'Neil, who was brought in to play keyboard and make the sound bigger. This didn't work out but it led to the hiring of Johnny B Great and the Quotations, who became our backing group. The last I heard of Jimmy, he was living in Las Vegas and still part of the music scene. He was a nice person and his having to leave the group was upsetting for us all.

The Quotations were indeed great, as Johnny's name suggested. He was a lead singer in his own right, and as big as a sumo wrestler. We had a wonderful time on the tour buses and travelling all over Europe. Johnny and the group helped no end to make us famous, and I'm sure that the boys would like to thank Scott for getting them into some very nice hotel accommodation, and then dragging them up early in the morning to play tennis.

In July, riots erupted at Walker Brothers concerts, and the fan mania began to get out of hand. Shows could not be completed; our clothes were ripped, our cars vandalised. Privacy, for us, was now a thing of the past.

When we started to play on the circuit, we did so mostly in small halls, where it was hard to get adequate security. The girls would rush the stage and sometimes jump up on it and, when they did get you, it would take about four men to drag them off. We always had a lot of girls doing this, and often they would rip our shirts or pull our hair. The bouncers' job was to grab the fans and throw them back in the crowd, which would always lead to the show being stopped, because of the safety factor. Even when we began to play the big theatres, it was the same, except that they had safety curtains that could come down in case of a fire. The curtains afforded some protection, but not much.

We began to experience the kind of fan mania associated with The Beatles. We were told by three or four promoters that even they and The Rolling Stones never got the kind of hysteria we inspired. Our being a bit more physical on stage, dancing and gyrating and even writhing on the floor, may have accounted for that. The whole concept of our shows was rock'n'roll, as it was pointless to do the slow numbers for which we were more famous. We found ourselves devising all manner of ingenious plans to enter and exit theatres and hotels safely, enlisting the services of John Wolfe, our first road manager. John – whom we called 'Wiggie' because he had lost his hair when young and wore a wig – looked just like John Lennon and was mistaken for him on many occasions. He took care of our security. He would come into our dressing room many a time and say, 'Boys, I want you to do this. I've had a word, and it's all sorted.' And we would do what he asked. But, no matter how good each escape plan was, it never worked. We would speculate that even the Secret Service would have trouble facing what we called the FBI (Fan Base International). The fans knew all the tricks, and, as a lot of them worked for the telephone, electricity and gas companies, or the Post Office, they knew how to use the system to find us.

Wiggie was later fired by our management because he was concerned about some of the things happening to the group, and management didn't like that. He would often warn us that Maurice was keeping our money and not telling us. Sometimes Maurice told us that we would get, say, £1,000, when the original fee was £1,500. We always said that, if we just got our one million, they could have their five million; it wouldn't have been right, but at least we would have got something. Once our managers found out that Wiggie was spilling the beans, it was time for him to go. The good part of the story is that he went on to become the head road manager for The Who. He also put on one of the biggest ever holographic laser light shows in the Royal Academy in London, which broke attendance records. Later he was hired to do the laser shows for others, including Paul McCartney and The Who. Wiggie and I remain the best of friends and try to see each other whenever we can.

At first, the fan mania was terrifying, but soon it became a normal part of our lives. We all had a great time – at least to begin with. It was like one endless giant party, and we got to the stage where nothing was a surprise. At the Hammersmith Apollo, there was a girl who climbed up above the stage to the catwalk, where the lights were, and threatened to jump if she didn't get to meet one of the Walker Brothers. The police and the fire brigade were

summoned, but by then the girl was in such a state that the officers were afraid to go up and grab her; instead they came to the dressing room and appealed to us for help, whereupon I said I would go up and say hello, which hopefully would persuade her to come down.

I climbed up to the catwalk above the stage. She saw me coming. Suddenly, I felt really mad at her for causing all this trouble, and yelled, 'What are you doing? Get off that thing and get down from there!' Meekly, she did as I told her, but as soon as she had descended she ran and grabbed me, and had to be pulled off and restrained.

We began devising all kinds of strategies for getting in and out of hotels and theatres, including one totally unique method of escape. We were performing at a vast old village hall outside London, which held about 1,200 people. When the crowds started arriving, the promoter came to say that the show was sold out. We asked him if he had enough security to handle the job, and he said yes, he had hired three extra bouncers, giving him six in total.

'Will that be enough to handle the situation?' we asked anxiously.

'More than enough,' he told us. 'We have a lot of pop stars playing here, and there's never any problem.' That was the first clue that they didn't know what was coming.

We had Wiggie check out all the escape routes in and out of the venue. We were on the first floor, and knew very well that that could mean a major problem. We just looked at each other: we didn't have to say anything.

'Gary,' said Scott, 'you'd better tell him that we have very enthusiastic fans and that things can get out of hand.' But I got the stock answer, 'Don't worry, it will be alright.' Johnny B Great and the Quotations went on to play the first set, then there was a 15-minute break before the compère introduced us. This was when the hysterical fans became more frenzied, just moments before we were due on stage. The chants started – 'We want Walkers!' – over and over again. 'We want Scott! We want John! We want Gary!' It got almost hypnotic, starting quite low at first, working its way to the apex of vocal terror. From the side of the stage, you could see the hot, sweaty bodies swaying in the compressed crowd. 'The eyes – look at their eyes, big, staring into oblivion,' we would say. To induce more excitement, the compère would draw out his introduction, and cruelly incite the girls to fever pitch. At last, he said, 'And now, here they are: John, Scott, Gary – The Walker Brothers!'

The Quotations, who were already on stage, started to play the opening music – the James Bond theme – and I was the first one out. The place erupted in screams of goalscoring volume, if not louder. Then the other two came on, and the needle went off the scale. The crowd surged forward towards the bouncers and the stage, and all logic and reasoning went out the window. At times, the girls seemed to be flying across the orchestra pit and the security men to the stage, but miraculously they were grabbed and thrown back into the pulsating mob. At this point, Wiggie appeared and told us to leave the stage, which we did as fast as we could, escaping to the safety of the dressing room. The safety curtain had been lowered and it was made clear that the show was over.

In the dressing room, we could still hear the yells and chaos from within the hall. The promoter was in total panic and didn't know what to do. He had never seen anything like this before. Wiggie said he was going to try to find a way out, if he could get through the crowd outside. We wished him good luck, and hoped to see him again. He returned after about 20 minutes, and informed us that, because the village was small, there weren't many police, so we couldn't expect much help there. But he did have a plan. As we listened to the unfolding of what sounded like the maddest of plots, it started to make sense – or perhaps we were losing it too. Wiggie had managed to hire a coach that would pull up to the hall outside our window, and we would exit through the window, which, being on the first floor, was the same height as the roof of the coach. This roof was concave in the centre, and could accommodate the three of us. We thought this was the ultimate plan so far.

Wiggie got us onto the roof of the coach and we were safely driven away. The band packed up and left, as normal, and we all caught up later for a late-night breakfast and a quick chat in the café as if nothing had happened. It was quite surreal.

It got to the stage when everybody knew who we were. One day, Scott and I stopped at a flower stall in Old Brompton Road in

South Kensington, and the old lady there asked us, 'Aren't you The Walker Brothers?' I looked at Scott and he looked at me. This was a total shock to both of us; we had never expected anything like that to happen.

During the summer of 1965, we began recording our first album, *Take It Easy With The Walker Brothers*, the title of which Scott and I immediately changed to *Take It Greasy*, because we were not too happy with it, and later to *Take It Cheesy*. We also had our first recording session with producer John Franz at Philips Records, the beginning of an enormously successful creative partnership with Franz. It's fair – and important – to say that we would have evolved our unique sound regardless of who we worked with, but Franz's input was crucial alongside our own unique production and musical skills. You may hear the song in your head, but then you have to try to get it onto the tape; the only thing that stopped us from doing it all on our own was that we didn't know how to use the studio equipment. But we would listen to a track and say what we liked and what we didn't, and then we'd decide how to make it better.

John Franz was a great help and a close friend, and he was very easy to get along with. He had perfect pitch, which means that if you rang a bell he could tell you what key it was in. Sometimes, listening to 25 to 30 strings, he would stop the orchestra and tell one of the players that he was playing the wrong note. Sometimes, I would go to the office and find John at the Steinway, with Scott standing at the foot of the piano, singing the old songs they both loved. It's a real shame that there was not a tape recorder there on which to capture it all. It was pure magic.

John Franz passed away in 1977, aged 54. He was a very special friend and, through his help many an artist became very successful.

From that summer of 1965 onwards, without exception, the choice of material was exclusively ours, as was the final mix of each song. Because the record company finally came to accept that we knew what we were talking about and could pick hit songs, things got a lot easier. They let us spend as much as we liked, knowing they would recoup it all from our royalties, although of course by the time we had paid for everything there wasn't much left. This happened to a lot of groups.

These were the sessions during which our third single, 'Make it Easy on Yourself', was recorded. We had wanted to do Burt Bacharach's 'Don't Make Me Over', and the only reason we didn't was that we thought Dionne Warwick had got there first. Scott was really pissed off when we found out that her version was released only in the US, so we would have had no problem putting it out in the UK.

'Make it Easy on Yourself', backed with our version of the Clarence Frogman Henry standard 'But I Do', was released on 6 August, the same month we were signed for our first ballroom tour. Unfortunately, when we played the smaller places, they just didn't have enough security and the sound was terrible. Contrary to what has been reported, Scott didn't have any fear of performing on any of these shows. In fact, they were quite fun, and most of the time we weren't on stage for that long anyway.

In *A Deep Shade of Blue* it's alleged that Scott sometimes went missing for days at a time, and that he found it hard to cope with a growing 'load of responsibilities' as 'the leader of The Walker Brothers'. Scott didn't disappear or go missing: we were together almost all the time and, as far as responsibilities went, there weren't any. All we did was go on stage, as we'd done in the clubs, play the best we could, and hope the sound was halfway decent. In the recording studio we made the decisions, not Philips, and it was important that we get everything right. We were all involved in any decision-making process, except when it came to recording or performing our individual songs, and then we each made up our own minds. Most of the serious career moves were discussed in private between just the three of us.

By now, I had become the group's unofficial spokesman. I just started taking over that role, as it seemed that Scott didn't want to and John was often busy. However, newspapers, radio and TV often wanted all of us together. It just seemed that the media were crazy for anything they could get their hands on. All it took was a picture of us on a magazine's front cover it would sell out.

When 'Make it Easy on Yourself' reached Number 1 in September 1965, we knew we were doing all the right moves, and we were really chuffed. After that, of course, things started to get harder because there was pressure on us – and we put pressure on ourselves – to have more Number 1 hits, which caused not a little

anxiety. For now, though, we were celebrating, and more than likely we would have gone out to a club. Contrary to what has been written, Scott did not end up in a police cell (I knew we should have paid those parking fines).

ENGLAND CHANGED MY LIFE
JOHN WALKER

We arrived at Heathrow Airport at six in the morning on 17 February 1965. It had snowed the night before, and as we were coming in for the landing I remember asking Gary, 'What's all that white stuff?' As soon as we got off the plane we knew it was definitely snow, for it was freezing cold outside. None of us had dressed for this weather and, to make matters worse, the seat of my brand-new pair of cords ripped wide open as I was leaving the plane. I had no idea how it had happened; I just hoped that my long shirt would cover it.

We were all too exhausted even to talk, having been through that long flight. We left it to Gary to get us into London (Scott and I would become quite impressed with Gary's savvy knowledge of how to do things in the UK). After he and the cab driver had talked for a bit, we headed straight to Earl's Court. Scott and I stared quietly out of the windows of the cab, taking in the dreary, bleak surroundings. I think he was as shocked as I was by what we saw. All the buildings and homes looked old, worn and smoke-stained. I was starting to wonder what I had let myself in for. The discussion among us was limited to where we were going to find a place to stay, and how tired we all were. There was a lot of yawning. It was a painfully quiet trip apart from Gary's occasional humorous outbursts. My only impressions of England were from old movies, so I was waiting to be engulfed in the famous London fog, and was actually disappointed that, despite the dreariness outside, there was absolutely none to be seen.

The situation did not improve much when we got to Earl's Court. We found a building with a sign outside advertising rooms to let. The address was 13 Courtfield Gardens. The neighbourhood was rough, and many of the buildings were in dire need of attention. The only saving grace was that our building was across the street from a beautiful church with well-kept grounds. Unfortunately, the church bells rang loudly at all hours of the day and night.

The four of us shared one tiny room with a small window. There were four beds, a washbasin and a two-bar electric fire. The toilet was on our floor, the bathroom was on the next floor up, and the halls were bloody freezing, so none of us bathed too much that first week.

The four of us hit the streets to find food. It was still quite early in the morning. I think we ended up at a Wimpy Bar about a block away. After we had eaten our eggs and chips, we all just crashed back in the room. As I recall, there was very little conversation – we were all so tired.

After a nap, Gary informed us that it was our lucky day: we were right by the Tube station at Earl's Court so we could easily get to Piccadilly Circus. He was anxious to show us around – and we couldn't wait to see what was out there. Scott and I had never been on the Tube (or subway), and again we quietly took everything in. The Tube station was incredibly noisy, windy and vibrating. There were people everywhere, and the maze of lifts, escalators and stairs to get us to different platforms was unlike anything I'd ever seen.

We followed Gary through the Tube network, and eventually popped up in the middle of Piccadilly Circus. It first struck me as being like a miniature Times Square in New York City: there were people everywhere, lots of advertisements on buildings, billboards and marquees, with the streets emanating from what was obviously the central hub of the West End. I knew right away that this was where the excitement was, the place where we would discover, little by little, the great boutiques, restaurants and theatres we had heard about.

Scott, too, was taking everything in without much comment. That afternoon, after nearly getting ourselves killed as we wandered for hours up and down the streets and alleys, Gary taught Scott and me two very important lessons about London traffic. Number one: the pedestrian does *not* have the right of way. Number two: the traffic comes from the right, not the left!

By now, jetlag was setting in and, when we made it back to our rooms, we crashed for the second time. All of us woke up in the

middle of the night, starving to death. The Wimpy Bar saved us again, although the tiny Wimpy burger with fried onions and strange ketchup that they served us was probably the worst meal Scott and I had ever had. I was very hungry during that first week, until we finally discovered some little shops selling food that we could bring back to the room. There was a lot of sitting on our respective beds, snacking on whatever food we had, drinking Cokes and talking about getting a better place to live.

Walking around and exploring really lifted our spirits and by the second day, after some sleep and food, we were all really glad to have made the decision to come over. We went to Piccadilly Circus a lot and hung out at pubs and the big music store, the Rose Morris Showrooms, on Shaftesbury Avenue. We discovered Soho and other parts of the city, stopping in the pubs for a beer to break up the sightseeing.

Wherever the three of us went anywhere together, people asked us what the name of our group was, and we told them The Walker Brothers, knowing full well they'd never heard of us. But they still seemed impressed with our presumed stardom, maybe because we were American. People would often mistake me for Brian Jones of The Rolling Stones. We both had very long, fair hair and similar jawlines, with long fringes hanging over our eyes. A little over a year later I was holidaying at the Don Pepe hotel in Marbella, Spain, sunbathing on the beach, when three members of the Guardia Seville approached me with rifles in hand, motioning for me to go with them. They were very aggressive and of course I had no idea what was going on. I kept telling them I was American, but they wanted to see my passport. We went back to the hotel to get it, and there I asked the concierge to confirm who I was and find out what they wanted with me. After a short discussion between them in Spanish, he explained to me that Brian Jones had been detained just a few days earlier, and had been asked to leave the country because he had been found with an illegal substance in his possession. Someone had just reported seeing Brian at the beach – but it was me. The Guardia apologised for their mistake, I was released, and they all wished me well and a pleasant stay while in Spain.

It was Gary who introduced us to the Marquee Club on Wardour Street in Soho. This was the place where we saw our first live band in England – The Who. The other two hot clubs we began to frequent were Ronnie Scott's – a jazz club – and the Flamingo, where the featured guest artist was Georgie Fame. Later, while Scott hung out a lot at Ronnie Scott's, I preferred the Marquee because it had the latest rock and pop acts.

I did get homesick in the UK, but didn't want to pass up the once in a lifetime opportunity. Phone calls home were expensive, so Gary sent his girlfriend tapes through the post. I know Scott called his mother fairly often. I wrote to Kathy and my family regularly about our adventures, and they in turn wrote back, letting me know what was going on at home, and that they were still annoyed I had left. I had terribly mixed feelings about the whole thing: on one hand I was really enjoying hanging out with the guys and exploring this whole new world, and was determined to stay long enough to see what, if anything, the outcome of the trip would be. On the other, I was very homesick and felt quite unsettled. I wasn't used to being broke all the time either. Aside from missing my family, I missed my 1957 Thunderbird, the beach, cruising around – and especially playing in the band, and making lots of money.

Within a few weeks, we moved to 1 Onslow Gardens, near Earl's Court. This was a great location. The four of us shared one huge ground-floor room with a very high ceiling and a big bay window. There was no kitchen or private bathroom, no television, radio or refrigerator. We just had a double burner and a sink, four beds, armchairs and a dining table with four chairs around it. Again we had a two-bar electric heater, and I think it required a shilling deposit to get it working.

I walked for miles in those early weeks. Our flat was not far from Hyde Park, Buckingham Palace, Park Lane, Marble Arch and Oxford Street. Scott did even more sightseeing than I did, checking out all of the famous art galleries. I was content to keep discovering new areas. I found a terrific restaurant inside Lyon's Corner House on Oxford Street, called the Seven Stars, where roast dinners were served along with Mâcon Rouge wine. They served huge portions for about £2 per person, including wine. It became our favourite hangout.

I also loved walking around Hyde Park and watching equestrians ride through the impressive avenue of elms, which sadly, much later on, had to be cut down due to Dutch Elm disease.

In fact, for years I always made a point of being in Hyde Park in autumn to see the spectacular display of colours, and was heartbroken when the massive elms had to come down.

England changed my life. It would make me see a lot of things in a different light. To start with, I was fairly naïve when it came to my relationships with the opposite sex. I'd had very little experience with women socially, and even less in a physical sense. The first thing I noticed was how comfortable the English girls seemed to be with themselves.

The next important discovery was the Cromwellian Club on Cromwell Road, a five-minute walk from our flat. There was dancing, gambling and lots of girls. I was invited to become a member, presumably because I had the right look and had told them that I was in a group called The Walker Brothers – even though we were still relatively unknown at the time. The first time I went to the Cromwellian Club in March 1965. I met a girl there, we had a few dances and drinks, and the next thing I knew she was staying the night with me. I certainly hadn't expected that to happen, and nothing of the kind was on my mind when I went out that evening. I had definite ideas and views on moral issues, but my earlier opinions about relationships with the opposite sex seemed suddenly to have changed completely, and I wasn't uncomfortable with that. But here I was, engaged to be married in the next few months, having sex with a girl I hardly knew and not feeling guilty about it. It didn't even seem like I was cheating on Kathy, but seemed to be a natural part of life. I still can't explain that.

As unfamiliar as it felt to me, I realised that I liked the forthrightness of the girls I met. I never saw that trait in American girls. The other thing that really stood out was that the English girls were very cool, yet sophisticated at the same time. That really impressed me.

I began to venture into other clubs in London. I would always meet some terrific girls and nature would take its course. Things continued like that for some time, and then I met the girl I shouldn't have. She worked as a secretary in an office I had to frequently visit and, after some persuading, she agreed to go out for a drink. We started seeing quite a bit of each other and I really got to know her well. I had never seen how an English girl actually lived. It was amazing to me that she shared a small flat with her friend and took the tube to work. She didn't earn a lot of money, but she managed. The girls I knew in America still lived at home and had a car and an allowance, so this was very different from what I'd been used to, and I thought it was wonderful. After a while I found that I began to care deeply for this girl, but it couldn't go on. I knew I would have to stop seeing her.

In mid-March 1965, I had to go back to California. My first priority was to get my hands on lots of cash to bring back to the UK, as I was tired of being cold, broke and dependent on someone else for money, and determined to make a success of our opportunities. Back in LA I visited with everyone, but being in California felt strange and odd to me. I realised that I quite liked being in England, even though I complained about everything every chance I had. I didn't like being cold, but I preferred the fresh, chilly air to the LA mixture of sunshine and smog. Everyone in LA appeared casual and a little sloppy compared with the Brits, who looked as if they'd stepped out of a fashion magazine. I actually found myself anxious to return to the UK.

I also realised that my engagement to Kathy might have been premature, and I seem to have blocked out my memories of the time I spent with her and my family during that trip. I do know that it became increasingly difficult for me to deal with the emotional turmoil I was going through. I was committed to Kathy, and she had no reason to think that anything had changed.

The group's recording schedule meant I had to get back to England. After I'd spent ten days in California, Judy saw me off again at LAX; this time I had plenty of dough and my Fender Esquire. I got a cab at Heathrow back to Onslow Gardens and knocked on our flat door – only to be told that Scott and Gary had moved. They had assumed I wasn't coming back. Fortunately, Hilda the landlady knew they had moved to Chelsea. They had definitely decided to stay in England; I found out later that they had cashed in their return tickets. I asked Hilda where I could stay, and was told that she had actually kept a little garden flat in the building available for my return. The basement room was tiny, but I did have my own private door. For me, the best and most significant part of this arrangement was that, for the first time in my life, I finally had a place of my own.

Soon after we'd arrived in England, Claude called Philips Records (who were affiliated to our company, Mercury, in the United States), and let them know that The Walker Brothers were in town and would like to stop by the office. But Philips had heard 'Pretty Girls Everywhere' and weren't the least bit interested in us. Before the end of March, John Franz, an A&R man and producer at Philips, gave us a call out of the blue, asking us to come into his office for a meeting. He'd been impressed with a tape of 'Love Her' sent over by Mercury and wanted to release the record. There was a lot of hassle involved because we had no work permits and were running out of cash; there had been no game plan from the start. Nevertheless, in April 1965, Philips released our recording of 'Love Her'/'The Seventh Dawn' in the UK.

In the meantime, Nick Venet had flown over hoping to find a position with a record company in Britain. He ended up saving the day for us. It was just lucky for us that he happened to be in town, and that we got in touch with each other. Having always been the leader of the band, I was the one who met with him. I went to see him at the Hilton Hotel on Park Lane to discuss business, and what we could get going. Nick said he would have a chat with Philips to let them know that we were held in high regard in America, hoping that would create more interest in promoting us in the UK. When Nick found out that we were really low on cash he immediately, without hesitating, took bills out of his pocket and handed them over to keep us afloat.

Soon after that, Johnny Franz called us for another meeting with the head of Philips promotion, Paddy Fleming. Paddy was a jolly Irish guy and we all instantly hit it off. More importantly, he was crazy about 'Love Her', telling us he thought it had a very good chance of being a hit.

It was Gary who introduced Scott and me to Arthur Howes, a promoter he knew from his Proby days. We also met one of Arthur's agents, Jimmy O'Neil, who became very instrumental in our early careers. Jimmy was a tall, elegant Irish gentleman who had fantastic presence; he entertained us with showbiz stories and could hold more booze than anyone I'd ever met. We were really pleased to have him represent us. Paddy and Jimmy were going to work on a promotion plan for us while Philips sorted out the work-permit problem.

Out of the blue we were contacted by a magazine – I think it was either *Valentine* or *Mirabelle* – to do a photoshoot. The three of us were met by a photographer at Marble Arch; he wanted some shots of us climbing around the arch and doing the silly poses typical of pop photos at that time. We just went along with it; we wanted the press. Through Philips' promotional department we had also hooked up with Dave Cash and Kenny Everett from Radio London, and started hanging out with them. They gave our music and interviews a lot of airtime. In fact, I credit them with our initial success because they promoted us so heavily on their show. I remain good friends with Dave Cash, although sadly Kenny Everett is no longer with us.

As I recall, it was Jimmy O'Neil who arranged our first television appearance, on *Thank Your Lucky Stars*, which was televised in Bristol. We sang 'Love Her' and were very nervous the whole time. Thankfully, my migraine headaches never bothered me once I got to the UK, so I didn't have to worry about those. Mike Mansfield, the producer and director, came up with an innovative presentation: he showed close-ups of our faces throughout most of the performance, rather than the standard long shots of the stage and band. There are reports that this show started the whole fan mob scene. Certainly, after we appeared on the show, people recognised us wherever we went: on the streets, in pubs, everywhere. Even the flower lady on the corner started calling me 'Mr Walker'. I really got a kick out of that. We immediately became members of the 'in' clubs.

Gary, Scott and I enjoyed this instant success and recognition, contrary to the many erroneous reports through the years that we – and Scott in particular – shunned the spotlight and viewed it as the start of a personal nightmare. We all loved the attention we were getting and hoped it would continue. I never heard him say this, but it's been quoted that Scott described our appeal as 'neurotic romanticism'. I think our image and music conveyed to the audiences an approachable romanticism that they could relate to; and our songs were loaded with drama.

After Paddy Fleming saw the show, he called Johnny Franz, urging him to get 'Love Her' in as many stores as possible, predicting it would be in the charts within two weeks. By May 1965, 'Love Her' had made the Top 50, and it reached Number

18 in June. In fact, it stayed in the Top 50 for three months. Thanks to that, The Walker Brothers' sound was firmly established in the UK.

We started getting a lot of magazine interviews with the trade papers – *New Musical Express*, with Keith Altham; *Melody Maker*, with Chris Welch; and *Disc* (later *Disc and Music Echo*) – and with the top pop magazines, *Fab 208* and *Rave*. During this period, the press was fairly accurate in its depictions of us and in quoting us. Later that year *Fab 208* took Gary, Scott and me on our first trip to Paris, for a photoshoot, where we stayed on the Left Bank. The magazine arranged a lot of sightseeing, taking pictures of the whole trip. We met up with an old French gypsy woman in a marketplace who told our fortunes; she told me that my greatest wealth would lie in my family. It was not until many years later – in 2003 – that I would completely understand her prediction.

On the first night we were taken to a typical French restaurant to try out real French cuisine. It was the first time any of us had been served escargots, frog's legs and raw oysters. I loved the escargots, found the frog's legs OK, but couldn't go near the oysters. Gary tried them, turned a putrid shade of green after swallowing one and had to medicate himself with a giant gulp of cognac, saying to me, 'That was a close one, Thaus.' That was the name he and Scott had for me. From the early days, each of us had an exclusive nickname among ourselves that no one else used: I was Thaus, Gary was Beads, and Scott was Scooty. There was no rhyme or reason to these names, but that's the way it was and continues to this day.

Our next television show was *Ready, Steady Goes Live*. Ours was one of the first live performances on the show. Until then, most pop shows had featured artists miming to their records. We should have known that, if something could go wrong with a live television show, it would happen to us. Our performance of 'Love Her' was going along just great until suddenly, without warning, Scott's vocal disappeared. The backing track kept playing, but Scott wasn't there. He turned white as a sheet and gave me that worried look of his. I thought he was going to faint, which would have been inconvenient because I was about to have a heart attack. Just when we were sure that all was lost, Scott's vocal reappeared in the studio. I sang my harmony part, and thankfully the song ended without further mishap. We were utterly relieved that the televised performance hadn't been interrupted. There were definitely drinks all around back in the dressing room after *that* show!

Around this time we were introduced to Capable Management in London through a publicist named Allan McDougall, and Maurice King and Barry Clayman became our new managers. Our initial meeting was at Maurice's club in Finchley – the Starlight Club – and we were taken out to dinner afterwards to Barry's restaurant, also in Finchley. Maurice was a wannabe gangster, dressing and talking the part; he must have loved it when people thought he was connected to the underworld, but we never saw or heard any evidence of that. Barry Clayman was a very conservative business type without any affectations or showbiz flair. I trusted him, and he was the main reason why I agreed to sign with Capable. My intuition was right – in later years Barry looked out for me. Maurice was another story.

That year, at the height of The Walker Brothers' success, Maurice formed his own publishing company, Miracle Songs, with a German publisher. He led Scott, Gary and me to believe that we – as The Walker Brothers – could become part owners of the company; we were all quite impressed, so we signed all of the papers he had prepared. It would be several years before we would discover that we'd actually signed away our publishing rights, first to Maurice and the German guy, and then to the other companies to whom they eventually sold on Miracle Songs. Scott, Gary and I had been well and truly shafted.

On 25 May 1965, after a lot of pressure and persuasion from our new managers, we played together live for the first time at a sold-out show at the Odeon, Leeds, filling in for The Kinks. Three nights into their tour, they got into an onstage fight – their drummer Mick Avory hit guitarist Dave Davies with a cymbal – and had to cancel the last three dates. Our management slotted us in as substitutes.

The three of us didn't feel prepared for such an undertaking. We were concerned that the fans would be disappointed in not seeing The Kinks, especially since we were an entirely different kind of

group. More importantly, we didn't have the type of musical backing we needed to perform our material. We basically threw the show together, Scott and I sharing lead vocals and playing our instruments, and Gary on drums. Instead of attempting big love ballads such as 'Love Her', which needed orchestral backdrops and swooning voices, we reverted to playing the good old rock'n'roll songs that Scott and I had performed in Gazzari's.

To say that our performance was a success is an understatement: we walked on the stage, and within minutes the place erupted in pandemonium, which really surprised us. The fans took to us immediately, and went absolutely crazy. We couldn't even finish our first show. None of us had experienced anything like that back in Hollywood! It says much for Gary's professionalism and musicianship that he was suddenly on a stage with Scott and me – who had been playing together to Hollywood crowds for the last few years – performing with us for the first time, with very little rehearsal.

This was the beginning of 'Walkermania', and we played all three nights to hysterical fans. The girls mobbed us, security couldn't handle it, and we were in shock. Scott and I had never experienced anything remotely like this before. On stage, I was so overwhelmed with fear, exhilaration and adrenalin that my memories of some details are a blank, although I do remember having two very clear thoughts that night: I felt complete disbelief and bewilderment at the reaction of the crowd; then I became very aware of the dangerous situation arising from the proximity of the screaming mob that was outside at the stage door, pressing towards us as we left the theatre after the show, and I began thinking for the first time about the need for beefing up security.

A lot of press covered the first night, and the fan chaos was on the front pages of the newspapers the next morning. Back at the hotel, the three of us talked about the whole event and how excited we were about the crowd's response. We couldn't wait to see if we would get the same reaction the following night, and we were not disappointed.

Maurice King hired John Wolfe – 'Wiggie' to us because he wore a wig – as our first road manager. We hadn't had a professional roadie before, and the three of us learned the ropes together with Wiggie, formulating various plans and schemes to outwit the hysterical fans. We worked together for almost half a year before Wiggie left to work for The Who; he did all our first ballroom gigs with us. He took his job very seriously, was punctual and very dependable, and quickly learned how to handle large crowds of hysterical fans who would try anything to get near us.

Early that summer, we discussed making a new single (and hopefully an album) with Maurice and Barry. At that time bands made singles first and, if they were successful, would follow with an album. Philips gave their approval because 'Love Her' had gone into the Top 20. We knew our next recording would be expensive, and were relieved to have Philips back us completely. We didn't have an album title in mind yet. Our first challenge was actually finding material that would suit the new Walker Brothers style.

I was always the leader of the band. I was the one who said, 'Let's do this, let's do that.' I spent a great deal of time making sure that the group would make incredible music. Most people don't realise that it was I who chose the songs that would become The Walker Brothers' biggest-selling singles. After the moderate success of 'Love Her' I suggested the Bacharach–David composition 'Make it Easy on Yourself'. Later, I also picked 'My Ship is Coming In', 'The Sun Ain't Gonna Shine Anymore', 'In My Room' and a lot of others. I had a Jerry Butler album called *The Best of Jerry Butler* – one of my favourites – and I played Butler's version of 'Make it Easy on Yourself' for everyone to hear. We all agreed that it had great single potential.

Before starting to record the album, I planned another trip back to California to marry Kathy. This was no surprise to Scott and Gary, or to Capable, because I had already discussed it with them. Scott and Gary did voice one concern, that my marriage might affect my popularity, but Maurice and Barry didn't say anything one way or the other.

I was gone for about a week, just enough time to get married on 26 June and fly back to England with Kathy. In retrospect, given my doubts, it would have been a better idea to wait for a while, but everything was planned and all the arrangements were made. I couldn't disappoint Kathy or her family, so I didn't. The truth was that neither Kathy nor I was ready for marriage, or even understood all that it entailed. That proved to be true in less than three years.

I didn't make any public announcement, but I made no attempt to keep my marriage a secret either. Kathy and I moved into a flat in Ormonde Terrace, by Regent's Park, then it was back to work as usual.

It must have been a little strange for Kathy when she came to London. Apart from being in a foreign country, she had been a recording star in America but was unknown in the UK, whereas The Walker Brothers were becoming increasingly popular. Things were considerably different from the days when I had played guitar for her. We had to do things around my schedule. I was very busy with The Walker Brothers at that time, recording, doing one-nighters, press and all the rest of the things that had to do with the group. Kathy and I didn't have a lot of time together as I was always going somewhere. When I was home, we'd do the usual things: have dinner out, go to the latest 'in' club or the cinema. I knew the manager at the Leicester Square Theatre, and he would close off the balcony to the public so that we could see a movie without causing any commotion. The Walker Brothers' popularity did impose some severe limitations on what one could do. Going out was really difficult, but I made deals with restaurant and cinema managers so that we could go to certain places without any hassle.

Kathy and I decided to get a dog. I wanted to get a German shepherd puppy. It was always my favourite breed and, because I lived near Regent's Park, it seemed like the perfect time. I told Barry Clayman what I wanted, and he said he knew a breeder. I got my first puppy when she was about four or five months old, and named her Brandy. Her real name was April of Stapleton. I have no idea where either name came from. Brandy cried a lot when she was left alone, and didn't want to sleep by herself. Fortunately, Angela of Stapleton, Brandy's sister, was still with the breeder, so I bought her, and it worked out great. I had to choose the name Scotch to go with Brandy, of course.

The dogs decided who their owners were: Brandy became more attached to Kathy and Scotch was crazy about me, following me everywhere – room to room, chair to chair – wherever I went. I even had to lock the bathroom door. *Rave* magazine did a photoshoot of me with Scotch and Brandy for their cover in October 1966. They were beautiful dogs, and somehow instinctively knew how to pose for the photographer.

At home with Kathy and the dogs I tried to live a normal married life, and according to the press we had a fairytale marriage with no scandals, illicit affairs or juicy gossip. Like most marriages, everything started out great. It was pretty amazing to be living in London in the sixties; it was even more amazing to be famous and have a lot of money and everything that goes with it. My marriage did work well for a while, but things would start to go wrong within a year.

Scott, Gary and I had our work cut out for us, going through material for the album. We wanted romantic songs that had a lot of dramatic potential. In order to get ready for the studio sessions, I played guitar as Scott and I went through the songs, laying out each piece, with me arranging my harmony parts, and both of us practising any unique phrasing. Knowing that we now had a full orchestra to work with, Scott and I decided on specific musical sounds we wanted to hear in various parts of each song: big sweeping strings, horn parts, heavy rhythms, percussive sounds, and our new idea of using two basses – one acoustic and one electric. We both drew on music we had been listening to over the years; Scott was familiar with a lot of classical music, and I loved the Mantovani strings, R&B recordings from Ray Charles, Jerry Butler and The Drifters, and the early Motown stuff. We relied heavily on Gary to give us his feedback through this whole process – he became our objective audience.

While we were working on the album, Arthur Howes booked us for some summer concerts. They all seemed to be at the end of some seaside pier. Getting to end-of-pier theatres always presented monumental challenges for us. Once, to avoid the mobs of fans, we actually tried to get a boat to deliver us there, but no one cooperated. We knew we had to talk to management about changing our whole approach to playing live, but in the meantime we just kept showing up for our dates. Because fans continuously rushed onto the stage each night, we realised that it was completely impractical to carry on performing with our instruments, and we also wanted a bigger, more powerful accompaniment on the stage, including two drummers, to help us recreate The Walker Brothers' sound and to also enable us to be heard above the screaming. Capable Management found The

Quotations, led by 'Johnny B Great' Goodison, and they became our backup band.

Johnny, a singer and keyboard player, was a huge friendly guy who loved Motown music, as did his band. We rehearsed with them at Maurice's club in Finchley. We all got along well right off the bat, and they were very enthusiastic about backing us. They would open each night with their own set before we came out, which added a lot to our shows.

I was aware that things had changed a lot: Scott had become the lead singer of our group and, for all practical purposes, stopped playing his bass. Gary and I really admired Scott's dedication to developing his voice and taking his new role very seriously. Now that he was singing lead, I enjoyed the opportunity to create some unusual harmonies, something I had never done before. We knew that we each had an important role, and felt responsible to each other, with one goal in mind, which was to make good records that were unique for the time. I don't recall any animosity among us as The Walker Brothers evolved – at least, not at this time.

As time went on, I had to figure out how to perform without a guitar in my hands. Now that we had no instruments to hold, Scott and I had hand mikes. I can't speak for Scott – who did more of a Dusty Springfield pointing-finger motion with a twist of the wrist – but I tried to use my own hand motions to describe the lyrics of the song. I wanted the audience to 'see' the words, as I was sure they couldn't hear us over the screaming. I also used other parts of my anatomy at the appropriate time to convey other meanings. From the first night, it felt completely natural for me, although I did miss playing my guitar.

Informally, we worked out new choreography for our act. Scott liked to tease the fans, and at the beginning of each show he'd walk up to the end of the stage, touching outreached hands, and playing around a little bit. I'd move around the stage a lot, dancing my ass off – maybe subconsciously creating a subterfuge for evading any aggressive fans. My battle plan never worked. The audiences always went wild, often pulling Scott and me off the stage. After one of the performances, I got the shit beaten out of me and ended up rolling around the dressing room floor in pain.

We learned the hard way what not to wear. One night in Dunstable, some fans got a hold of me from behind, and were pulling so hard on my polo-neck sweater, choking me, that I passed out. The next thing I remember was lying on the floor of the ballroom, with my road manager helping me up and trying to get me back to the dressing room while trying to protect me from the mob. I had to be carried back; all I had left on were the remnants of my trousers, which were in complete shreds: no shoes, no socks, no sweater, nothing but crushed ribs, bruises and bloody scratches. There are famous photos of Scott being mobbed by girls during that same show. From that night on, I always wore clothing that tore easily, but it wasn't always proof against the fans. My most embarrassing moment occurred at the Rawtenstall Astoria in 1965. Everything was ripped off of me, except for some shreds left on my waistband. Shirt, socks, shoes, shorts – all gone. It's a good thing nobody took that picture.

Our roadie always drove us back to the hotels after the shows; we stayed mostly in smaller places without any extra services. Most of the big hotels frowned on hosting pop or rock singers, with one outstanding exception: the Manchester Piccadilly. At the time, it was a super-modern hotel with a grill that was open until 3am. One of our biggest after-show challenges was finding hot food in the wee hours of the morning, so we often ended up at some Chinese or Indian joint, nothing fancy. We'd get back to the hotels, have our booze brought in by Bobbie (Scotch for Gary, Scotch and Coke for me, and vodka for Scott), or hang out at the bar, chatting up girls and talking about the show and stuff until we got tired. There was no television or radio in the middle of the night. Scott got tired earlier and would disappear, but Gary and I were the late-nighters so we usually shared one of the two rooms. The fans were starting to hang out at the hotels, and some even checked in to be near us.

In August, we began performing in ballrooms and clubs. Now there would be no orchestra pit as a barrier between us and the audience, and we'd have to play on stages that were on, or close to, the ground, with ineffective security. We were told over and over again by venue managers, 'We've had them all here,' as they reassured us that The Rolling Stones and other top groups who had played at their venue had encountered no problems. We were to learn over the next few months that, every time security gave us this line, we were in big trouble. At each performance, as soon as

the three of us began playing our instruments, the girls ran onto the stage and attacked us, ripping our clothes and hair, knocking us and everything in sight over, pulling out cables and wreaking havoc everywhere. We were never able to finish a show, nor could we hear each other or our band. By the end of each performance, we were a mess and so was the stage, night after night. We all suffered injuries. It was complete chaos and mayhem.

This became the pattern for all our ballroom appearances. The security people were simply unable to deal with the fans. It became an increasingly frightening situation, so we would devise quick escapes, cutting the show short after a song or two, running to our dressing room and locking the doors. Things got more and more out of control, and increasingly dangerous for both us and the fans. At a show in Belfast, we told the Irish police and security that we were really worried about getting past the fans and into the theatre, and we ended up following them through the fire escape that led up to the roof of our hotel, walking across the roof, climbing down an emergency ladder outside the building to another roof, then crossing that and clambering down to an alley. When we got to the second roof, we asked the police and security if they'd ever tried this route out before and they said yes, with The Rolling Stones. Gary asked them if it had worked, and one man cheerfully responded, 'No – but you'll be alright.' We finally arrived at the side door of the theatre, but the secret knock we had agreed on didn't get any response. The door wouldn't open, so one of the security guys had to go around the front and have somebody let us in. In the meantime we were sitting ducks, waiting outside the door for several minutes. Thankfully, it opened in the nick of time, as the perceptive fans had put two and two together and figured out that something was going on in the alley after they saw the security guy breathlessly running from there. We watched in terror as the screaming mob turned in our direction, getting closer and closer.

Despite such hair-raising incidents we kept showing up night after night, hoping for the best. Not once did we request the cancellation of any shows. If we never showed up for a date it wasn't our decision to cancel, but our managers', as at the Portsmouth Birdcage (we heard that a riot broke out over that). We just went where we were driven, and played where we were told to play. One night, at the Colston Hall in Bristol, the police had to be brought in because security was so inadequate; the show lasted less than 15 minutes. The problem at Colston Hall was lack of security, not a dispute over lighting, as has been falsely reported.

Our most horrific experience occurred at a ballroom on the south coast. The roadie told us there were handicapped people in wheelchairs in the front rows. We immediately warned the theatre people that these folks were vulnerable sitting there in the front, and told them what had happened at other shows. The theatre security people smugly informed us that these people had as much right to sit in the front rows as anybody else, ignoring our pleas and jeopardising our front-row audience. We were really concerned, and threatened not to go on until the people in wheelchairs were moved to a safer place. We waited it out, but the fans were getting loud and very restless, so we finally had to go out on stage. Just as we predicted, within five minutes girls were storming it, knocking over everybody and everything in sight. The next thing we saw was a sea of overturned wheelchairs, the wheels spinning ominously, and lots of people helplessly lying on the floor. We never could have imagined such an awful sight. We ran off the stage, panicked and traumatised over what we had just seen. That whole experience still haunts me. By the time we got in our car and headed back to the hotel, we were really pissed off. For us that was the last straw. The next morning, we called Maurice and Barry and told them we wouldn't play any more shows without proper security in place. The outcome was that, after they had contacted the upcoming venues and related the story, security was heavily beefed up.

Within a few weeks, we presented all the tracks we had chosen for the album to Johnny Franz. Scott was the spokesperson, as he was better able to describe exactly what we wanted. Starting with this album, without exception, we would always choose our own material, and approve the final mix of each track.

Johnny Franz hired Ivor Raymonde to be the arranger and musical director for the new album, and made sure Ivor knew what we wanted. For 'Make it Easy on Yourself', we actually used the same arrangement that was on Jerry Butler's album, but with a bigger orchestra and a more dynamic rhythm section. The most

noticeable difference was obviously Scott singing lead, and the addition of harmony, which I created and sang. The rest of the material mostly comprised covers of American pop songs; again, the basic original arrangements were enhanced with a bigger orchestra. Gary wasn't on the album; we were already signed to Mercury/Philips when he'd become involved. Neither Scott nor I played on it either. The decision was made to use studio players who had been working together for years as that would expedite things, and arrangement we were all quite happy with.

Of the other songs on the album, 'There Goes My Baby', was originally a big hit for The Drifters, and it suited our style perfectly. We chose 'First Love Never Dies' because of the poignant lyrics and beautiful melody. Scott wanted me to do 'Dancing in the Street', a terrific song that he thought suited my voice. We came up with 'Lonely Winds' because it was similar to 'There Goes My Baby', but more driving and uptempo. David Gates, who later became the lead singer of Bread, wrote 'The Girl I Lost in the Rain'. His publisher sent it to us, and it stood out from all the other material we had received. The three of us really liked it. Bob Dylan had written and sung 'Love Minus Zero', and, although it was different from everything else, it seemed to fit in. It's one of my favourites on the album. Scott needed a solo, so I chose 'I Don't Want to Hear it Anymore' for him, because I knew it would be perfect for his voice. 'Here Comes the Night' was more challenging than the other songs for both of us, but we had fun recording it. I chose 'Tell the Truth', a Ray Charles classic that I had always wanted to record.

Philips came up with the name of the album – *Take It Easy With The Walker Brothers* – a name we didn't care for, even though we didn't have any better ideas. The three of us agreed that we wanted a big, dramatic musical backdrop, but not in the Phil Spector style: we wanted our own unique sound. To achieve this, a massive orchestra was used, instead of overdubbing a small orchestra, which is what Spector did. Our approach would normally be a sound engineer's nightmare to record, but Peter Olliff was a master, and with this album he set the technical stage for our future recordings, helping us to enhance our signature sound. He overcame the challenges of the crammed studio space, and the orchestral sections leaking into each other, by using strategically placed directional microphones. Aside from Peter, Scott made the biggest contribution to the sound, offering specific ideas about what we wanted, with Gary and me making suggestions from time to time. We were with Peter in the control room as he got the orchestral sound balanced during the run-throughs.

Scott and I shared one microphone – a Neumann U47 – and felt a lot of pressure because we needed to carefully blend our spontaneous performance, as it wasn't feasible to use two microphones. Separate tracks weren't available for editing or alterations either, so if one of us made a mistake we had to start over again. We recorded three songs in daily four-hour sessions, balancing our sound after a few takes.

John Franz was always in the studio, listening to each track, and pointing out things such as a violin playing the wrong note. Some people have falsely concluded that John became a father figure to Scott, and collaborated with him to develop our 'wall of sound', but that is totally untrue. John and Scott had a mutually respectful relationship, and of course John admired Scott's vocal abilities, as did we all. The 'wall of sound' was a result of our ideas combined with Peter Olliff's technical expertise, and John Franz accommodating us; and of course, credit is due to Nick Venet and Jack Nitzsche for steering us in that direction with their arrangement of 'Love Her'.

I particularly liked Scott's version of 'I Don't Want to Hear it Anymore'. It was a very demanding piece and, during the recording, he shot me that look that I had come to know meant he was uncomfortable or nervous – it was a certain expression in his eyes that inevitably ended with a questioning look at the end of a performance, waiting for feedback from Gary and me. I would always keep supportive eye contact with him whenever this happened, aware of the pressure he felt. Gary did his famous vibe sending, concentrating very hard on Scott's performance, and hoping he was getting the positive vibes. It was comical and touching to see Gary so quiet and serious and intense. He had done the same thing for us when we recorded 'Love Her'. There were many times when I needed an encouraging nod from Scott, too, reassuring me that what I was doing was working. The three of us relied on each other for candid opinions, and we had our own unique interactive support system, which we each needed

whenever the pressure was on. We had an intense work ethic and did whatever it took to get the results we wanted, in the studio and on the stage. Above all, we had a strong musical bond. The professional relationship between Scott and me was crucial to the group's success. Whether recording or making music, musicians know when something good is happening. We had a relationship of mutual respect.

Neither Scott nor I would tolerate inadequacies in the other, whether in the recording studio or during live performances. When we went on stage to performed 'Make it Easy on Yourself' we didn't have the luxury of the sound equipment we had in the studio, so to recreate the record we had to know that we could replicate live exactly the same performance as we had on vinyl. The problem was, we couldn't hear each other on stage, so our performances were based on trust, as the person singing the harmony has to be able to rely on the other person. Scott never deviated from his original performance, and that enabled me to do my performance.

Professionally, Scott was always very focused, especially in the studio. It never mattered to him how long it took as long as he got the recording the way he could hear it in his head. But he was aware from very early on that, with his voice and reputation, the critics were just waiting to shoot him down.

By now I was married, so I spent time at home, rather than hanging out like I used to with Scott and Gary. There's no way of knowing what effect, if any, this had on us as a group. The three of us still spent more time together – touring, rehearsing, recording or discussing things after a session – than we did at home. If Scott and Gary felt that I had in some way abandoned them, they never mentioned it to me.

As time went on, I became increasingly aware of the pressure Scott was under. I blamed the press for this because the media focused primarily on him instead of the whole group, which made him feel more and more responsible for the success of our projects, which he wasn't comfortable with. The Walker Brothers' popularity was the sum of all their parts, but the press chose to ignore that. The truth is that none of us achieved anywhere near the success in our solo careers that we did when we were together. Scott ended up not wanting anything to do with the press because

they seemed to be setting him up for failure over and over again. It would be fair to say that, at the hands of the media, and so-called authors, the public has been subjected to many misrepresentations and lies about us. It really used to piss us off. Thankfully, though, there are still a few credible journalists and members of the media around.

After being released in August, 'Make it Easy on Yourself' reached Number 1 on 23 September 1965. I think Capable Management called to tell us the good news. That night, we were playing a show in either the Buxton Pavilion or the New Brighton Tower. We celebrated – wherever it was – with a lot of booze, as usual. I was elated, of course, and, knowing me, I probably reminded everyone that I had found the song. However, the excitement was short-lived when we realised we'd have to come up with another one to follow its success. There's a weird rumour that Scott ended up in some police cell around this time, but I never heard a thing about that – and I'm sure I'd know about it if he had. Our management bought us all gold bracelets inscribed with our names to mark our achievement. I kept this and all my other awards and memorabilia for years but, one day, my third wife got really angry with me and threw everything out.

CHAPTER 4

TOPPING THE CHARTS

CLOUDS OF MASS HYSTERIA
GARY WALKER

Having earned our first silver disc, The Walker Brothers were now one of the top groups in Britain, with our popularity rivalling The Beatles and The Rolling Stones. This was probably more thrilling for me than for the other two because the venture had been my idea. We would sit around and wonder how this had happened to us. Paul McCartney and I were in a club in London and talking about how incredible it all was. I asked him, 'Why do you think this is all happening?' and he looked me right in the eye and said, 'Do you believe in magic?'

Looking back, I realise how lucky we were. We were young and believed no one could touch us. As we became more successful, we decided that we would go with whatever we felt was right, and stick to it, regardless of any plans made by our record company, agents or management. When we recorded songs, Scott would fight for the overall sound we wanted and for what we needed to achieve it. Scott's perfectionism often led to very long and very costly recording sessions. This task naturally fell more on Scott than on John and me, but, if he needed backup, more musicians, more studio time or whatever, we would be there on his side to support him, and often he would find that our advice was good.

He did the same for us when we needed it; we were a pretty good team. Because Scott had a bit more power, being more the frontman than John and I were, the plans that our record company and management had for the future were more in his favour than ours, but for now they wouldn't jeopardise anything in case we all walked out.

Scott's musical gifts made him especially vulnerable. Of course, once the management and record company got hold of him their entire focus was on marketing him as a product because they knew they had a special talent on their hands. Naturally the hype got to Scott, magnifying his insecurities and making it even more difficult for anybody to get to know him. The only person I ever knew Scott take an instant liking to was Marc Bolan. Marc really made Scott laugh in a way that broke down all his barriers.

If we had an image, it was created by ourselves through our stage act and the clothes we liked to wear, not by our managers, our publicist or the record company. If anything, they would try to get us to dress more upmarket, but it wasn't my thing or Scott's, although John could be a bit of sharp dresser. I think we got the reputation for having a sexy image as a result of the wild dancing we did in our live shows. I remember that a lot of people thought we wore wigs but it wasn't true – we just dried our hair with a hairdryer that also straightened it at the same time, a look we brought from America that could have been mistaken for a wig. We had to hide our hairdryers from everyone, press and fans, in case they thought we were cissies or gay – men just didn't use hairdryers then. We called ourselves 'The Walker Sisters' behind closed doors.

We were the new guns in town, and we did spend a little too much. It seemed we had to buy everyone a drink or be called tight-assed like Rod Stewart, who has a reputation for taking it with him – just ask Elton John. It was lucky that we did spend a lot of money, because we were not going to get any later. I think we did what most young people who made some hard cash would have done. We bought fast cars, lived in some nice places, got good tables at restaurants. What more could three young men want at such an early age? We enjoyed it and felt we were truly blessed. Most people have to work all their lives to get to anywhere close to that point.

The press had a field day: they could not get enough of three good-looking boys who came from a different country and had new things to say. We only had to do a photo cover or article, and the paper would sell out. We were big business. Scott was increasingly portrayed as the intellectual one, and he was in fact interested in Jean-Paul Sartre and existentialism, Albert Camus, Ingmar Bergman and jazz. John and I found all that a bit – dare I say it? – boring.

As for the music we were recording at the time, it had to be in keeping with where we were at, with the big orchestra and romantic lyrics. It wasn't until we came to record our final album, *Nite Flights*, in 1977, that we could do whatever *we* wanted. Still, in the sixties, the songs we recorded and performed were chosen by the three of us, and – for a time at least – it didn't matter who or what anyone else said, as we seemed to get it right all the time. The main aim was to move the group forward and hope that we would remain famous without sacrificing our unique lyrics and music.

The makers of TV shows loved to have us as guests because we could sing live, whereas most of the groups would mime. But we found out that the rerecordings were not as good as they should have been, so Scott put a stop to the live singing. We wouldn't do prerecorded TV shows because we knew we would be performing with poor-quality sound, which is why so little TV footage of The Walker Brothers survives today.

A lot of TV directors were 'one camera, one shot' guys, and had we known that John and I probably wouldn't have shown up, as the one shot always focused on Scott. We complained about it, but it never changed anything. The only time they screwed up was when we were on a TV show in Vienna, and the camera remained on me most of the time – and I wasn't even singing!

A lot of the groups had their performances taped for use in different countries, but the acts never got anything for it while the TV companies made a fortune out of them. We were aware of this and whenever we did anything we signed an agreement that it would be wiped, another reason very few of our TV appearances survive.

Then there would be the dreaded interview, and they would ask us very youth-oriented and silly questions. That was our chance to have a bit of fun with the presenter. One regular question would be: 'If you weren't a pop star, what would have like to have been?' I would say, 'A gynaecologist or a taxidermist.' 'What's that?' would be the reply. 'It's stuffing birds.' You get the picture.

There were a lot of rumours circulating about us. Scott was supposedly arrested in Oxford Street, while another had Maurice King putting a tail on him for six months. It's also been said that he began to drink heavily at this time, but to my knowledge Scott was not arrested in Oxford Street and Maurice didn't put a tail on him (I was with him most of the time and we both would have spotted it). I have to admit, though, we did start our drinking a little early in the day and this would lead us on to the good times, which often didn't end until three or four in the morning.

The fan mania was intense and we were lucky to get in and out of the venues. Because of the rampant hysteria, leaving a theatre could create a dangerous situation, and sometimes the car might even bump one of the crowd.

Bobby Hamilton had taken over from Wiggie as our road manger. He was good at his job, and a bit of a crooked angel who got a kick out of selling our shirts to the fans and occasionally forging our signatures, which he would also flog.

One night Bobby brought the car to the stage door, where we managed to jump inside. We then had to drive around the corner from the theatre and up a hill to freedom. There were about 100 girls at the stage door, all of them hysterical. As we approached our turning, followed by screaming fans chasing the car, Bobby steered to the right but failed to see an oncoming bus, which had to make an emergency stop. At the top of the hill was a young policeman, with a dog, waving at us to stop. Bobby pulled the car to a halt, and the policeman said sternly, 'Do you realise that you cut up that bus, and that you could have caused a terrible accident?'

Bobby tried to tell the policeman what happened, as 30 or 40 girls were running towards us. I watched them getting closer, and Scott and John said to me, 'You'd better tell the policeman that it could get very exciting in the next couple of minutes.' I tried to talk to the policeman, who carried on ranting at Bobby. However, the dog had heard the threatening chants of the pack, and started to bark. On came the fans, eyes glazed with intent, hair blowing out of control. There was nothing that could stop them. Closer, closer

they came, louder and louder. You couldn't hear the dog any more. The policeman was minutes, seconds from catastrophe, yet he was still going on about the bus. Then they were on us. A human tidal wave came crashing over the policeman and the dog, followed by the thundering hammering of hands on our car.

'Get us out of here, Bobby!' we yelled, and as we began to pull away, I looked back to see no policeman or dog in site, just a police helmet lying at the feet of the mob. We had tried to tell him, Lord knows we tried.

When we played Blackpool Pier, Bobby had a few ideas as to how we should attack the problem of getting in and out of the theatre. John suggested that we pull up as close as we could to the pier entrance. 'Bobby, let us out and we'll run down the pier and into the stage door,' he said.

'It's not in the plan,' came the reply.

'Look,' John persisted, 'if we can't outrun those girls, we might as well jump off the pier, let alone run down it. They can only be about 14 or 16 years old, and they look fairly small.' Bobby capitulated.

We ducked down in the car as low as we could, so as not to be seen. We pulled to a halt to one side of the girls; it had been agreed that, on the key word – 'bollocks' – we would run for our lives. Everything happened in microseconds. As the door flew open, John was the first to go, then Scott, then me. It took a few moments for the girls to realise what was happening, but at least we'd had a head start. John was in the lead, followed by Scott and me very close behind. All we could hear was this thunderous, ear-piercing wall of hysterical sound from behind, and the stampede of pounding footfalls on the wooden-plank pier. At the time, we didn't realise how long the pier actually was, and how far we would have to run. It seemed like miles at the time, as the pier is over 1,600 feet long and we were wearing Anello & Davide boots, the ones they designed for The Beatles with two-inch heels. I couldn't resist looking behind to see how we were doing. To my shock, they were right behind us, which goes to show what people are physically capable of when driven by hysteria. We kept on running, with screaming to the left and right of us, onwards to the open stage door and out of the clutches of the autograph hunters from hell. John in particular amazed us with his turn of speed fleeing the fan mania. We christened him Runnolis Mausolus, a nickname he loved because he was into dinosaurs, and it stuck for about a month.

The dressing room conversations, unsurprisingly, were of the astounding marathon we had just run. There was just one problem: how were we going to get out? There would be a lot more fans this time. Bobby told us not to worry, he was working on another strategy.

When the show was over and it was time to leave, we could hear the fans outside through the walls of the theatre.

'What are the plans, then, Bob?' we asked.

'You're going to love this one. We're bringing around a cart that they use for taking equipment back and forth on the pier for the shows. You three will get in the cart and we'll take you to the car, which will be waiting at the end of the pier. The cart is enclosed and no one will see you, so you will be laughing.' It sounded good – for once. The cart pulled up at the stage door and we entered the enclosed tomblike chamber. It was very dark in there and a bit of a tight fit. We quickly realised that we didn't like tight dark places.

We could hear the fans outside the cart talking, and some banged on the side, as young people do. When we set off, the cart felt as if it were moving at a rate of one foot a week, and soon we were starting to lose it. Panic would have erupted if we hadn't made it back to the car when we did. Thankfully, Bobby was there, waiting to take us back to the hotel. One to us this time: zero for the fans.

On 16 October 1965 we played our last ballroom date at Grantham Drill Hall. As security in ballrooms was insufficient, it was announced that we would play only theatres in future. The safety aspect had increasingly become the main issue, and we decided that playing the bigger theatres would give us more control over the security arrangements. In reality, the only thing different was that in the theatres we had 2,000 or more hysterical fans instead of 500. You can't win.

A Deep Shade of Blue claims that Scott was now suffering from horrendous stage fright, and that the singer Jonathan King, a close friend, had to be summoned repeatedly to persuade him to go on stage. I don't know where this came from, as we actually had a lot of fun on stage, and if for any reason things didn't work as well as they should, then Scott would be more concerned than horrified.

We did BBC's *The Billy Cotton Band Show* one week, and it was so successful that we were asked back for a second week, then they asked us again for the next week! We were worried that we were becoming a little overexposed and should back out, which would have been difficult, because the Cottons, father and son, were very powerful in the TV industry, so we agreed to do the third show. On 22 October, during rehearsals, Scott swelled up like a balloon after taking a prescribed medicine containing aspirin, to which he was allergic. He looked real bad, so we said we couldn't do the show. It had to be scrapped and an angry Bill Cotton Jr vowed that The Walker Brothers would never appear on the BBC again. This unofficial ban lasted until 1975, when we appeared on *The Vera Lynn Show*.

That autumn, *Fabulous 208* flew us to Paris for a photoshoot for a special issue of the magazine devoted entirely to The Walker Brothers. The editor went with us and took us to all the famous landmarks: the Arc de Triomphe, Notre Dame and the Eiffel Tower. Scott and I skived off to the Louvre; it was the prospect of visiting this famous art gallery that had made Scott want to come along, otherwise he might not have done the shoot. We had expected, like so many others, that *The Mona Lisa* would be larger than life, but instead it was very small, something you could miss very easily.

In November 1965, our fourth single, 'My Ship is Coming In', backed with 'You're All Around Me', was released. The A-side was one of the few optimistic songs we recorded; it went to Number 2 in the charts. This was one of our favourite songs, and I think it just gets better with time.

December saw the release of our first LP, *Take It Easy With The Walker Brothers*, which reached Number 3 in the album charts. It kicked off with 'Make it Easy on Yourself' and also included 'Land of a Thousand Dances', which I talked Scott into recording, although it didn't really suit his voice. 'Love Minus Zero (No Limits)' was written by Bob Dylan, then an up-and-coming star. One of my favourites on the album is 'You're All Around Me', co-written by Scott and his good friend Lesley Duncan.

The authors of *A Deep Shade of Blue* claim that I 'threw a fit' over my lack of coverage on the Christmas edition of *Ready Steady Go!* Back then, the fans often complained that the other two got all the attention and that I was overlooked. As far as wanting the lion's share of the attention was concerned, that just didn't come into it: I wasn't bothered. What it did for me was create more fans who wanted to see more of me on TV, and repeatedly wanted to know how come they didn't get their wish. We would get lorry loads of letters about that, so Scott said he would change places and play the drums because the more famous we got the less he liked it.

As time went by John and I got less exposure during TV appearances than Scott because our management and record company had other ideas about the direction in which we were going, but I don't think Scott was aware of this at the time.

On 11 December 1965 I went to see The Beatles at the Astoria, Finsbury Park. John and his wife, Kathy, were with me. When we first arrived at the dressing room, we were ushered in to see The Beatles and say hello, and everything was fine, but The Beatles ignored Kathy and behaved as if she weren't there, not even saying hello to her. John looked at me, and we were both thinking that this was strange. So John decided to introduce Kathy, saying this was his wife, and the mood changed in a finger snap. Ringo was first out of the chair, saying what a pleasure it was to meet her, followed by the others paying similar respects. I suppose a lot of girls seized the opportunity of attaching themselves to people who knew The Beatles, just to get the chance to meet them, and they had got wise to it and didn't acknowledge the girls unless they were genuine. Anyway, they were now behaving like perfect gentlemen, and the mood changed for the better.

As I was talking to John Lennon, it seemed to me there was a kind of anxiety about him. When I went to the toilet next door, he came with me and asked me not to go back as he had he had something he wanted to tell me. I wasn't quite sure what was coming next. It transpired he had been told that Helen Shapiro was somewhere in the building and wanted to see him. However, he didn't want to see her, and said he would hide in the toilet until she had gone and George had given the all clear. He said he and Helen – she had then been the biggest female singer in Britain – had a thing going when they had toured together in 1963 and she was top of the bill. John and Paul had written a song called

'Misery' for their first album, and had given it to her to record, but EMI decided not to let her do it. So here we were, stuck in the toilet, waiting for George to show up and tell us that Helen had gone so that we could return to the dressing room. When we finally got there, we watched TV and tried to decide which club we would go to after the show.

When The Beatles went on stage, I sat on the floor in the wings, where I had a good view of what was going on. This was the first time I saw them play live, and I got some idea of what our fans must have felt when they watched us. Of course, no one could hear anything, and the girls tried to climb on the stage no matter what it took to get to their favourite Beatle. There was one girl who seemed to soar over the orchestra pit, past the three Beatles in the front and straight to Ringo, securing him in a wrestling hold that would have beaten anyone in the ring. It took two good-sized bodyguards to get her off; I would have guessed she was only about fourteen or fifteen, but girls like her had a strength that we always found unbelievable.

We undertook a five-day tour of Scotland in February 1966 that stretched the security guys to the limit. We stayed at the Caledonian Hotel in Edinburgh, which was located near the railway station, so getting into it was not too difficult. We were to spend two nights there and perform the following day at the Empire Theatre. We had a few interviews with the radio and press, and all went well. Unknown to us, the clouds of mass hysteria were forming for the coming show, which was to rock the town. The police suggested that we go into the theatre around five o'clock. We thought that sounded OK, until they told us they meant five in the morning. We were told that, because the fans were extremely enthusiastic – to put it mildly – for their safety and ours, extreme measures had to be taken. The streets around the theatre were roped off to keep people away from the stage door until near the performance time. The police took pride in handling the situation, but were surprised by the frenzy we were generating.

We entered the theatre as suggested, and found makeshift camp beds in case we got tired, so we could rest. The dressing room was full of food and if we needed anything else they would have it brought in. The show was to kick off at 7.30 that night. It was all smooth sailing until about 4.30pm, when we started to crack and one of us said, 'Why don't we have a wee dram?' As everyone knows, drinking in the late afternoon is fatal, but we developed some bad habits on the tour. Deep down, we were probably very nervous, and unfortunately drinking seemed to help. By the time we got on stage, we were speaking Scots! As always, once the curtain went up, the girls were screaming louder than the band was playing, and no one could hear anything, but we were all having a great time. And we would have to say that the Scottish fans were the loudest and most enthusiastic we'd heard.

The next stop was Glasgow, where we had another whole day to kill. This time, we started drinking a little too early in the afternoon, and by the time we got to go on stage we were like wax dummies from Madame Tussaud's. I was the first out, as always, followed by the other two. The crowd were deafening and you couldn't hear anything, thank heavens. John came on and was facing the wrong way; fortunately, he realised his mistake and turned around to face the audience. Scott followed; he was looking at me and laughing, which made me laugh too, and I thought we would never stop.

The crowd were getting louder and louder, and I thought they were going to call time on the show, but we got through about 20 minutes of it, after which I think they brought the fire curtain down and that was it. We were told that the ambulance crews treated 30 or so girls for hysteria and fainting, a typical number for one of our concerts. We did have a great time, however, and the people were very good to us. Back at the hotel, we went to the bar and I noticed that, on the shelves behind the bartender, there were at least 50 different whiskies. I asked the him, 'Has anyone ever had all those?' And he said, 'Yes, but she didn't finish the last two.' Loved that Scottish humour.

On 11 February 1966, backed by a group called The Vibrations, I released a solo single, 'You Don't Love Me/Get It Right' on the CBS label. The record was produced by Scott and his friend from Hollywood John Stewart, and it reached Number 26. Our management and the record company wanted me to capitalise on our popularity and release the single, saying it would be good for

business. I picked 'You Don't Love Me', which I'd heard a group play in a Hollywood club, and liked. My making solo recordings didn't cause any conflict because Scott and John were always behind me, and it also gave Scott a chance to produce, which he really liked doing.

At last, I could do my own thing: write, sing, play or take my clothes off if I wanted. I was always a rock'n'roll person and didn't go for a lot of the stuff that we did as a group.

When I started to make my own records, I told Scott that I didn't like recording. I felt I had a terrible voice, and because he and John had these brilliant voices, I didn't like to sing and show myself up.

'You have a great voice,' Scott said. 'All it is, is that people have to get used to it. A lot of people think I have an incredible voice, which is true – only kidding! Do you think, for example, that Neil Young has a good voice, or Tom Waites?'

'Yes, I do,' I said.

'And a lot of other people think they have great voices, and some really like them and maybe hate mine. It's the sound, the tone, and what you're saying that comes across. Once people get to hear you and know what you sound like, and hopefully like it, you'll be OK. After that, they'll always know it's you, because there's only one of you, and that's the way you sound.'

This reassurance helped me out, and impelled me to move further forward, but I was still nervous. However, Scott let me do whatever I wanted in the studio, and would sit there and not say a word. This, of course, was an artist's dream, as most producers would try to do what they wanted. But Scott just let me go with what I was hearing in my head, focusing on the originality of what I could do. He told me that I had a good feel and a style of my own; the tracks would have my own stamp on them. I felt much better after that, and the big bonus was that my single became Ringo Starr's favourite record. I never got over that.

Around this time Scott told us about some rumours that Andrew Oldham, who managed The Rolling Stones, wanted to manage us, too. Changing managers was fraught with difficulties: you had to be careful because you could end up with a succession of lawsuits, the last thing you wanted, so didn't pursue the matter.

Brian Epstein certainly expressed an interest in managing the group and, thanks to Brian Sommerville, who had worked for

Epstein and was responsible for the publicity that boosted The Beatles' success, we were able to make a connection.

We had several meetings at Epstein's London office near Green Park Station. I remember that it was dark, with the blinds half closed, which felt quite intimidating. The only time Scott and I had been in a gloomy room like this was when we'd had a few late nights and a worse hangover than Gig Young.

Epstein was well groomed, dressed very nicely in a dark pinstripe suit with tie and shirt; he had what Scott and I called the 'Savile Row' look, after the famous street of upmarket tailors in London. He came across as a quiet man, almost to point of shyness, yet he put us at ease at once. He said he liked the group, having been to see us at a few shows, and said he'd like to work with us and see us move forward, which was very flattering. However, after many late-night conversations, Scott, John and I decided that, because Brian's first and foremost loyalties were to The Beatles, they would always be number one with him, while we needed someone with that same commitment to us. I still wonder what would have happened to the group if we had been able to go with Epstein, and where we'd be now.

During the period we were meeting with Epstein, I recorded 'Get It Right' with Scott producing. If you listen carefully to the instrument solo in the middle of the song, you can hear Scott say, 'BE', our name for Epstein. My path would cross Brian's again, but that belongs to a later chapter.

A couple of weeks after my record came out, on 25 February, our biggest single, 'The Sun Ain't Gonna Shine Anymore', backed with 'After the Lights Go Out', was launched; it went to Number 1 and stayed there for four weeks. Philips gave Scott a big TV set to mark the occasion, while John and I just got bracelets with our names on.

On 9 March 1966 – by coincidence my birthday – a man called George Cornell entered the saloon bar of the Blind Beggar pub in London's East End, ordered a light ale, then sat down at the bar to drink it. Around 8.30pm he was approached by Ronnie Kray, one of the notorious Kray twins. Kray walked towards Cornell, took out a nine-millimetre Mauser and calmly shot him once in the forehead, just above his right eye. Cornell slumped against a

nearby pillar, the bullet having apparently passed straight through him, although he was in fact fatally wounded. Moments earlier, the barmaid, who was later to become a key witness in the trial, had put a new record on the jukebox – 'The Sun Ain't Gonna Shine Anymore' The weird thing was that, after Cornell was shot, the record stuck on the word 'anymore . . . anymore'. Again, our record made the headlines, but it was publicity we could have done without.

In March, we undertook a week of cabaret at Stockton's plush Tito Club, where we received the biggest ovation in the club's history. It was an experimental idea suggested by our management, but Scott and I were upset with the idea of our playing in cabaret – I more so – because we were not a cabaret group. Management, however, were pushing us into doing that type of show, and there can be little doubt that this was to be the direction they wanted Scott to go later. On the bright side, I did a drum solo and got a marvellous reception. Scott would sometimes tell me that he'd forgotten how good I was.

That month, I was 'kidnapped' and ransomed by students of Harrow Technical College for Rag Week. I agreed to do it, and it was arranged that I would meet them at a secret location and go with them to get the ransom. It all went fine and would have been a lot more fun if I could have stayed on with them at the college afterwards, but I had other commitments.

On 26 March our first package tour (with Roy Orbison and Lulu) opened at the Finsbury Park Astoria in London. It was manic. Wherever we stayed, the fans were breaking through back doors and climbing in bathroom windows. It got to the stage where, when we returned to hotels for the second time, the staff would say, 'You'll be on the fourth floor, and you'll be the only ones on the fourth floor.' They insisted that we remain on the assigned floor and not go anywhere else, with all our food and drink sent by room service. At a lot of the hotels the girls who cleaned the rooms and had keys would come in early, trying to get a peek at us in the nude. I even had them pull the covers off me when I was still half asleep.

We were delighted to have a whole floor to ourselves, where we could string a net across the hall and play badminton. The hotel manager even joined in to make up the teams, and we had Scott, me and the manager on one side and John, Bobby and the bar girl on the other. We won! Increasingly, though, we were becoming more and more isolated from the world. Young as we were, I don't know how we got through it. We survived, I believe, because we were pretty grounded and just didn't fall for all the hype.

At Birmingham, John was badly hurt. As we approached our hotel Bobby told us that when we left the car the three of us should run straight to the centre door and not stop for anything. The hotel staff would be ready to receive us. We could see that there was a crowd of 50 or 60 screaming fans waiting for in front of the hotel, but Bobby told us not to worry because he had talked to them and everything would be fine. It wasn't.

'Remember,' he said, 'go straight in. Don't stop.' The car drew up to the drop zone, and the door was quickly opened. The first to make for the safety of the hotel entrance was John, because he was the fastest runner. In seconds we realised Bobby had been far too optimistic. The fans were like caged animals. You knew that, if you moved a fraction too fast, they would start a riot. They had glazed eyes. If you looked into them it was frightening, like looking into the eyes of predatory lions and tigers in the zoo.

I was second out of the car, Scott last. John was racing ahead of me through the press of screaming fans trying to grab him, but unfortunately he was running at such a rate that when he went through the hotel door, where there were three or four descending steps, he ran straight forward in midair, plunged down and smashed his head. There was blood everywhere. I was right behind John and I saw it all. But the fans were after me too. I could see a wheelchair ramp to my left and made my escape that way, avoiding the stairs. I ran past the fans, turned quickly to the left and hurried down the ramp to the bottom, then saw two blue eyes widening in an elderly face framed by blonde hair. It was Marlene Dietrich, the movie star. I smashed into her with some force, but luckily she twisted to the right, dulling the impact, yet she still went down. I glanced over my shoulder to see that people had come rushing to her aid, then disappeared through an open door, thinking the police would be coming to take me away for assault. Nothing of the sort happened, and I heard later that although Miss Dietrich didn't know who we were she said she found the whole incident very exciting. As for Scott, I still don't know how he got in.

Fortunately, although John was badly hurt, he didn't miss a performance. The girls were still screaming and yelling as Bobby was helping him to a chair and calling for a doctor.

On another occasion, John hit a girl of 15 in the face. She was hysterical and had got hold of his hair. He could not get her to let go, so he slapped her hard to calm her. She went, 'Ooh!', started laughing and finally let go. The fans would always grab us by our hair whenever they got close enough. As things got tougher, and our hair began to disappear, we came up with a solution: we wore motorbike helmets. Later, we would find that these had a major disadvantage, because the hysterical fans rained down blows of retribution on their surface.

On the last night of the tour, it was traditional to do whatever you wanted, within reason. This would terrify the promoter, as he didn't know what was to come, and safety was the most important thing. There was an infamous incident when Tony Marsh was compèring a show with The Rolling Stones, and on the last night he pulled his pants down, exposing his bum to the Stones and the audience; he never worked again. But we just had a lot of fun: on 2 May, when our tour ended in Coventry, Scott appeared on stage riding a bike, John was on piano and I did lead vocals. It was probably one of our best shows.

Around this time Tower Records issued an album of old recordings by Scott and John Stewart as The Dalton Brothers, on which they were incorrectly described as 'original members of The Walker Brothers'. I'd had calls from my dad in America, telling us that one of the record companies was releasing this as a Walker Brothers album and warning us that it would be bad for our careers. Tower Records were just trying to cash in on our fame, which would have been detrimental to us. We were going to sue them, but because John Stewart was a good friend of Scott's we didn't go ahead. It was fortunate that this record didn't impact on our success in any way.

According to *A Deep Shade of Blue*, Scott, 'the great perfectionist', began complaining about his workload and the increasingly hedonistic lifestyle that John and I were supposedly leading. 'I was working like a badger,' he is supposed to have said. 'The other guys were just enjoying things.' If he had said something like that, it must have been taken out of context. We were all working like badgers, and it would be equally right to say that Scott was enjoying a nice lifestyle. We were no more hedonistic than any pop stars of the time, and not at all when we were touring and losing eight pounds in weight each a night on stage, putting up with Spartan conditions in theatres and freezing hotels – once I had to heat my bed with a hairdryer. I didn't spend huge sums of money – I wasn't given any. My flats were paid for by the management, and they gave us all a salary as they kept control of the purse strings.

We would often eat out at the Lotus House, a Chinese restaurant on the Edgware Road near Marble Arch, or at La Loggia, an Italian place on the Bayswater Road. Barry McGuire, who had a hit with 'Eve of Destruction', was sometimes in there, and Cliff Richard. Cliff was alright, very clean and young-looking. Whenever we did *Top of the Pops* he was there, with four or five singers, and they would rehearse for about two hours – Cliff had an obsession with rehearsals.

When we did the TV show *Sunday Night at the London Palladium* he was just the same. Cliff's people got scared because they knew we were going to get more screams than their artist. So they put about 40 girls in the upper circles of the Palladium to scream at him, but Brian Sommerville knew that outside there were 80 girls waiting for us, which was fine. Anyway, Brian went out and opened the door, and they came running down the aisle. It was all captured on film for the show but when it was televised, on 12 June 1966, that had been cut and all we could hear was the screaming for Cliff. He was right in there with Bernard Delfont and Lew Grade because he was doing just what they wanted: an album, then a summer season, and so on. I don't think it mattered to us: it was just kind of a shock that they did that.

The media scrutinised everything we did, although a lot of the things that were printed about us were just made up. We were rarely out of the press. It got so that we were accused of believing our own publicity, but we were too down to earth to fall into the trap of not being able to distinguish what was real and what was not. You don't believe in your own publicity when you are the one making it.

We didn't try to manipulate the press, and it was never Scott's

intention to create an air of mystique about the group. He just didn't like doing any press and on occasions it got a little too silly, being asked what was his favourite toy, or what colour socks he wore. To be fair, he did do a lot of interviews, as did John. At one time we all were doing something every day.

That summer, John, Kathy, Barry Clayman and I went to Marbella, Spain and stayed at the Don Pepe Hotel, a new hotel that was the place to go, and they wanted the top people to be seen there.

Susan and I had continued dating and became closer, although we were still hiding from the ever-prying media machine. But things went wrong after I promised her that she would be able to come along on this holiday and then discovered that she couldn't: the management wouldn't pay for her to go, and I couldn't afford it. I don't know if she was more hurt or mad.

Scott was meant to come but refused to fly and decided to drive there. I can't remember if he ever made it. Meanwhile, back in England, Susan was cheating on me, either to get even or just to make me go berserk, and when I returned we had a horrible row that lasted for days. I just couldn't see how she would cheat on me, Gary Walker. How many girls would have given their left arms to be with me? If I had been just Gary Leeds, it wouldn't have been so bad. I left her, saying I would never have anything to do with anyone who cheated on me. The truth is, I'd also cheated on Susan, but that seemed to be OK when I did it.

I wasn't happy just breaking up with her: I was going to broadcast the truth on a TV show called *A Whole Scene Going* that that stared Barry Fantoni, Mike Quinn and Wendy Varnals, who later became my girlfriend. When Mike asked me, 'What do you want to talk about?' I replied, 'Have you ever been cheated on?' As the camera panned in to a close-up of my face, I described the cheating incident to the whole of England, concluding by saying that I would never trust any girl again. It was one of the best shows in the series and got a lot of letters. The funny part was that when I was going around with Wendy she kept telling me that I should get over it as it happens to everybody at one time or other. But, all the time we were together, she was seeing Bruce Johnston of The Beach Boys. I miss Wendy; the last I heard was that she lives in America. Susan and I kept in touch, but not very often.

In May, I released a second single for CBS, 'Twinkie Lee'/'She Makes Me Feel Better', which reached Number 26. I felt the A-side was a bit weak, but later it became something of a cult record, which typified the pop music of the time. It has been compared to the songs of The Blues Brothers and has that kind of energy.

On 28 May 1966, we went to West Germany for club and TV dates, then to Copenhagen, where we were reportedly refused entry to a hotel that the Stones had trashed the previous week. Not true – this was the kind of story that attached itself to all the famous groups at that time. In fact, in order to ensure that we would not to be refused entry to the hotel, the Dutch record company took the whole top floor.

One time that the Walkers went to do TV in Amsterdam, we stayed in the Marriott Hotel, and Scott and I were drinking in the lounge. There were a few girls staying in the hotel, and when Scott and I asked some of them if they wanted a drink, they joined us at our table. As Scott and I continued down the yellow brick road to happiness, we asked some more girls to enter our parlour for drinks. They must have thought us mad. In the end, there were at least 20 of them at the tables we'd pulled over to accommodate them all. The hotel must have loved us. We did hear later that the record company was very upset with us about the cost of it all, but Scott said, 'What's the problem? They got a Number 1 record out of us.'

Scott was going out with a model, Irene Dunford, at the time. Irene and Scott were very good friends. They kept themselves pretty much to themselves and I didn't get to talk to Irene until long after they stopped seeing each other. I found her very nice and very humorous, which I hadn't been aware of when she was with Scott.

In June 1966, back in Britain, we recorded the EP *I Need You*, with Reg Guest as musical director for the first time. Some believed 'I Need You' should have been the next single, but I fought for '(Baby) You Don't Have to Tell Me' because following 'The Sun . . .' was going to be impossible, so I felt we needed something different and more upbeat. *A Deep Shade of Blue* asserts that Guest 'realised an inescapable truth . . . Scott's persona had grown to such an extent that John and Gary were little more than passengers . . . In the studio, The Walker Brothers were as

manufactured a group as The Monkees proved to be six months later.' Guest is even quoted as saying that he never saw me play drums. None of this is true. We were never a manufactured group as we'd evolved to become one of the top draws in Hollywood, then in the UK – and indeed the world. In the studio, Scott and John had the responsibility, and I of course put in many ideas – Scott wouldn't do anything without first asking my opinion. Reg Guest never came to our shows or watched our TV appearances, so obviously he never saw me play drums.

The EP was released on 8 July, along with our new single, '(Baby) You Don't Have to Tell Me'/'My Love Is Growing'. We all liked the song, but a lot of people weren't so keen, and of course it didn't do as well as 'The Sun . . .'. Perhaps if we had recorded another song in the kissie-smoochie Walker Brothers style it might have been a hit. As it was, it only reached Number 13. But we were still on top so it was felt that there was room to cope with that.

In fact, at the time we were one of the top three groups in Britain. On the day our single was released, a whole edition of *Ready Steady Go!* – now sadly wiped – was devoted to The Walker Brothers. We performed (among other things) The Beatles' 'We Can Work it Out'. It was one of the best TV shows of us ever filmed, thanks to the efforts of the show's producer, Vicky Wickham (who later became Dusty Springfield's manager), and director Michael Lindsay-Hogg.

We were also among the leading acts in the *New Musical Express* polls, and that summer we performed at the *NME* Poll Winners' Concert at Wembley. We were now more popular than The Beatles: our fan club was certainly bigger at this point. There was a rumour that we topped the Best Group poll and that Brian Epstein paid *NME* a large sum of money to put The Beatles at the top instead, because the concert was to be shown in the USA, and it would not have looked too good for The Beatles to come second, after all the time and money that had been spent on making them the biggest band in the world. How true that was I don't suppose we will ever know. We came in at number three after the Rolling Stones.

We were increasingly enjoying some fame and fan adulation in America; 'Make it Easy on Yourself' had reached Number 16, and

'The Sun Ain't Gonna Shine Anymore' got to Number 13. But, after coming to England in 1965, we never played live in our homeland, despite having hit records and featuring in the top ten in fan polls. I was aware that Scott had some problem over the draft, but not that it was a reason for our not making it big in America. We were offered a slot on *The Ed Sullivan Show*, but turned it down because we wanted an offer for three shows, the same as The Beatles had got. They came back with two, and they were so keen to have us that they would have sent a film crew here to film us, but we turned that offer down as well. As far as I know, had we got the three-show deal, Scott would have gone, draft worries or not.

I knew I had arrived when I bought my Marcos sports car. John got one too: mine was red and his was blue. *Rave* magazine featured us racing around Brands Hatch, and I did it faster in 54 seconds. John came close to crashing.

When John and I made a public appearance at Brands Hatch that summer, we flew there by private plane. There were quite a few photographers waiting, each trying to get that special shot, and one tried a little too hard and backed into the propeller blade. The pilot went wild, but the guy was miraculously not injured, and just carried on as if nothing had happened. We heard a thump, but we weren't aware at the time what had happened. Brian Sommerville was much more shaken up than we were, but mainly because, going over Brands Hatch, I had put the plane into a spin and pulled the nose up – I was just showing off!

That summer, for a publicity stunt, I sat in a cage in Chessington Zoo dressed up in a gorilla suit. It was one that had been used in movies and really looked like the real thing. I waited in the cage to see how people would react to my picking up a magazine and pretending to read it, or pouring some water into a glass. Most of the time I sat in the corner while the baboons next door went absolutely crazy and tried to break down the door between us. I did get a little nervous about that.

Meanwhile, a crowd had gathered and stood staring at me, and some of the children were saying, 'That's not a real gorilla!' and their parents would reply, 'Don't be stupid, of course it's real.' But the children kept insisting that I was a fake. I was in there for about half an hour, during which the crowd got bigger, and I began to

wonder how I was going to get out. The only way was to exit through the door where the people were standing, then the zookeeper could grab me and take me away. So I got up, pushed the door open and jumped. At that moment there was obviously no doubt in anybody's mind that I was for real because suddenly the 30 or 40 people who had gathered were gone. The zookeeper hurried me off to the toilets, which were the only place we could go. Anyway, it was a very successful exercise; it reminded me of the werewolf incident, and it made the centre page of the *Daily Mirror*.

In August, there were reports that we were planning to star in a movie. Scott and I would have loved to do some shooting and directing, and John would have enjoying starring roles, but although we were we offered a few film deals nothing ever came of them.

That month, when Scott was found unconscious in his gas-filled flat, there were widespread reports that he had tried to commit suicide. According to *A Deep Shade of Blue*, he had been labouring long and hard on the next album and was under stress. After he himself hinted at a 'personal problem' some papers claimed that Irene Dunford had either dumped him or turned down his marriage proposal, when in reality they just drifted apart. It was also rumoured that the attempt had something to do with Jonathan King, who has been described as Scott's greatest friend in the mid-sixties; they went on holiday together after Scott left hospital.

This so-called suicide attempt was, I think, just another publicity stunt to increase record sales. I was under the impression that Scott was too strong a person to do that kind of thing, or maybe I don't know him as well as I thought I did. He did work hard on the album, and wouldn't let anything slip, which can be a lonely road to travel. The bottom line is that if he had wanted to kill himself he *would* have done so because he was a perfectionist.

During the mid-sixties, I shared a house with Graham Nash of The Hollies. Graham and I had met in 1965 when The Walker Brothers and The Hollies were on the same TV show. We hit it off right away and became good friends. The fans would gather outside and wait to catch a glimpse of Graham or me; they would ask for autographs and sometimes we would chat with them. This didn't go down too well with the neighbours because the crowd, which sometimes numbered up to 30 teenage girls, was very noisy and boisterous. The police were regularly called, and would take the girls away in their Black Marias or scare them off. Usually they would run off in all directions at the sight of a police car, but ten minutes later they'd all be back again. We eventually had to move on because the neighbours got up a petition demanding that we leave.

Graham and I would often meet up with John Lennon or Paul McCartney in the various clubs we frequented: the Ad Lib, the Scotch of St James, the Speakeasy, the Cromwellian or the Bag O' Nails. These places opened about ten at night, and stayed open until about three or four in the morning. We would stay in the clubs until closing time, go home and sleep all day, and then get up the next night and go to another club. That was the routine, because we did all our work at night – writing a tune, rehearsing or whatever we had to do. You always knew that the next tour would be coming around soon, and that that would be the end of the clubs for a while.

The clubs also became part of the show routine. You would arrive at the theatre, fight your way in, do the show, fight your way out, go to a club, get drunk, meet girls, then go home. It got to the stage where I thought it would all be in our contracts.

We went to clubs to get drunk and get women – and they all looked pretty good after a bottle! Scott and I would meet lots of girls in clubs, and because we were famous they would talk and flirt with us all the time. If we liked one in particular, we would invite her back to our flat.

None of us had any problem in pulling girls; in fact they came onto us. That reversal of the traditional roles threw you off. It didn't feel right, but it did make us appreciate what girls go through. The other issue was that the girls seemed to be after us for what we were rather than who we were. Even so, we didn't look a gift horse in the mouth.

Some girls would come up to you and say, 'You're so famous, I bet you can have anything or anyone you want – but you can't have me.' I'd say, 'That's not true,' and a big argument might ensue. It would end with our retreating to the bar. Other girls

were too scared to come near us, furtively watching us instead. The last thing we wanted to project was that we were big, show-off stars – through it all, we remembered our manners and treated girls with respect. Unwittingly I was building on my reputation as the 'Casanova of Pop', which was increasingly getting out of hand, but it was my own fault. When we went to a restaurant, and the waitresses recognised us, I would ask them to come to the flat. 'Leeds, you old Casa!' Scott would tease. You get the picture . . .

It got worse. Fans would push nude photographs of themselves through our letterbox, hoping to capture our attention. All those stories about girls wanting us to sign their boobs and bums were true. We only stopped doing it because we started to get embarrassed, and someone had said that, if they got cut, it might cause blood poisoning. Well, that's what we told them. A lot of the time we would get panties through the letterbox, and girls would also throw them on stage during our shows; occasionally there were even Y-fronts in the pile. In our flat, we had a little room that wasn't used for anything, so we kept all the panties in there, along with the Gonks (egg-shaped soft toys that were all the rage in the sixties). The Gonks we gave to children's homes, but try giving used panties away! In the end, when the security around us tightened up, my Casanova nickname became redundant, as we hardly got to meet or see any girls.

Of course, there were a lot of recreational drugs on the scene. Everybody was experimenting at that time and, if you didn't try anything, you'd be thought really uncool. We never got into any of the real heavy stuff, and anyone who was smart enough didn't need it, but we all smoked a few joints. Scott, a nonsmoker, didn't like it because it burned his throat, so he gave it up after a while. The stuff just made me laugh and feel hungry. In America, the dangers of harder drugs had been repeatedly rammed home to us, and so we avoided them. The warnings were justified, as I've seen friends die or lose their personalities as a result of drug abuse.

I smoked about 40 a day at this time; I had never smoked or drunk alcohol until I was about 22. In England everybody was smoking and drinking and, as The Beatles did it, we felt we should follow suit. I often drank too much Scotch, but was young enough to handle it. This lifestyle became so nocturnal that I wouldn't see the sun for days. It was an awful feeling – you feel ill when you get no daylight – and I didn't like it at all, so I ended up setting the alarm to get myself back to normal.

In 1966, rumours began that The Walker Brothers might split. In May 1967, *Melody Maker* referred to the 'constant air of insecurity' that had surrounded the group over the past 12 months. It was just press speculation.

On 3 September 1966, our second album, *Portrait*, was released and hit Number 3 in the album charts. I wouldn't agree with the critics who called this The Walker Brothers' finest album; that's a nice opinion, but I prefer *Nite Flights*. The opening song on *Portrait*, 'In My Room', is one of my favourite tracks. There was almost a problem with 'People Get Ready', as Curtis Mayfield would not normally allow anyone who wasn't black to record his songs, but he made an exception for us, which we found very flattering. 'Summertime' was a standard and I think Scott and John were showing off when they did these kind of songs because they found it so easy, and did them so well.

That September, we returned to Paris to play at the Alhambra with Bill Haley and His Comets and The Spencer Davis Group. I couldn't get over being there with Bill because, when I was around 15 or 16, I had roller-skated to his 'Rock Around the Clock' at the local park in Sunland-Tujunga in California. But, when I met him, he seemed old enough to be my grandfather, and didn't really have much to say to me; in fact, I don't think he even knew who we were. I was very disappointed, as I would have loved to have told him how I'd admired him when he was younger.

In September, we released another single, 'Another Tear Falls'/'Saddest Night in the World'; disappointingly, it reached only Number 12. There were the first murmurings of criticism that The Walker Brothers' records were becoming too repetitive. Keith Altham at *NME* blamed John Franz for this, saying he had had too much control for too long, and stated his belief that Philips' 'reluctance to change a winning formula hastened the group's demise'. I would agree with that. I think they thought, 'Why fix it if it's not broken?' I'm sure that was our management and record company's only concern. We were always aware of that, but we also thought that one day we would be able to change our style.

That, however, would not happen for many years. I guess that John Franz did have too much control, but I still maintain that we three had the final say, although maybe he influenced us more than we realised.

Just prior to our second package tour, Scott had his hair cut very short. It could have been a clever move to draw more attention to himself while maintaining the image of the loner who didn't want publicity. Scott was good at scene stealing. If John and I were having individual colour photos, he would have black and white, as on the *No Regrets* album. A nonsmoker, he would go to the extent of posing with a cigarette. Whether instinctive or totally planned, it was a good way of self-promotion.

Between 1 October and 6 November 1966 The Walker Brothers played 33 shows on a UK tour. We didn't tour 'out of greed', as Scott was quoted as saying, but because we needed the money, since we never got given enough of it by our managers; and, of course, we did it for our fans – on my part at least. Also on the bill were Dave Dee, Dozy, Beaky, Mick and Tich, The Troggs and Clodagh Rogers. It's not true that Clodagh Rogers walked out after a row with Scott because he refused to allow The Quotations to back her; he would certainly have let them play for her.

One night I was shattered and Dozy gave me some tabs – uppers – to combat the tiredness. Did they have an effect on me! When I went out on the stage to play the drums, the only one who could have competed with me would have been Buddy Rich. There wasn't anything I couldn't do on those skins. Everyone was saying that that was the best they ever saw me play. But I was awake for almost two days and never took anything like that again.

At Chester, we escaped from the ABC Theatre disguised as policemen, and at Ipswich Gaumont on 6 November, the last night of the tour, we were dissuaded from doing something startling on stage to surprise our fans, which artists often did at the end of a tour. We hadn't planned anything definite, but the theatre management were scared to death that we would do something terrible, so we allowed ourselves to be talked out of it, to everybody's great relief.

SOUGHT-AFTER AND SUCCESSFUL
JOHN WALKER

After the short tour, I returned home to my flat in Regent's Park to find that the fans had found out where I lived and were waiting outside to congratulate me on the Number 1 record. The crowds grew and seemed to come and go in shifts – there were always people waiting outside, day and night. Finally I had to ask my upstairs neighbour, Phil, to take my dogs, Scotch and Brandy, outside for their walks.

It became increasingly difficult for us, and our neighbours, to move about freely. Even so, none of the neighbours ever complained; in fact, they were all very accommodating and seemed a bit amused at having an American pop star in the building, and all the attention that went along with it. There was very little parking, so my Bentley was usually parked outside on the street. Although the fans would leave notes on the windscreen, I was surprised – and very grateful – that there was never any damage to the car. I thought that was very cool.

I became more and more cautious and cunning when leaving the house. For one thing, I couldn't just spontaneously go outside without feeling the pressure to be the pop star that the fans expected me to be. Just to get a pack of cigarettes, I always shaved, did my hair and put on some cool gear before stepping outside. I quickly learned how to dart out to my car, barely nodding, or giving just a few waves so that, by the time the fans got organised, I was gone. Of course, both they and I knew I had to come home at some point, so I always stayed out very late – till at least two or three in the morning – and by the time I got home, the waiting fans were either sound asleep or hesitant about making a loud scene.

The biggest challenge at this point was grocery shopping. People would follow me around as I tried to buy food at my favourite shops in St John's Wood. The store owners and managers were polite, but definitely annoyed with the mobs that descended upon them but never bought anything. I finally solved the problem by getting the telephone numbers of the fishmonger, butcher, baker, greengrocer – everyone – and calling them with my orders. I would make appointments to pick up the food, double parking outside each place, then running in, grabbing the bags, and paying for

everything by practically throwing the money at the cashier. I was in and out like a flash.

Scott, Gary and I handled the fan situation pretty much the same way, except that after a year or so Scott was less interested in signing autographs, and avoided the whole thing as much as possible.

We had quite a team of people working with us at Capable Management, whose London offices were at 185 Bickenhall Mansions, right off Baker Street. The fan club, run by a woman named Alex, was also in this office, but I never got involved with it that much. It was impossible for the three of us to read every piece of mail that came in – and it would have been unfair just selecting a few to respond to from time to time. It was an all-or-nothing situation there, so we left it in the hands of our staff. However, we did read all the fan letters that came to the venues where we were playing, and we signed all the autograph books and fan pictures that were delivered to our dressing room. The letters were very complimentary, enquiring if we would stay in the UK, what songs we were working on, what our future plans were, and so on. We really appreciated the support that we got.

All the money that we earned went directly to our managers, Maurice King and Barry Clayman. We never actually saw any of it, didn't think about it at the time, and never questioned Maurice or Barry about our finances. I didn't have a bank account, but had accounts everywhere I shopped and ate out – with the bills going directly to Capable Management for payment. We never knew how much cash we each had at our disposal because we were happy and busy, and everything seemed to be taken care of. When any of us needed a larger sum of money we had to pick it up at the office.

Gary and I were described in *A Deep Shade of Blue* as 'the new lords in London's pop aristocracy' who were 'spending money as if there was no tomorrow'. That book also claims that I bought a Lamborghini, for example – it's all completely untrue. I was too restricted to have the freedom just to go out shopping whenever I wanted to. The most expensive item I bought was my Marcos sports car.

Looking back, it was completely out of character for me to not get involved in the financial side of things, or at least not to insist on an accounting of our income and where the money went. After all, Scott and I had just come from Hollywood – otherwise known as 'rip-off city' – and were overly wary of scams, yet here we were, unquestioning. Later, sadly, we would find out that, like other artists in the sixties, we never saw all the money that we were due.

Arthur Howes was our primary promoter. The three of us always commented about how un-English Arthur looked. He actually reminded us of an American Indian with a crew cut. Bobby Hamilton became our second roadie, replacing John Wolfe. Bobby was a heavy-set guy with a wonderful sense of humour. The three of us really loved him. After several months of working with him, we decided we needed our own car for the gigs. Much to the dismay of our managers, Scott, Gary and I asked Bobby what *he* wanted, and he said he'd always wanted a Mark X Jaguar. So the three of us went in to see Maurice and Barry, and said we needed a Mark X Jaguar. After a big argument with us, they bought one.

Once, in winter, we had to go to Manchester to do a television show, but we'd missed the last train available and couldn't get a plane. Maurice knew a rally car driver named Paul, who kept a barely roadworthy Mini Cooper S that had been customised to the hilt for speed. Paul was quite an amazing guy; he had driven Christine Keeler out of the country during the Profumo affair. Maurice now hired him to get us up to Manchester, which was usually at least a seven-hour drive at that time. It was snowing that day, but we got there in a little over four hours. It was a ride I'll never forget. Paul told us, 'Don't look, just hold on and let me drive.' It was like being on ice skates, with the car sliding sideways much of the time. Scott and I had somehow squashed ourselves down in the back, while Gary was in the front, looking as white as a ghost; we all remained intensely quiet and terrified, as the racing engine blared away under the bonnet. The one time I looked all I saw was a vortex of snow hurtling at us, but Paul never stopped. He was totally skilled and never broke into a sweat. Altogether, this was the most frightening and hair-raising experience that any of us had ever experienced in a car. We thanked Paul for getting us there on time, and headed to the nearest bar very quickly.

I remember playing a show at the Blackpool pier, where there was a huge electric-driven box that was used for transporting stuff from one end to the other. We hopped in it after the show, but someone in the crowd suspected we were inside and we had to

jump out of the box – with me going first – and run for our lives. We were only 10 or 15 feet in front of the mob, with Gary yelling, 'I didn't know girls could run this fast!' We leapt over the barrier at the end of the pier, but the car was nowhere in sight, and as the fans jumped over the barrier, they jumped on us. Just then, the car miraculously appeared, and Bobbie sprang out and started wrestling us away from the fans and into it. Somebody picked me up and tossed me into the car. Gary got tossed in next. Scott was already in. Then the door slammed shut and some very big guy we had never seen before was sitting in the front seat next to Bobbie. The fans were literally crawling all over the car – on the roof, everywhere. Bobbie sounded the horn and pulled away slowly.

He now asked the fellow in the front seat what his name was, and he replied, 'Arthur.' We asked what he did for a living. He said, 'I wrestle.' We asked him if he wanted a job, and he said, 'Yes.' We hired him on the spot, and he stayed with us for years. He and Bobbie were our dynamic duo, and we totally trusted the two of them to look out for us.

There was the mandatory full-time publicist hired by Capable Management, a man named Brian Sommerville, who had his own office somewhere in London. Brian was considered to be one of the best in the business, along with Derek Taylor, The Beatles' publicist. His job was to ensure that The Walker Brothers were kept in the press and the public eye at all times, and to arrange all the interviews, photographers, articles and publications. Brian and I got along really well, and he also liked Gary, but as time went by Brian leaned more and more towards promoting Scott in the media, increasingly giving him priority over Gary and me; and he was very influential in creating the image of Scott Walker as the reluctant star who shunned fame and fortune, an image that still informs the public's perception of Scott to this day.

In all the years I've known Scott, he really never changed from the way he was when we first started working together in Hollywood. Always very artistic, he liked classical music and jazz, art and films, but I don't remember his being absorbed in anything experimental or avant-garde at that time. It didn't surprise me that he got into this later, as he always wanted to produce records and had a certain idea of how he wanted the recording to sound, whereas I was interested in the technical aspects of how the sound was created. Scott, Gary and I always chose standard, commercial songs that we each liked for the albums – and Scott never suggested anything out of the ordinary.

Of course, in the sixties it became very common for pop singers and entertainers to create or perpetuate some type of image, and there were some real scene stealers who captured the public's imagination and pandered to the press. For example, Mick Jagger became Britain's naughtiest boy, John Lennon was the cynical Beatle, and PJ Proby started ripping his trousers on the stage. I didn't give the press a lot to work with, so they never did present an accurate portrayal of me. I had lost a lot of trust in journalists, and also preferred living a quieter, more private life.

We didn't consciously decide on an image for The Walker Brothers or for ourselves as individuals. We all remained pretty much the way we had always been – but we now had more money and were living in the middle of Swinging Sixties London with lots of attention focused on us at all times. It was awesome to be sought after and successful, especially when we were doing what we loved to do. What young man wouldn't be flattered by all the attention we received?

Of the three of us, Gary was always the easiest-going, most approachable member of our group, being very friendly with a great, dry sense of humour, and I think the press portrayed him pretty accurately as the fun-loving Walker Brother. Gary and I always liked clothes and boots, and in England we got into the whole Carnaby Street fashion revolution, spending large amounts of money on the latest gear. After a while, I had everything custom-made at Lord John in Carnaby Street, the boutique owned by the Gold Brothers. Scott only fussed about clothes once, when we did the Royal Gala at the Palladium in November 1966, and needed to have tuxedoes made. Scott decided on the style of the tuxedoes he thought we should all wear, and since it was the only time he ever got involved with how we looked, we happily went along with it. I remember his telling me once that one of his girlfriends remarked to him, 'You always look like an unmade bed.' The only thing he really cared about was his hair – like the rest of us.

Hair back then was an incredibly important statement, often becoming a person or group's trademark. Long hair for men was in fashion. Contrary to what some press reports alleged, I never

wore a wig, but I did have the longest hair of anybody I knew at the time – including many of the girls! I started going to John Isaac, the hairstylist, because I could never get my thick hair to look good. He was a miracle worker, solving my problem, and I followed him when he went to Michaeljohn's (Michael John was the hairstylist to the royal family at the time) and stayed with him through the seventies. I went through a few fashion phases: while in the Walker Brothers, I wore mostly black trousers and long-sleeved velour pullovers with Anello & Davide boots; when I went solo in 1967 I liked the military look; then I got into the more formal tuxedo look. I also loved the Edwardian and Regency frock coats with lace cravats and cuffs – which seemed to launch a trend. Finally, by the seventies, I got back to my basic jeans and denim shirts, also favouring deerskin suede shirts at that time.

We worked with several photographers, among them Cecil Beaton, who was celebrated for his portraits of the royal family, and Dezo Hoffman, who shot several of our album covers, along with those of The Beatles.

The press had a field day when my marriage was finally made public in October 1965. I hadn't seriously considered the impact it would have on the group, or on Scott and Gary. Hell, John Lennon was married, and that hadn't seemed to affect The Beatles. I guess I didn't really think about how it would impact on my own popularity. I just carried on regardless.

I now realise that my new, marginalised status in the group put a lot of unnecessary pressure on Scott. All of a sudden he had to deal with more than he should have. I think he may have felt abandoned by me. I didn't back off from my commitment to the group, but I guess it had to seem that way. When we first came to London, Scott, Gary and I had really hung out a lot together. After I got married the time we spent together was mostly work-related, for meetings, rehearsals, tours, recording or photoshoots. Except for going to check out new clubs or having the occasional dinner, we didn't see each other often. Gary, too, had to work out a new role. I guess he felt that he had to do more in the group because I was perceived to have distanced myself a little by my marriage.

In at least one book it's written that Scott was arrested at least once, that Maurice put a tail on him, and that he started drinking heavily around this time. If any of this happened, I didn't know a thing about it – except for the drinking, which we all did, like so many of the other bands who had to be hidden away from the public until show time, and had to find something to do. Day after day, we were cloistered for hours in hotels and lounges, without the freedom just to come and go as we used to. So we'd spend our time drinking. My drinking had started back in Hollywood and by now was a habit. Miraculously, I usually sobered up before going on the stage – probably due to the adrenalin rush and, occasionally, a little cocaine.

Contrary to what has been widely reported, Scott never expressed any fears of performing – ever. In fact, he teased the audience and went all the way up to the front of the stage night after night. It was also falsely written that Scott's friend, Jonathan King, was summoned to persuade Scott to go on stage, which was totally untrue. In fact, I don't remember ever seeing Jonathan King at any of our shows.

Surprisingly, we never developed stage fright, or worried about performing on the stage – but we did have constant concerns about security. What we really wanted was just to go out and do the show. In the end, we had to abandon the ballrooms. Our management decided that the risk was too great and that we would play only theatres and bigger venues in the future. Our travelling car, the Jaguar Mark X, also sustained damage countless times: the fans prised off the mirrors and anything else that they thought was a noteworthy souvenir.

In November 1965, we recorded 'My Ship is Coming In'/'You're All Around Me', which reached Number 2 soon afterwards. Although I was featured very little on 'My Ship', I really liked it and thought we should record it, although John Franz, Scott, Gary and our managers had misgivings. In December our first LP, *Take It Easy With The Walker Brothers*, was released, and reached Number 3 in the album charts. It was a standard-setting, groundbreaking album; we were the first to do those big orchestra and harmony sounds in the pop business.

By then, we were preparing for our next tour, and life was rather hectic. We all stayed in England over Christmas 1965, working through December and January, with no chance of taking time off even if we had wanted to. The story that Scott and Gary bought

me a ticket to go home for the holidays because I was dreadfully homesick is another one of those written untruths. We were busy, appearing on the *Top of the Pops Christmas Show*, which was televised on Christmas Day, *Thank Your Lucky Stars*, shown on 8 January 1966, *Now TV* on 12 January, another *Top of the Pops* on 13 January, and a show at the Floral Hall, Stockport, on 22 January. We were also preparing for a short tour of Scotland.

The Walker Brothers' third big hit was 'The Sun Ain't Gonna Shine Anymore', which remained at the top of the singles charts for a month in the spring of 1966. Frankie Valli had recorded the song, but with little success. Bob Crewe, who wrote it, told me many years later that he had sent the song to me in England because he thought The Walker Brothers should do it. I guess it went to our management's office, as I never got it. Coincidentally, Scott, Gary and I all had the Valli recording and had decided early on that we wanted to record it, but first we wanted to wait to see if Valli would have a hit with it.

On 'The Sun . . .', Scott and I switched parts on the chorus. The first version we'd recorded had been a complete failure: unless one has the weirdest vocal range in the world the song cannot be sung by one person. Scott is brilliant in the opening but the hook is out of his range, so on the chorus he sings the harmony and I sing the melody from that point. If we were recording that today, it would be apparent but, back then, you couldn't tell: even the guy producing thought Scott was singing the lead.

When the conductor counted off, and the track started, it was already magical. Scott sang the opening lines – and we knew we had a Number 1 record. Even today, I can be sitting in a restaurant or shopping in a store and when the song comes over the PA system it reminds me of the day we recorded it, and still puts a smile on my face every time. The B-side, 'After the Lights Go Out', was written by Scott's friend, John Stewart. The three of us wanted to help promote John at the time and thought the song was good, and also appropriate, because it was in the style of 'The Sun . . .'. John wasn't present at any of the recordings, so we arranged the piece to our liking with Reg Guest.

In March 1966, our management decided to experiment, putting us in cabaret for a week at Stockton's Tito Club. It was a very high-end deal with tickets selling for £10 to £20 each, compared with 12 shillings (60p) at the theatres. The club held 2,500 to 3,000 people, and I think that our playing there paid off very handsomely for our management, although who knows what we made from it?

We were very nervous. We would be playing live again, trying to imitate the massive sound that our audience had come to know from our recordings. We didn't know the monitor or sound systems at the club, and that caused us even more anxiety. Our band had to do its best to reproduce the big, sweeping sound that we got in the studios with a huge orchestra, as back then there were no synthesisers to simulate the strings. The whole thing felt bad. Thankfully, the audience loved our show, giving us the biggest ovation in the club's history. The people who came to see us there were more mature – there was no hysteria – but they were very exuberant, and there was lots of whistling and applause. Even so, by the end of the week the three of us knew that, although cabaret was an incredible financial move for our management, it was in every other way a bad move for us as a group. I felt that, at this point, we should have been on big stages with an orchestra backing us, because that's what the fans expected.

In March 1966, we began our first major tour: Roy Orbison was top of the bill, and we were second. Lulu was also on with us. Our first show of the 30-date tour began at the Finsbury Park Astoria in London. The package tours in the sixties usually included three well-known groups or artists, and there were two shows a night. Because we wanted certain lighting effects Bobby had to go over the lighting plot with each new technician, and he even ran one of the spotlights because he knew the cues. Even though he wasn't in the union, or even a bona fide light guy, there was never any problem with that.

We had our own car, driven by Bobby; most of the others on the show went on the tour bus. Ron King was the tour manager. He was very experienced after doing tours with The Beatles, and Arthur Howes, our promoter, always used him. We invariably stayed in the theatre once we got there, having food, drinks and anything else we needed brought in. Food was sandwiches, fish and chips, or whatever Bobbie could find. None of us liked to eat before the first show at 5pm or so, so we ate between shows. We

wore stage clothes that could travel well, as we didn't yet have a valet to fuss over our wardrobe. We also knew it was very likely that our clothes would be ripped to shreds each night, which still often happened even at the bigger venues. Somehow the girls figured out how to climb over the orchestra pit and land on the stage, and then the whole place would go wild. The stages were always extremely hot by the time we came out, so we wore what was comfortable – nothing theatrical.

Towns were more isolated back then, with fewer motorways, so we travelled no more than an hour or two each day. We'd wake up, take our showers, hop in the car and try to find food. Pubs and restaurants stopped serving food around 2pm each day. Many days we didn't get a proper hot meal, unless Bobby found an Indian or Chinese joint. Sometimes there were cafés along the routes, where we got sandwiches. Bobbie could always find food. We all hung out at the theatres, chatting with the other people on the tour, reading or dozing off. Our dressing rooms had only one sink, so the three of us took turns at washing our hair and shaving. There was a lot of 'hurry up and wait' after that.

I was injured quite badly during this tour. We had to get from the car to the door of our hotel in Birmingham, and although Bobby thought things were under control, all hell broke loose when I emerged, the first of us three. There was a human barrier of bobbies keeping back the fans, but I sensed danger and bolted towards the door. Gary was behind me, then Scott. A fan somehow got her hand through the scrum and grabbed my hair, pulling my head back. Gary told me that he slapped her to make her let go. She did, and I got myself balanced again, still running – but not anticipating the few steps that went down to the hotel entrance. It all happened in a split second: I went into the air, plunging down onto a hard floor, hitting my head on the edge of a revolving door. I was knocked unconscious and the next thing I knew Bobby was picking me up and requesting a doctor. There was blood everywhere, and I had to be taken to hospital for treatment. Then I carried on with the tour with a huge, bloody cut down the back of my head. I wouldn't let the doctors cut my hair, so they actually used glue and clamps to hold me together. As a result, our management decided that the three of us should wear crash helmets to get in and out of the theatres, a rule that we adhered to.

Capable Management also decided to take out a life insurance policy on us, with them, of course, being the beneficiaries.

The rest of the tour went off fine for all of us, even though there is a false account – written in at least one book – that Scott had the flu, Orbison had a leg injury and appeared on stage in plaster, and Lulu had laryngitis. All totally untrue. The three of us put on our same performance each night, and – contrary to another inaccurate statement that has appeared in print – I did *not* dance to divert attention from Scott. I like to dance.

During this tour we didn't spend much time with Roy Orbison, although I was very impressed by him: he enchanted the audience with song after song, just standing there, practically motionless, singing and playing his guitar. I watched him each night from the wings, wishing that I could get to know him, but for the most part we were kept isolated from everybody, and then whisked off immediately after our performances.

Through the grapevine, I found out that Roy had just been reunited with his wife Claudette, but not long after the tour was over she was killed in a motorcycle accident in America while they were out riding their bikes for the afternoon. I got to know Roy much better in 1967, on our second tour together. Tragedy struck him after that tour as well when his two young sons were killed in a fire that destroyed his home.

Lulu was the only girl on the show, and she kept to herself most of the time. She was a nice girl, very young and quite vivacious on stage, and of course she went on to become one of Britain's most beloved female pop singers. I felt that the first hit she had – 'Shout' – didn't showcase her vocal abilities as well as the hits to come. A year after this tour, when I was living with Barry Clayman, I met her again with a group of friends at a pub, and we all ended up going back to Barry's place for a party in one of the other flats. It was then – the last time I saw her – that Lulu told me she'd had a big crush on Scott during the tour. I did remember her always gazing at him with longing in her eyes.

We were now enjoying some fame and fan adulation in America. 'Make it Easy on Yourself' and 'The Sun Ain't Gonna Shine Anymore' had got to the lower reaches of the Top 20 and, in 1966, we were featuring heavily in US teen magazines. But we never

returned to play live in our homeland, despite having hit records and charting in the top ten in fan polls. At the time, touring was a necessary part of perpetuating a group's success with the public. It was Scott's fear of being drafted if he returned to America that prevented us from touring there. As a result, our popularity never reached its full potential in the US. Neither Gary nor I ever pressured Scott into overcoming his discomfort with the draft possibility. We respected his position, and let it go at that.

More and more, in our personal and professional lives, our thoughts and actions were dictated by where the fans might pop up, and what they were capable of doing. We always had that to consider before making any decisions. At first it was flattering to have so much attention, but that was short lived. After a while it was a terribly frustrating burden to feel like we were always on television, with people staring at us everywhere we went, or hiding out, lacking the freedom that most people enjoy. Scott tried several disguises so he could go out in public, but it never worked. Somebody always spotted him. We'd laugh every time he told us about the latest outfit, like when he wore some old hat with scruffy tennis shoes and a huge jacket and scarf. It must have been the signature dark sunglasses that gave him away. We all had to move many times; I finally chose obscure locations, such as Sanderstead, in south London, where only a handful of people would know me and the rest would leave me alone.

I rented all the flats I lived in, and never stayed long enough really to get too attached – except perhaps to my flat in Haverstock Hill, which had been decorated by the landlord in very bright, unusual colour combinations, such as the turquoise, orange and black scheme in the kitchen. Every room was like that, done up in weird shades. I lived there for most of 1967. I had my Morris 8 car then, a 1938 model that looked like a baby carriage. It was tiny and wonderful.

I moved to Sanderstead in 1966. The house was semidetached, so I was able to play my guitar into the wee hours of the morning – something unheard of in my former residences. The place had big rooms, one of which became my studio. I remember picking up a stray cat while living there, whom I called Sir Winston; he harassed my dogs Scotch and Brandy but they were very patient with him. My main requirement when moving was to be near a park, or to

have a back garden, so that I could take the dogs out. Until I moved into the Water Gardens in Edgware Road in 1968 I never had what I would consider to be a terrific flat. That place was really cool; it was a rather luxurious split-level apartment with a balcony overlooking the actual water gardens.

We travelled by small planes to get to some of the gigs; one year, we actually logged over 120,000 miles in the air. We had some terrifying experiences on planes, which left Scott and me particularly uncomfortable with flying. Eventually he would only get on board after taking Valium, and maybe a sleeping pill if it was a long flight, while I needed at least three whiskies before boarding. Gary, however, loved flying, and actually had a pilot's licence, so he always looked forward to the flights and it never seemed to bother him when things got rough. He would lecture us on the technical details relating to the plane's structure, G-force and so forth, to the point when we told him, 'Shut up, Leeds! Who cares about the stress on the wing when it's going to bloody fall off?'

Gary noticed on one flight that oil was leaking from the engine. Scott went berserk, yelling, 'Don't tell me that, Leeds! Don't tell me that! Get the booze and Valium!' He reached for his bag and got out the Valium tablets, downing them with shots of vodka, while I called the stewardess and ordered four whiskies, which I quickly downed. Gary would snicker at us, muttering under his breath, making sure Scott and I heard every word – 'Burial at sea is good. Now they'll buy all the records 'cos we'll be dead. I can see the headlines tomorrow – "MYSTERIOUS PLANE CRASH . . ." '

On another flight, the three of us were all hanging out, drinking and talking, Gary and I smoking, while Scott was bitching about the cigarettes. Leeds got up and we just continued on with our party without him when, suddenly, Scott and I looked at each other, wondering where Gary was, for he had been gone for over a half-hour. We asked the stewardess if she'd seen him, only to be told, 'He's flying the plane.'

Gary was quiet during just one flight, in 1967. We were in New Zealand, travelling from Christchurch to Wellington, and an announcement was made that, due to severe wind and weather, the airport was closed to air traffic but we would be the last plane

allowed in; we were told to buckle up as severe turbulence was expected. The stewardesses quickly gathered up all drinks and food while we braced ourselves for what was to come. The plane's descent to the runway was the scariest ride we'd ever had. It was tossed around like a little kite in a hurricane, then suddenly plummeted hundreds of feet as the pilot fought to rebalance it. For 20 minutes, it rolled and plunged again and again, dropping suddenly and going this way and that. We could see huge, white-topped waves crashing below us as we plunged towards the water, then up we went again. The loud groaning and creaking sounds that the plane was making were too horrible to describe. All of us were holding on for dear life with no talking or joking, not even screaming, just an intense quiet among the passengers. It was like being on a terrifying out-of-control roller coaster. Miraculously, we landed with the plane and everyone in it intact. Roy Orbison got out and kissed the ground, and everybody shook hands with the pilot, thanking him profusely. As always, we headed for the nearest bar, Scott and I already being somewhat tranquillised – he with Valium, and I with Serenid – but nevertheless traumatised by the whole thing.

We were always happy to get home after touring. We all liked going to the Scotch of St James, which was located down a little alley behind Piccadilly, and the Bag O' Nails. This was where all the major groups hung out. One night we were at the Scotch when Wilson Pickett performed his Number 1 hit, 'In the Midnight Hour'. He was super-popular with all the musicians, so that night, watching with us in the audience, were The Rolling Stones, The Beatles, The Hollies, The Animals, Long John Baldry, John Mayall, Eric Clapton, Manfred Mann, The Yardbirds, Jeff Beck, a few guys from The Who, some supermodels and, basically, anyone who was anyone in the music industry. The Brian Auger Trinity were also playing, with Julie Driscoll singing lead; they later went on to have a big hit with 'Wheels on Fire'. If somebody had dropped a bomb on the place, the entire British Top 30 would have been wiped out.

Of course, the press always printed mostly erroneous accounts of deep rivalries between some of the groups and artists – such as Mick Jagger being jealous of Scott, for example. The rumour was that Mick's girlfriend at the time – Chrissie Shrimpton, Jean's little sister, who was also a top model – remarked that Scott was good-looking, and from that point on Mick became jealous. Another report asserted that Scott had supposedly complained that Gary and I were leading increasingly lazy and hedonistic lifestyles while he 'worked like a badger', which was completely untrue.

In the spring of 1966, Tower Records released an album of old Dalton Brothers recordings made by Scott and John Stewart, falsely describing them as 'original members of The Walker Brothers'. Eventually the record company had to publicly correct their statement, but they had probably sold a lot of records in the meantime. It got to the point when I read fewer and fewer magazines and papers because I had lost confidence in most journalists. I'd read too many articles that had been twisted out of shape or blatantly made up in order to mislead the public and sell more papers. Increasingly, the three of us guarded our privacy and led quieter lives. We were certainly not 'out and about' all the time, or nonstop partying like many other groups and artists we knew. It was, perhaps, for this reason that there was an air of mystique about the group.

I had noticed that Kathy was becoming increasingly uncomfortable with the fan mania. I can't blame her, as the fans were always everywhere, and some of the girls who came round to my flat made it clear that they wanted more than an autograph, which didn't help matters.

Even though I had been faithful since we were married, it didn't seem to matter because, within the first year we were together, near the end of the Orbison tour, Kathy began to suspect that I was up to no good every time I was away from home. At first I was really upset about this and tried to set things straight but, as time went by, it became a big issue.

I am very sensitive to the people around me, and can usually tell when something has changed or if things don't feel right. Then all it takes is an inappropriate comment or action to create cause for concern in me. Right after the Orbison tour, I began to think that all Kathy's fussing wasn't right, and that something was going on, which set me wondering about what she might be getting up to. I didn't have any evidence, but when your new wife tells you that she may have made the wrong choice it doesn't need a lot of imagination to start thinking that something is up, and I wasn't

going to play that game again. I had not forgotten that Kathy had broken off our relationship before we were married. I'd known she was no stranger to sexual activity when I met her, so that wasn't an issue; but, when she also began to mention that she'd enjoyed having sex with her former partners, it became one, and I started believing that, at some point, she would start to look elsewhere. It became a fixation, and I knew that emotionally I would not be able to deal with that situation when it occurred. Kathy was a lovely girl and a lot of guys found her a pleasure to look at. I didn't mind that; it was the looking back that bothered me. This, more or less, was the beginning of the end for me. I've always needed someone to care for, it's in my nature, but I do expect the same in return.

This situation put me in an unenviable position. I ended up doing things and saying things I wouldn't normally do or say, and eventually paying for it. I didn't have enough life experience or skills to deal with this. I no longer felt safe in our relationship, so – as immature as it may sound – I had to erect a barrier between Kathy and me. We were still married, but I was no longer emotionally committed. I'd more or less put up an emotional wall between us. It allowed me some kind of peace. I knew, from before the end of the first year, that the marriage would end in divorce. I should have ended it then but I didn't, and I don't know why. Maybe I viewed it as a kind of personal failure, and of course there were other things to take into account: divorce was to be avoided at all costs, and there were 'the family', 'the friends' and 'the embarrassment' to consider.

I didn't actually know what to do at the time but, having distanced myself emotionally from Kathy, I discreetly found some comfort with several other girls, with no strings attached. At first it was purely sex enhanced by some drugs and too much alcohol. Soon, I was looking for someone I could be with, with no strings attached. I don't believe that anything I have said excuses my behaviour at that time, but I didn't know what else I could do.

I was drinking in pubs a lot then, and taking drugs. When I'd first got to England and started going to clubs, I met a lot of people who smoked either hash or marijuana. Early on, I tried both and liked them, particularly hash, which I enjoyed as a recreational drug. It enhanced any sexual encounter. Then, in 1966 or 1967, someone in a club asked if I wanted to try cocaine. I did, and it made me feel alert and awake – very energised – so after that, I used coke occasionally. Cocaine also played a practical role in my life: if I drank way too much and had to be ready for something, all I had to do was snort a couple of lines of coke, and it completely sobered me up.

The drugs I never tried were those that involved needles and chemicals, the ones that led to hallucinogenic episodes. I just wanted to relax and have a good time – at all times. Nobody ever complained to me about my substance habits, but I'm sure I missed out on some things, particularly business-related issues. I didn't get any more excessive than Gary, Scott or most people around me but for some reason if there was any talk of immoderate behaviour on the part of The Walker Brothers, fingers pointed at me – and I got 'the look'. Back then, everyone I knew was doing something. However, after the group split up in 1967, I had a lot more time on my hands to get into trouble.

The casual-encounters phase didn't last long. I felt very guilty, and disappointed in my behaviour, and it seemed pretty pointless to continue, but I didn't feel that I had any other options. I was very lonely and nothing was helping very much. It was at this time that I started drinking really heavily, particularly when I was home; I didn't see many sober days or nights. I don't know how Kathy felt about all of that, because my memories of that time are a little blurry. I am sure of one thing, though: I wasn't a very nice guy at the time.

I wasn't the only member of the group with problems. There was general shock when, on 15 August 1966, Scott was found in his gas-filled flat, unconscious – an event that is still referred to in press articles today. But there are still unresolved issues about this episode.

I want to state something that I consider to be a significant fact regarding the alleged suicide attempt: in the three-plus years that Scott and I knew each other professionally and worked together in California, and well into the first few UK tours, neither I nor, to my knowledge, anybody else involved with us, knew of anything peculiar or out of the ordinary regarding Scott. He was just like everybody else, a bass player and singer, without any eccentric behaviour or tastes. But, starting in 1966, a new and increasingly

dramatic series of events associated with Scott began to 'feed' the press, so I've always wondered what came first, the chicken or the egg, regarding the press and Scott.

From my understanding, roadie Bobby Hamilton was supposed to pick up Scott at his flat at a predetermined time. When Bobby got there, Scott didn't answer the door. Bobby said he smelled gas, which is questionable because, according to Bobby and Scott, the windows and door were sealed with tape. Bobby said he broke down the door and found Scott 'close to unconscious'. Bobby turned off the gas and opened all the windows to clear the air. I can't recall if an ambulance was called.

If this was a publicity stunt – which I always thought it was – I don't know whose idea it was. Maurice King and Bobby Hamilton were very vague about the whole incident. I'm not sure that Bobby knew completely what was going on, although I am sure he was told to be at Scott's flat at a certain time. This was significant because under no circumstances would Bobby ever be late – he could always be counted on. I am sure Maurice knew about the whole plan. I also felt that, if Maurice thought Gary and me could be convinced, then so could everyone else, especially the fans and the press.

Of course, if Maurice did not know what was going on, then the whole event may have been a ploy on Scott's part to make the management treat him with a great deal more deference – as in 'Before we do anything else, we'd better check with Scott first.' In a sense, that would mean that our management could no longer manage us.

But if neither Bobby nor Maurice knew about any secret agenda, then Scott was completely responsible for the event. Yet it is unlikely, in my opinion, that if there was indeed a suicide attempt, gas would have been the first choice: access to booze and drugs was easy, more certain and a lot less painful.

Scott now garnered particular curious attention and speculation, partly because of the so-called suicide attempt, but also because Brian Sommerville and the press definitely put a 'spin', as they say in politics, on him. For the most part, this wasn't the Scott either Gary or I knew. There were all sorts of false or questionable rumours around the alleged suicide event, some created by those I consider to be opportunists looking for their moment in the spotlight. For example, it was said that Scott had been labouring too long and too hard on the next album; or his girlfriend, model Irene Dunford, supposedly reported to the press that she had turned down Scott's marriage proposal and dumped him; and, finally, there was speculation about his relationship with Jonathan King.

I went to see Scott immediately after the alleged suicide attempt was reported, and he answered me only vaguely about the whole event, clearly wanting to move on to a new topic of conversation. He was acting completely normally, not agitated or upset in any way, so it was back to business as usual. To my knowledge, Scott did not make any attempts to commit suicide, contrary to what may have been written in books or the press, or supposedly reported by Jonathan King, whose credibility is questionable: in 2001, he was convicted of sex offences against young teenage boys, and served time in jail. Because I knew Scott so well, I'm quite sure that I would have known about any suicidal tendencies.

Later that summer, Kathy and I took a holiday in Marbella, Spain, and stayed in the famous Don Pepe hotel for a fortnight. We ran into Lulu and her manager, Marion, in the village, and all had dinner together. Lulu and Kathy became quite good friends.

Then it was back to work. The group went to Sweden for a concert and television show, then on to Holland, Switzerland and Germany. Back in the UK we recorded an EP called *I Need You*, after the title track, with Reg Guest as the musical arranger. Unlike Ivor Raymonde, who basically followed the arrangements of the original tracks and beefed them up a bit, Reg was far more imaginative, creating tailored arrangements to enhance our recordings in every way possible, always taking what Scott and I did into consideration. In this way, Reg enhanced the quality of our records and performances. He and I became quite good friends. He always made sure that I got what I wanted, understood my vocal intentions right off the bat, and wrote his arrangements accordingly, to complement my style. There are some erroneous quotes, attributed to Reg, that suggest that Gary and I were merely 'passengers', 'playing second fiddle to Scott'; that we were becoming 'increasingly tetchy', with our 'insecurity manifesting itself in the studio'; and that we were 'as manufactured a group as

The Monkees', along with other demeaning and completely false statements depicting rivalries and snubs between us. The fact is that all of us had a very professional and respectful relationship with each other, which was maintained over the years.

On 8 July 1966, our new single, '(Baby) You Don't Have to Tell Me'/'My Love Is Growing' was released, along with the EP *I Need You*. The single reached only Number 13. You are always disappointed when you record something you think is good and the public doesn't agree. I think we both gave a really good performance with this song, but that all the key changes made it hard to remember. Unlike 'The Sun . . .' and 'Make It Easy . . .', '(Baby) You Don't Have to Tell Me' was not immediately easy to sing along with, so I guess it just got lost. The choice of songs was always democratic, but I can't remember who suggested '(Baby) You Don't Have to Tell Me'. Scott had more pull because he had John Franz's ear. I told Scott and Johnny that the track 'I Need You' could be a stronger piece of material for a single if we redid the vocals and lifted mine out of the track more, which would have made for a dynamic recording. But it didn't happen. Johnny was already starting to distract Scott away from The Walker Brothers with material and ideas intended to showcase his talent. I thought – and still think – that 'I Need You' was wasted on an EP, but Philips was hoping that it would go into the singles charts.

The other three tracks on the EP were 'Young Man Cried', which I really liked, 'Everything's Gonna Be Alright', which wasn't done as well as it should have been, and 'Looking For Me'. I don't even know why we did that one.

In June and July we started a series of television appearances, topping the bill on ATV's *Sunday Night at the London Palladium* and performing on an edition of *Ready Steady Go!* that was devoted entirely to The Walker Brothers. We also won awards, and performed at the *NME* Poll Winners' concert.

Gary and I liked cars, and I saw an incredible sports car in *Road and Track* magazine, which I read avidly. It was called a Marcos 1800. This car was not common at the time in the UK. It was an English car with great styling – a cross between a Ferrari and an E-type. It was made more for racing than street driving, which also appealed to me. I bought one in a beautiful silver-blue, but because I wanted it to be a left-hand drive car – I still wasn't comfortable with a right-hand drive – it had to be custom-built, and therefore I had to wait for it. Gary bought one too, but his was bright red, and because it was a right-hand-drive model he got it right away. When mine finally arrived the first thing I did was drive out to Stonehenge, in the middle of the night, to run it in. Gary came too, in his Marcos.

During a photoshoot for *Rave* magazine we were asked to drive around Brands Hatch and hang out on the track so that photos could be taken of us and our new cars. Gary and I decided to take things a step further, and ended up racing each other. I had the bigger engine, but was at a disadvantage because of my left-hand-drive car. Gary was doing fine going around the track, but I pushed hard during the second lap on the straight away, reaching up to about 140mph, then trying to slow way down to about 40mph to make the curve. I couldn't do it, and my car started sliding off the track and towards the dirt wall. I mistakenly touched the brakes, which made matters even worse. My stomach felt as if it were up in my throat and I was squeezing the wheel as hard as I could, bracing for a bad crash. Yet somehow I managed to recover and get up the hill, finally stopping and getting out in front of Gary, who had watched the whole thing. I was as white as a ghost and shaking so badly that he had to light my cigarette, making some Gary crack. We hid the near-fatal incident from the photographers and reporters, but when word got back to Capable Management they forbade me to take part in any activities involving race cars in the future.

We recorded our second album, *Portrait*, in autumn 1966 and it went to Number 3 in the charts. The critics loved this album, and so did we. There were 12 tracks, all chosen by the three of us, and the album was named (by Philips as usual) for the unique black-and-white photograph that was used for the cover, and reproduced on an inset card. The country-rock material I was writing at the time wasn't suitable for this album, but Scott had a few originals on *Portrait*. The three of us chose 'People Get Ready' – which had been recorded in the mid-sixties by Curtis Mayfield's group The Impressions, and was basically a gospel song. 'Old Folks', one of

Scott's solos, was an old classic standard that our parents had probably listened to, and a song he'd always wanted to do. We got extremely dramatic with 'In My Room', a powerful piece that I chose, which had been recorded by Verdelle Smith in the US and Julie Rogers in the UK.

On the lighter side were 'Living Above Your Head', in which I added a harmony line that carried the song way beyond the original by Jay and the Americans, and 'Saturday's Child', Scott's original composition written for the album. He wrote this as a dance song, and it has been said that it's reminiscent in parts of 'River Deep, Mountain High', but the similarity is more in the arrangement than the actual song. Scott also wrote the easygoing 'I Can See It Now'. 'Hurting Each Other', which was sent to us by a music publisher, was more serious but uptempo; this song would later be a hit for The Carpenters. 'Where's The Girl' – originally recorded by Jerry Butler – was a song I suggested for Scott as one of his solos. 'Just For a Thrill', a Ray Charles track, was one of my solos, another extraordinary piece that I simply wanted to record, and remains one of my favourites of all the songs I've recorded.

I had written the vocal arrangement of 'Summertime' when I performed it back in California, many years before Scott and I recorded it, and it was thrilling to record it on this album with Scott and a big orchestra. I played it for Reg Guest on guitar while we sang, and he then wrote the orchestration. 'Take It Like a Man', originally recorded by Gene Pitney, was a song Scott thought I should perform, so that was my other solo on the album. 'No Sad Songs For Me' – written by Tom Springfield, Dusty's brother, and recorded by The Springfields – struck Scott and me as the most beautiful love song we'd ever heard. I sang lead on that, a departure from our usual format.

That autumn, Capable Management lined up a second tour, which would play at 33 venues, with us headlining. Also on the bill were Dave Dee, Dozy, Beaky, Mick and Tich, The Troggs and Clodagh Rogers. There was a myth circulating that Scott told Clodagh that our band, the Quotations, would not back her, and that she walked out because of this. That's not true.

This tour was terrific for all of us. Despite the cloak and dagger stuff we had to go through to escape the chaos and fan hysteria, we really enjoyed ourselves, and everything went quite smoothly.

The Troggs were real characters and we all got along well, while Dave Dee and I became lifetime friends on this tour. What I really liked was that everyone was relaxed. We all hung out in the hotel lounges after the shows, drinking and badgering the management for food well into the wee hours of the morning. Even Scott would stay up, lurking about and looking for something to fill his glass. Generally, there was a great atmosphere backstage, and each show was sold out, which also put us in very good moods.

One black cloud at the time, however, was when I was badly misquoted in a music paper, which insinuated that I regarded Scott as 'a pain in the neck' and 'a lead weight'. Although I did grow weary of constantly being compared with Scott, I had a high opinion of him and never said any such things. Comments were always being made about friction between us and our management but, at this time, there weren't any difficulties.

At the show in Chester, the police decided to outfox the fans. They had us dress up in full uniform, with our hair stuffed up into our helmets. After the show we went out, hoping to blend in with the large police presence, but all of a sudden we heard, 'There they are! They're dressed up as bobbies!' Thankfully, we were fast and got to the car in time, but the poor bobbies were attacked by the girls and we saw them falling to the ground, struggling, and crawling to get away. We were never asked to use those disguises again.

Another night, up North, a big guy rushed the stage and I saw him heading towards me and I got out of the way quickly. Bobbie saw him coming, ran out, restrained the guy and somehow removed him. We just carried on with the show. Afterwards, I asked what the deal was, and Bobbie said, 'The guy wanted to smash you one because his girlfriend won't stop talking about you.' That was scary.

Unfortunately, by the end of our second tour, Scott had become terribly disenchanted with performing as we could not be heard, which was frustrating to him. He said to me one night after a show, 'What's the point? No one can hear us anyway'. So his mood did start to change, and on the third tour, in 1967, he was miserable. Although I didn't ever feel disillusioned about being on stage I didn't like the hassles, or the travelling, but I loved performing. Playing to thousands of screaming fans felt a bit

glamorous, and satisfied my ego at the time. I was only in my early 20s, after all.

My personal life, however, was not getting much better as I worked on straightening out my drinking and my emotional unrest without a great deal of success. Life at home wasn't as it should be, but that was not going to change, and the group were also starting to have problems. I was uncertain and uncomfortable. My only thought was of what was going to happen next. The strange thing is, I wasn't looking for any excuses for myself or anyone else, nor did I blame anyone for anything good or bad; I just wanted some way to escape, and I was determined to find it.

I was in such emotional turmoil that to this day I can't be sure whether I acted on impulse doing the things I did, or if I was just trying to protect myself. I don't talk a lot about my marriage to Kathy because for me there isn't a lot to talk about. I think the press had more to say than I did: after all she had been a star in America, she looked like a model, and she was married to one of the Walker Brothers. From my point of view it wasn't the 'fairytale' romance it was made out to be. Unfortunately, it lacked its most important ingredient, apart from love – trust.

There were two very attractive young ladies who came to see us on tour quite frequently. I had met one of them, the girlfriend of a guy I knew, at a club in London. She introduced me to her friend, who was married to a member of a successful UK group, a great-looking girl from the North with a straightforward personality. I liked her right away.

After a show – I think it was before the second tour, in Manchester – we had a few drinks together back at the hotel before they had to leave, although they said they'd be back another night. I actually found myself looking forward to seeing this great-looking girl again. We became very good friends and shortly afterwards, during the second tour, began an affair that lasted quite a long time, meeting nearly everywhere I played for the next year or so. It became an on-and-off kind of thing: when we were together it was on, and when we were apart it was off. I wouldn't say it was a love affair, but it was more than just sex. I felt comfortable when I was with her, something I needed then.

In October 1965, The Walker Brothers were invited to appear on *The Billy Cotton Band Show*. Being on this show was a prestigious opportunity but, during rehearsals, Scott complained of having a bad headache. We sent one of the television staff to get some tablets, specifying no aspirin, as Scott would have a terrible reaction to it. They came back with the tablets, assuring us that they were aspirin-free. Within minutes of his taking them he was having difficulty breathing and his face began to swell up. We had no choice but to leave, because obviously we would not be able to perform on the show. Reportedly, Billy Cotton Jr, who would later become the head of light entertainment at the BBC, remarked that we would never appear again on the BBC – another fabrication by some press hack.

Unfortunately, shortly after this episode our work permits were about to expire, so Gary, Scott and I had to come to terms with the fact that we were going to have to leave Britain if we wanted to continue working.

CHAPTER 5

ANATOMY OF A GROUP BREAK-UP

GOING TO THE FAR OUT
G A R Y   W A L K E R

That autumn, when our work permits expired, we were barred from working in Britain for six months. I wasn't worried about this, and in fact the uncertainty about our future that it generated only seemed to boost our popularity. Maybe the fans thought we might not return.

We took the opportunity to tour Europe, doing TV shows in countries where there was huge interest in our success in Britain. One night we were to play at an outdoor concert in Sweden. It was held in a vast open space somewhere in a forest, and the huge audience had to stand in a big clearing. This was a kind of forerunner to the big open-air concerts we have nowadays. The promoter who put on the show was very excited that we were there, and that he had pulled in such a big crowd. He told us that our latest Number 1 single was his favourite, and he couldn't wait to hear it live. It turned out that he wasn't talking about 'The Sun Ain't Gonna Shine Anymore', but my solo release, 'You Don't Love Me', which – unknown to us – was Number 1 in Sweden at the time. We just looked at each other in shock, then Scott said, 'Well done, my boy!' and John just said, 'Leeds!' in the his usual manner. The funny part was that our management didn't know about my record being Number 1, nor did the record company, and none of them ever said anything about it, either.

It was in Denmark that Scott met Mette Teglbjaerg, whom he would later marry. Mette came from a wealthy family and was a strange girl, really possessive and jealous. She and Scott used to have terrible fights, and I'm sure that jealousy was a factor in their eventual break-up, but that was several years in the future.

We did a TV show – *Beat Club* – in Germany, and the record company, Polydor, wanted to show us around. One night we were taken to a street with big gates at both ends that were shut behind us when we entered. It was a quaint little street with about ten or twelve houses on each side of the pavement, and in these houses there were girls sitting in the windows, looking to get our attention any way they could. As we walked along, sometimes exchanging a word with them, one of the gentlemen in the street recognised us. The Germans are very big fans of most pop groups and it is the guys, not the girls, who rush the stage which, if you're not prepared, comes as a shock the first time it happens.

When the other men realised who we were, they all came over to meet us and get our autographs. The girls in the windows went wild and were screaming and swearing, 'Get them out of here! They're stopping all the trade!' It got so bad they were throwing things at us, among them beer cans. They even called the police to get us out of their street, which they did. The record company said they were sorry, and that it had never happened to any of the other groups they had taken there; they hadn't realised how popular we were.

We got a call asking if The Walker Brothers could record the title song for a forthcoming movie that was to be filmed by Betty Box, the British film producer who was responsible for the highly successful 'Doctor' series. She was making a film called *Deadlier Than the Male*, one of the James Bond pastiches that were all the rage at the time. Scott and John Franz put together a nice track that Betty liked, then Scott and I went to see her. She lived just outside London and her house looked like a stud farm, with stables and white fences. We found Betty very approachable and professional, and gained the impression that she was a fan of The Walker Brothers.

This period – autumn 1966 – was an extraordinary time for us, with a lot of good things happening. We were asked to play before Prince Philip at a royal gala at the world-renowned London Palladium. We heard later that Princess Anne was a big fan, and wondered if she was responsible for our being booked. Bernard Delfont, who put on the show, and our managers wanted us to wear straw hats, carry canes and do a vaudeville number, which would have been fine if we were Frank Sinatra or Bing Crosby, but it was definitely not our thing and our refusal to do it caused a bit of a stir.

We had the best dressing room; it came with a chaise longue, our own toilet and a TV. We could easily have lived there. When we thought of all the famous people who had occupied it before us it just seemed unreal. We were three boys from California who were big fans of many of those big stars, and here we were, sitting in this shrine that had housed their talents. It was too hard to take in.

We watched some TV and had a bit of chitchat to ease the unbearable tensions that were building up as the time for our appearance before Prince Philip and the 'angry villagers', as we would call them, approached. To this day, I still don't know how Scott, with his uncontrollable nerves, made it onto that stage without passing out.

When Prince Philip came backstage to meet the artists, they put us at the front of the line. The press printed just one photo of us with him. It was taken by a royal photographer and I was really upset because, although they took a lot of pictures, he picked the one where I was blinking.

The Prince asked me, 'Why did you come over to England when you've got such great weather in California?' I told him, 'I like the rain.' I wasn't taking the piss, I was telling the truth, because it never rains in California. Scott and John didn't say anything, they were just standing there, so I had to do all the talking. Prince Philip was a real gentleman. He made me feel comfortable.

Another integral event in the mythology surrounding Scott was his famed retreat to Quarr Abbey on the Isle of Wight in December 1966. For three weeks beforehand we had been listening to Gregorian chants on record, and Scott was intrigued by the vocals and the structure of these pieces. In my view he didn't go there with the idea of generating publicity but genuinely wanted to study them more, and told me that this was the reason for his visit. Unfortunately, the press found out and hounded the monks, as well as Scott, which he hated. The only option was for him to leave. He might still be there otherwise! He made such an impression that the community gave him a key to the door, so he could come there any time. It's the one he wore on his belt.

On 9 December Philips – without our consent – put out 'Deadlier Than the Male' as an unofficial single, backed with 'Archangel', a song composed by Scott. The dramatic Gothic backing was recorded on the organ of the Royal Albert Hall, not at the Odeon Cinema, Leicester Square, as was reported, and it's likely that Scott based it on a Bach fugue. 'Archangel' was about a woman called Claire he had met at one of Maurice King's parties. She was the ex-wife of a peer, who later married an art dealer of some sort, a nice girl but totally mad. She used to hang out with Scott and had taken to bringing soft drugs to his flat. None of us used them, but Scott based this song on that. We were all angry about the A-side being released as a single as we were not consulted and would not have chosen it.

That month, The Walker Brothers came third after The Beach Boys and The Beatles in the World's Best Group category in the *NME* polls – we should have come first!

When I think of the *Images* album, recorded in late 1966, the first thing that comes to mind is the front cover, which we all hated. It was done by the art department at Philips and was meant to look like an Andy Warhol study, very much in keeping with the times. The original design shown to us by the record company must have looked a lot different or we would have vetoed it. We were to take a lot more care with album covers in the future.

As you record more and more, working in the studio starts to become more of a punishment than a pleasure, what with the pressure of trying to get the vocals right, finding new songs, costing it all and keeping the hits coming. In the end, you are never sure what's good or bad, and there's no one to ask. This happens to all creative people at one time or another, and it might have started to happen with that album.

Early in 1967, we went to see Lew Grade, a very powerful figure in the TV and entertainment world. He was shaped like a chubby penguin, was bald on top and smoked a huge cigar. He was famous for his quick one-liners, although Scott wasn't too sure about his saying, 'Don't give them art, give 'em what they want!' But I felt it was an honour for the three of us to be in his office. He said there was a lot of interest in us in Australia and New Zealand, and wanted to know if we would be interested in doing a tour there with Roy Orbison and The Yardbirds. We said we were keen, so the deal was done.

We were looking forward to touring again with Roy, the 'Big O', and to performing with The Yardbirds, who had Jimmy Page (of Led Zeppelin fame) on lead guitar, replacing Jeff Beck, who had gone solo. I knew Jimmy from the time when I had come to England with PJ Proby. As one of the top session guitarists in Britain he had played on a lot of PJ's songs, and on many other people's too.

On 15 January 1967, we left Britain for a major tour of the Far East, which was to take in Australia, New Zealand, Singapore and Japan. Two thousand fans saw us off amid chaos at London Airport, with the terminal roof in danger of collapsing. Inside the terminal, we were causing all kinds of problems. At one point, the security guards had to put us in the ladies' toilet, which was the only place to hide from the fans. All the papers printed the picture of us going into the toilet, 'confirming' the gay rumours about 'The Walker Sisters'. In fact, the airport security people were caught with their pants down (excuse the analogy), because they hadn't realised how popular we were. We were finally taken to the VIP suite, which was reserved for MPs and executives, and things got back to normality.

We ordered two whiskies and one brandy, and Scott took some Seconal that his doctor had prescribed to reduce the fear of flying – to which I might add the fear of most things. Scott insisted that we all take them, so we did, timing them to kick in as we boarded the plane. Because the alcohol made them work faster, our speech became slurred, we started to go to sleep, and as the plane left to go to the Far East, we were going to the Far Out. Unknown to us, the aircraft developed engine trouble over the English Channel and had to turn back to Heathrow. Because of the state we were in, John and I had to be held up, but a stretcher was needed to carry Scott into the building.

We then had no choice but to take the replacement flight, which would take 48 hours to reach our destination, stopping in many places along the way; it had four changes of crew, all cheering us on. After Paris, we flew on to Egypt. It was dark as we were coming in to land and I asked the stewardess if I could go up to the cockpit with the pilots. She returned and said it was OK. I was allowed to because I was a Walker Brother. When I got to the cockpit we all introduced ourselves and I told the pilots that all I had ever wanted to do was fly. They were a bit shocked because they said they'd give anything to be a pop star and have all those girls chasing them. When we were about 15 minutes out from landing I said I would go back to my seat, but the captain said that I could stay up with them in the cockpit. For a pilot, this is something you dream about.

We were all very impressed with Sydney. We wanted to know what that funny-shaped thing in the harbour was. 'That's the Opera House,' the bodyguard who was acting as guide told us. 'They ran out of money and can't finish the project. A lot of people don't like it, they think it's radical.' The three of us thought it was great, however, and were happy later when it got completed.

The first show was on the second night at a boxing ring that was used for big events; there was nowhere else that could hold big crowds. Scott and John had to move like boxers around the ring, so that the crowd who were seated on every side could get a good look at them. We found the audience a lot more subdued than those in England, but still got a good response. In fact, the show was a sell-out, and the grateful promoter invited us back to his house for some drinks. The next day, he took us out in his high-powered cruiser and got it up to 70 knots. That was an experience!

Before we left Sydney Scott and John had chased me around the pool where we were staying, and tried to throw me in. I jumped in to avoid them, but the builders had put the diving board at the wrong end. The bottom of the pool was four-feet deep, and I hit it with such force that it almost broke my ankles. For the next two weeks, I had trouble walking because of the extreme bruising, and was on painkillers waiting for it to subside. When I got off the plane in New Zealand it was so bad that I thought I might need a wheelchair. But the show had to go on!

The first impression we had of Auckland was that we had been transported back to 1940. The place looked is if it were caught in a time warp. We were taken to a hotel out of town, in a rainforest setting. It was built of brown timber, like a log cabin, the type you would see in a ski resort in the mountains. Off we went to the bar for some refreshments. I hung around with Robert, the drummer in Roy's backing group, who later went off on their own to form The Atlantic Rhythm Section in the USA. We got along real well, and later I would record 'Spooky', which they wrote. Because we had long hair, one of the gentlemen in the bar, a total creep, gave us a bit of a hard time, calling us 'homos'. Robert didn't like it and was going to flatten him, being over 6 foot and 14 stone, but the creep's wife jumped in saying he was drunk, just ignore him, and saved the day. The rest of the night passed uneventfully, and after a few cool ones we retired to bed.

We were to play the next night at the town hall in Auckland, an ancient building that looked like one of the old theatres in the West End of London, and held around 2,000 people. The show was to start at 6.30pm, which seemed a little early to all of us. We went over to the Town Hall about 3pm to check the sound and lights, and were surprised to find only five or six girls at the stage door – and that was it. So we went straight in. We saw the stage manager, and I asked him, 'How come the show is so early?' He told me that most of the townsfolk liked to get home by 9pm. This was a novelty for us: we were used to staying up all night.

I spent the waiting time talking to Jimmy Page backstage about the old days and PJ. The Yardbirds were to be the first to open the show, then us, followed by 'Big Slow', as Scott and I called Roy Orbison, but for some reason Roy had to finish his set early, leaving us to close the show. I was at the side of the stage watching The Yardbirds and it got to me just how good Jim was on the guitar; the group did a very good set. But the crowd just didn't appear to care for their music, and you could hear a few comments that weren't flattering. The Yardbirds ended their act to only light applause, and walked off, unable to believe what had happened.

I went back to the dressing room and told Scott and John how the audience had reacted, and they said that maybe our sound would be too much for the people here. Roy was on before us, and he did all his hits, but they didn't seem to care for him either. I ran

back to tell the boys all about it. To say they were both surprised was an understatement.

I said, 'This is going to sound funny, but I think that the audience is stuck in the 1940s, and that we should do the old standards and some Frank [Sinatra] thrown in for safety.' They both agreed. When we finally went on stage, we did 'Summertime', 'My Funny Valentine' and 'Over the Rainbow', plus a few more oldies. The crowd loved all the old tunes and success was ours. I hate to say it, but I really enjoyed it.

We said goodbye to Roy and The Yardbirds, then flew off to Japan, a place we really wanted to visit. On the way, we stopped in Singapore for a layover for one night. The promoters put us in a hotel on a hill overlooking the city, and took us out for dinner. Scott and I wanted to try typical local food, but John played it straight by sticking to the Westerners' menu that was suggested by our guide. Scott and I got through what we ordered, but we weren't quite sure what we were eating. It could have been one of three meats: dog, cat or snake, which I was later told were specialities at that restaurant.

As we were returning to the hotel, we saw some very attractive young ladies on the corner; they were stunning – and they were waving and shouting to us, so we told the driver to stop, as we wanted to talk to them. He smiled and shook his head, and continued on to the hotel. When we pulled up to the hotel, we were greeted by one of the reps who were looking after us. He asked if we'd had a good time out, as we made our way to the bar. We told him about the driver not stopping so that we could talk to those girls by the shop, and he started sniggering.

'Those girls you saw are some of the most beautiful in Singapore, but they're not girls, they're boys, "lady boys", and they work the streets,' he told us. Shocked as we were, we had to admit how great they looked.

The next day, I wanted to be taken to the famous Raffles Hotel, and the other two wanted to tag along, but it was closed for renovation. Even The Walker Brothers didn't always get what they wanted.

Japan proved to be a very exciting experience that would stay with us always. Around 200 hysterical fans lined up along the top of the upper observation walkways at Tokyo International waiting to greet us. We were driven to the New Otani Hotel, one of the best in Japan, and all the way there the fans followed us in taxis, beeping their horns and screaming and yelling. Sometimes they got a bit too close, which made the drivers laugh, as they found it quite funny, but Scott didn't think it was that amusing and was glad when we arrived at the hotel and checked in.

We had Western-style rooms, but found out we could have had Japanese ones, in which you sleep on the floor (which I did later opt for I came back with my group The Rain). The three of us had a security guard assigned to stay with us all the time we were there.

That night the record company took us to a geisha house for dinner. We removed our shoes at the entrance, were led into a private room where we sat on the floor at a table under which we could put our feet and were given Japanese overshirts to wear. A Japanese man entered, dressed in traditional clothing and accompanied by three girls in full geisha makeup.

They asked if any of us would like to take a bath, which is customary in geisha houses. I was the first to say yes, and was escorted to a room at one side of the dinning area. In the centre was a round wooden bathtub – the size of a very small swimming pool – and a girl attendant. She handed me a robe and asked me to change in the cubicle in the corner. When I came out, she led me to the bath and indicated that I should go down the steps into the water. It was like a whirlpool that bubbled up all around you. The girl took hold of one arm and washed it, then turned her attention to the other.

Curtains surrounded the bath in a half-circle at my back. I was wondering what was behind the curtains, but the girl didn't speak any English, so I pointed at them. Clearly she thought I was telling her to open the curtains as she stopped washing my shoulders, got up and walked to the other side of the room. When the curtains were fully open, I turned to look back over my shoulder and saw ten or twenty people walking by. To my horror, I realised they could all look in and see me taking a bath. The girl was now beckoning for me to come out starkers and wash my private parts in front of hundreds of passing people. I made some frantic gestures – and now it didn't matter if she spoke English or not – for her to shut the curtains, which thankfully she did quickly. Then she tried to get me to come out again, but I told her no, and motioned for her to turn her back, so that I could emerge without embarrassment. This bath was supposed to relax you and make you calm, so that you would enjoy your night out. All it did for me was make me order more drinks when I returned to the table. The other two wisely didn't take their baths. Shame – they missed out on all of Tokyo seeing them nude.

The geisha girls entertained us with old, traditional songs accompanied by Japanese instruments, and Scott asked to play the shamisen, a three-string, guitar-like instrument. To the surprise of all of us, he played all the music that the geisha had just preformed. She was very impressed. We had a lovely meal and tried many different foods.

The next day, we were to do a prestigious TV show. Beforehand we went to an outdoor market and discovered that we would not be able to disguise ourselves in Japan unless we dyed our hair black, had plastic surgery on our eyes, and cut our legs off at the knees. Still, we had no problem with the fans because they were well mannered and polite.

Scott noticed a jacket hanging from a market rack; it was black with no collar, and buttoned up to the neck. He admired it, and was told that it was part of a Japanese school uniform, but bought it anyway. The rest of the day was filled with meeting the fans and press interviews, which would lead up to the TV show, a popular late-night talk and chat format. We were to perform 'In My Room', which was Number 1 in Japan at the time, and Scott decided to wear the school jacket that he'd got in the market. The record company said it might not be a good idea as it might offend some of the people who were watching. The next caveat came from higher up, with the director saying it might not be a good idea to wear the uniform.

'Leeds, tell them I want to wear the jacket,' Scott insisted. So I informed everyone that Scott would prefer to go on in the coat, but they still thought it was a bad idea and hoped he'd change his mind. It fell to me to convey the studio's thoughts to Scott.

'Tell the record company no jacket, no show, Leeds – right?'

'Right,' I said.

'John?'

'Right,' said John.

There was a ten-minute wait, then the record company rep returned to tell us, 'Everyone says yes.' We did the show. The next day, we got a tremendous response to the TV show *and* the jacket, and it seemed that all the Japanese schoolchildren were proud to wear their jackets and thought it was absolutely brilliant that some famous pop stars would think they were cool and wear them on a famous TV show.

We all had a great time on the tour and – contrary to what has been written in other books about John and Scott not getting along – we all got on great. There were no disagreements, nor did I have to act as peacemaker between the other two. To be honest the three of us had one of our best times together.

On our way back to California, Scott and I stopped at Hawaii to see the owner of the club where Scott and John had once played with Judy, John's sister. At the time Scott was taking a lot of vitamins, 12 to 15 at a time, to keep himself as healthy as he could. The customs people stopped him and wanted to know what they were. He said they were vitamins, but they brought out a book so that they could check that he was telling the truth. This took about 30 minutes and was starting to get on our nerves. I think it was because of our long hair that we got the hassle; they had no idea who we were, but we probably looked suspicious to them. We thought it couldn't get any worse, but one of the porters asked if he could carry our bags to our taxi. Despite having a lot of luggage, we could have managed on our own, but it was hot and the porters had trolleys. When we were all loaded up and ready to go, I handed the porter a $10 note, and he asked, 'What's that for?'

'It's your tip,' I told him.

'That's not enough,' he stated, which really pissed us off, so I took the note back and said, 'Maybe that's better!' Hawaii is costly, and maybe he was used to getting more. We stayed a day and then flew on to California.

Our new single, 'Stay With Me Baby'/'Turn Out the Moon', was released on 3 February 1967 and got to Number 26 in the charts. The album, *Images*, came out a couple of weeks later, and got rave reviews, chiefly, I think, because of the great songs and the way they were performed, and the fine vocals and phrasing, which showed just what Scott and John were capable of doing. When you listen to this album, it's hard to think of The Walker Brothers as a group who were chased and screamed at, and mobbed wherever they went, but that's just how Frank Sinatra started out. This album contains one of my favourite tracks of all time, 'Just Say Goodbye'. I never found out until later that Petula Clark wrote most of it.

Between March and May 1967 we were to do the legendary tour to end all tours. It would star The Walker Brothers, The Jimi Hendrix Experience, Cat Stevens and Engelbert Humperdinck. Also on the bill were The Quotations, The Californians and Nicky Jones, the compère. I feel lucky to have had the privilege of appearing on the same bill as Jimi Hendrix, one of the greatest rock stars of the sixties.

The first time I met Hendrix was when I got a call from Chas Chandler (formerly of The Animals), who was to become his manager. Chas said he wanted me to come and see this guitarist whom he'd signed up at a club in London just off the Cromwell Road. He said that Paul McCartney would be there too. Jimi was virtually unknown then; he had first played in London at the Scotch of St James, jamming with another band and doing some blues numbers. Jimi and his other group members – Mitch Mitchell and Noel Redding – were playing together for the first time on the night I went to see them. The club was in a basement and rather small; they had a table set aside for Paul and me. After the Experience had played the place went wild; nobody had seen anything like this before.

Chas took us backstage to meet the boys and have a chat. I knew Mitch from the days when he was with The Riot Squad and we were on a show together. I'd borrowed his bass-drum pedal and broken it, and sent the roadie to get a new one right away. We got on, both being drummers, and he was surprised to discover how good I was at drumming.

Paul was impressed with Jimi too, and told Chas he thought the band would go far. Chas thanked us for coming; if you had a few really big names turn up to see a new group it could help them a lot.

After that first appearance, I saw Jimi a few times in the clubs, but somehow we were never introduced. Then one night he approached me and invited me to sit with him. He told me he thought The Walker Brothers were great. I was very flattered to hear that from him. I recall that he had a very quiet voice, verging on shyness, and that he would often giggle as he finished speaking – I would describe it as the kind of giggle that I'd experienced when young Japanese fans spoke to me.

As we were both musicians, the conversation inevitably turned to music. I told Jimi about my days playing with The Standells and various other groups in LA in the early sixties, and he talked about his experiences playing in New York and other East Coast places. We chatted for a while and had some more drinks, which he paid for. He would not let me pay for anything. He was such a gentleman and very well mannered.

Later Chas, with the help of Keith Altham, our publicist, who was also to become the Experience's PR man, asked if I could get Jimi on our tour. I said I would do all I could. As the tour package started to take shape, things got more bizarre day by day, with such diverse talents as Cat Stevens and Engelbert Humperdinck being signed up. Because the acts were so different, musically and in appearance and image, some people doubted that the shows would work. In the event, it was one of the most successful package tours in pop history.

It was when we began working together that I got some proper understanding of the character of Jimi Hendrix. The most vivid memory I have of him is of when we were touring. I arrived at the theatre in Bath late in the afternoon, and heard a commotion coming from one of the other dressing rooms. I went along the hall to find out what all the noise was about and found some of the backing musicians in there with a girl. They told me that she had somehow got into the dressing room earlier in the day because she was desperate to meet Jimi, and that they had found her hiding in a wardrobe. They were telling her that they could arrange for her to meet him, but only if she would fool around with them first, doing various unmentionable acts.

I spoke to her, and she told me she had been hiding there for hours just hoping to meet Jimi. I said I'd be right back. I knew he was just down the hall, so I went along and told him what was happening. He came back with me to the dressing room, and when he went over to her, the girl became quite hysterical. The other guys were urging him on to have his 'wicked way' with her, but instead he calmed her down, took her to his dressing room, signed some autographs and chatted with her for a while. Then he and I took her outside, where he invited her to come back later to see the show as his guest. He even put her in a cab to make sure she got home safely. From his image, his music and his wild stage shows you might not expect him to have had such integrity. He was a very special man, a true gentleman. I know I've often disappointed journalists who have come to me in search of a juicy story about Jimi, because all I could say was that he was one of the nicest, well-mannered people you could wish to meet.

I also struck up a rapport with Noel Redding, and we made up our own lyrics to the Experience's version of 'Wild Thing', which included such immortal lines as, 'Slag heap, you make my skin creep / Slag heap, you make everything runny . . .' That will give some idea of how unstable we were, hey, but we had some full-sized laughs together.

A lot of the time was spent travelling in the tour bus and in the dressing rooms, where John and Jimi would play their guitars all the time. Jimi had played on the east side of America, and John on the west, but they knew a lot of the same licks and riffs. We had such good times. In fact, we became good friends with all the other performers. Contrary to what has been often reported, there was no rivalry or jealousy. Anyway, we were too far ahead, with a solid, loyal fan base, and weren't the temper-throwing, jealous star types, which I think is one of the main reasons we made it though pop mania and lived to tell the tale.

Sometimes we would even suggest things that might get Jimi a little more publicity. One night, I was in the dressing room when Keith Altham said he'd thought of a little idea that would make Jimi a bit more famous. I always trusted Keith because he was one of the best in PR and knew what he was doing. He said, 'Can I borrow your lighter?' and I said yes, and didn't think anything more about it. Later there was a lot of yelling and pandemonium in the theatre; Jimi had set fire to his guitar and the place was in a panic. But he had been very careful with this stunt because of the risks involved. That was Keith's little idea, to set fire to the guitar, a trick that would become part of the Hendrix legend.

On a later occasion, I was in Hump's dressing room – I think it was in Wales – and we got onto the subject of Jayne Mansfield. We were both fans, and he said that he had a dinner date with her the following Thursday. After hyperventilating with laughter, I said, 'Are you serious?' He was. He had some good connections, he was with the Gordon Mills Agency, who handled Tom Jones, and they had set up the date. The next show was on Saturday, and I was going to give Hump the third degree regarding Jayne Mansfield, because the whole cast wanted to know what had taken place. Upon his return to reality, I asked him if he had had a good time.

'Well?' I waited.

'Well what?'

'You know, did anything else happen?' I prided myself on my self-restraint. But after a verbal tennis rally, I emerged with nothing to tell the rest of the cast. I did try for a week or so to find out what had happened, but to no avail: Hump would not budge from the 'nothing happened' story. He could have made something up, because he knew all of us were disappointed. Later, I found out that he had told John everything – although perhaps he was just bragging.

I was very thin at this time: we always sweated off pounds on stage. Whatever I ate, I never seemed to gain weight. I even saw a doctor – his name was Dr Kost, and we called him Kost-plenty – whose surgery was opposite our management offices at Bickenhall Mansions. I asked him if he could give me something to make me fat. He threw me out and that was that.

Maurice King arranged for Shirley Bassey to visit us in our dressing room; he was her former manager and thought our being photographed together would be good for all of us. When she arrived, though, she was made to wait in the hall outside because we were – I know it sounds awful – doing our hair, but she didn't seem annoyed or upset at all. Being an artist herself, she would have understood. We all found her very attractive and approachable. I told her that the last time I had seen her was on a show at the London Palladium with The Beatles. I had been in the audience with PJ Proby. Gloria Swanson, the actress, had made a guest appearance and kept giving PJ the eye; she even had a note sent to him, asking if he would like to go for a drink, which was music to his ears. I never got to see it and he never told me what happened.

Our shows continued, attended by the customary screaming and yelling, with all the acts receiving full attention from the fans and press. Everyone was a hit. But on 30 April, the last night of the tour at the Tooting Granada, it was announced that The Walker Brothers were splitting up.

I don't remember much about what actually happened. Maybe I blocked it out. I had not been involved in any disputes between John and Scott – if there were any – because I was not one of the main singers, but I would have helped to resolve matters if I had been asked, because I cared about both of them. I can't remember John and Scott being at odds on that tour. If anything, we would have made sure we got on with each other, just to get through it. It would have been hard for me to stop anything going wrong between the other two; I was caught in the middle.

I had no inkling beforehand of what was going to happen, and I can't even recall how I learned that the group was no more. There had certainly been tensions but I just couldn't believe that we were breaking up, and thought that the notion would be abandoned in a few days. I was wrong.

I still don't know all the reasons why The Walker Brothers split up, but it must have had something to do with the pressure on the group to maintain its success, and the management disagreeing among themselves about the different directions we should take. Each of us had an idea of what he would like to do to further his own career. Scott may have known which way he was going, although it may have been decided without his knowledge. John wanted to do his own thing.

One issue would have been creative differences. It would have been the same with The Beatles, or any group. A lot of groups would still be together if the record companies had let them do what they wanted – and the same went for us. For example, even back then, Scott wanted to do some avant-garde stuff like he does now, while John wanted to record rock and country songs and I wanted to have my own group side by side with The Walker Brothers.

The music scene was changing. The Monkees – actors who were brought together to play a pop group in an American TV series – were enjoying huge international success at that time, but the radical change was the hippy movement and 'flower power', which affected all of us, with its experimental music, drugs, colourful clothing and message of peace and love. This was a very special time in history, and its ethos struck a chord in me. I still can't think of anything better than everyone in the world getting on with each other. These sentiments would later inspire the music I recorded with The Rain – and we were given credit for it by a lot of the critics. Back in 1967, the new trends suggested that The Walker Brothers should take a different direction – but the policy was to stay with the successful formula.

For example, Paul McCartney once asked me and Graham Nash if we would like to come and play on the album that his brother, Mike McGear, was recording with The Scaffold. When we arrived, Jimmy Hendrix was there too, and several other pop stars. What a line-up that was! We got involved in this because we wanted to, but when our record company and managers found out they demanded to know how much we were going to get paid, so the whole thing got scrapped. Paul must still have the tape of those tracks, and I often think it would have been great if they had been released. In those days, however, if you wanted to record anything that didn't conform to what the record company wanted they wouldn't let you; the alternative was to go it alone.

The three of us were all suffering from one addiction or another. John was drinking heavily, to the point where he needed more and more alcohol for it to have any effect. It clouded his judgement, which added to the insecurities within the group, and particularly affected Scott, who thought the drink made John less reliable. The only time we tackled him on it, he said he would quit drink if we would stop taking tranquillisers. The difference was, though, that while drink made him irrational and argumentative, the tranquillisers kept us calm and didn't distort our capabilities.

As the drink problem escalated, John started to get aggressive. He was mixing with other people who were equally dependent. One evening, Scott and I were having a meal at the Lotus House when John turned up with Gordon Waller (of singing duo Peter and Gordon). Both were intoxicated. We invited them to join us, and they ordered some drinks but no food. For the first time I felt very uneasy with John as there was a new edge to his manner. Both he and Gordon were quite belligerent, trying to provoke Scott. Although much of what they said was incoherent I did think at one point that a fight might break out between John and Scott. Then, abruptly, John and Gordon got up and left. Scott turned to me and said he too had feared violence, even though we had never hit each other. That was the only time I thought that John and Scott might come to blows. I blamed it on the drink: had John been sober, it would never have happened.

Scott's dependence on Valium could have been a factor in our splitting up. One of the casualties of being a pop star was the impact it had on our nervous systems. Because of the unstable nature of our profession, our nerves were bad, and we were prescribed tranquillisers. It could have been much worse, of course: we could have sought refuge in hard drugs. Scott and I were hyperactives, and found that Valium both calmed us down and got rid of hangovers. We both became terribly addicted to it. The doctor had said that the drug was new and told us all the good things about it, claiming that the tablets were not habit-forming. They did help us, yet we became too dependent on them and later found out they were very addictive, and we'd face a lot of problems if we stopped taking them. In the end, it would take me six months to get off them.

One thing has always haunted me: because we were taking this drug increasingly, we were experiencing ever-higher levels of stress when we were not getting that fix, so I have wondered if this dependence was actually causing – or materially contributing to – Scott's nerves? If he hadn't been hooked on Valium where would the Walkers be now? I also wonder if Scott's much-publicised fear of going on stage – which has always been overstated – stemmed from his fear of the Valium wearing off during a performance.

Our managers were having problems of their own, and had been trying to talk each of us into going with them as a solo artist. John and I wanted to go with Barry, and Scott – God knows why – wanted to go with Maurice.

As all this was happening, Maurice and Barry were auditioning for a group to back me in my own venture, so the splitting up of The Walker Brothers didn't immediately impact on me as much as it might have done. That project came to nothing, and it wasn't until much, much later that I realised what the split had meant for me.

Should we have split up? I personally would have liked the group to stay together. I felt we had so much more to offer, not just musically but in films and different media. I still feel that way today. If our management and our record company had let us continue down the road on which we had embarked as a trio when we came to England, and had not been set on promoting Scott as the next Sinatra while sidelining me and John, it's anybody's guess where we would be now.

Financially, I came out of it with nothing – is there anything lower than minus zero? We owed the taxman thousands, and it took us about five years to pay it off. The split left me feeling shame and sadness. The thing that gets me now, later on down the line, is that we have since been offered big money – and I mean *big* money – to do some concerts. Not that the money is the only thing, but it is a factor when you don't have any! I would do it because, yes, I need the money, but above all it would be great for the three of us to get together and really have some fun, just as we used to.

THERE WERE NO GOODBYES
J O H N   W A L K E R

In autumn 1966 we signed up to do a tour that was to take place in January 1967, with Roy Orbison headlining, and The Yardbirds. Jimmy Page, the lead guitarist in The Yardbirds on this tour, later went on to form Led Zeppelin. This tour was timely for us, as our work permits were about to expire, although they would eventually be extended for a special performance later in the year.

In October or November of 1966, all sorts of rumours about us were floating around. There were reports that we were taking out British citizenship, but that wasn't happening. Capable Management had fed the story to the press, but the truth is that none of us ever discussed taking out British citizenship, although we did consider Britain to be our home. Another rumour was that Scott and Gary were supposedly going to marry British girls in order to get a green card – another press fantasy. We also heard that Maurice King was supposedly forcing Scott to sign an agreement not to marry, on pain of forfeiting £50,000 – a completely fictitious press story. There was further gross exaggeration in tales that Capable Management took out an insurance policy for £1,000,000 on our lives! I don't think so.

The expiry of our work permits meant that we were barred from working in Britain for six months. Even today, music journalists claim that this had an adverse effect on our career, but from our perspective it had little impact at all because we took advantage of the ban to schedule a highly successful world tour.

November was a busy month for us. We went to Germany, Denmark, Sweden and Holland for television and live shows. In Germany we did *Beat Club* and other TV. The record company had set us up with lots of radio and press as well. We primarily promoted 'Another Tear Falls' and that was featured throughout. I loved Stockholm, with its beautiful concert hall, and the Scandinavian countries in general with their gorgeous mountains and water.

The tour was horrendous, though, in terms of the travelling involved – there were huge hauls between shows, and we were stuck on the bus most of the time. Trying to eat, sleep, feel refreshed for the shows – it was a nightmare. Scott had the flu and went home after about a week on tour, and Gary and I finished the last few dates by ourselves. My electric-blue 1959 Stratocaster disappeared from the tour bus after the last show in Germany, and never showed up again. There were always so many people roaming around backstage and on tour. Thankfully, I wasn't overly fond of this particular guitar.

I had noticed one significant change in Scott, once The Walker Brothers had achieved stardom: he became quite distrustful of women. As a result of his celebrity, he could never be sure that women liked him for himself, or because he was famous – a common problem that all successful artists encounter. You don't know who your friends really are. Once he found a lady he trusted, he stayed with her for a long time.

Scott was dating a model, Irene Dunford, exclusively for quite a while. Then, when we were playing in Copenhagen while touring Denmark, we met a young woman named Mette Teglbjaerg, who had come to see the show with some friends. Both Scott and I noticed her, commenting to each other on how attractive she was, and we were all introduced to her. She may have been known to somebody connected to the show, because normally we didn't meet fans or audience. Contrary to what has been written in *A Deep*

Shade of Blue about that meeting, there was no coin toss to see who would take her out after the show.

Scott started dating Mette. One thing that set her apart from most of the girls whom he met was that she didn't idolise him; she wasn't starstruck but really cared for him. In fact, she took the mickey out of him when the occasion called for it. Also, she seemed emotionally stable, with a very even temperament, which benefited Scott as he threw himself into his projects completely and was usually either elated or worried about things, there was no middle ground.

I can't say much about Scott's girlfriends because he was very private about that part of his life. However, after the break-up of The Walker Brothers, and after Scott and Mette parted in the seventies, he did have three serious relationships that I knew about – but that's another story.

There were some terrible false stories circulating about, or attributed to, Mette, once it became publicly known that she and Scott were an item. The worst was an awful report that Scott had persuaded her to go back to Denmark and face up to a shop-lifting charge, no more than an unethical attempt on the part of some journalist to get press attention and sell more papers. The story was completely untrue, and Mette herself has refuted it.

The authors of *A Deep Shade of Blue* attribute The Walker Brothers' break up to Mette – again, there is no merit to this theory. In the same book, she is quoted as making unkind comments about Gary and me, which I am sure is something she would never have done, as we were all quite good friends. In the late sixties she would come over to visit my future second wife, Julie, hanging out at our flat at the Water Gardens and talking a lot about Scott and the things they were doing.

They had got a large dog – a St Bernard – which lived with them in their small flat nearby. The dog was named Rasmus, after Mette's father, but they nicknamed him 'the no-no boy' because he was always in trouble. They had to get a baby-gate to keep him in the hallway and out of the living room, and they kept it in place for about six months.

I was over at their flat one day, and Engel said, 'Come over here, you've got to see this.' Rasmus was loose, and he was huge – but the gate wasn't up any more. Scott then put it in front of him, and

Rasmus completely stopped in his tracks. No matter where he went, if they put that gate up, that huge doge froze. It was hilarious. Later, he got so big that they shipped him out to the country to stay with Mette's father on his farm. Rasmus actually had his own claim to fame – he was recorded as being the largest St Bernard ever.

In November 1966, Capable Management mentioned to us that EMI had released four of Scott's early Liberty singles on an EP. I actually never listened to those songs, and really wasn't that interested because they were recordings Scott had done years earlier as a very young man. Scott, who wasn't consulted about their release, was really angry about their being put out.

At the end of that month, we played before Prince Philip in a royal gala, which was filmed at the London Palladium and shown across Great Britain. Princess Margaret and other members of the royal family attended. After the show, the entire cast of artists was up on the stage, at which point a chap announced the names of those who were to be presented to the royal family. As we were organised into a line Gary, Scott and I were given quick lessons in royal protocol and etiquette. We were not to extend our hands unless royalty extended theirs first, and we were not to speak unless spoken to. We were also to do a small bow from the waist when we were presented. I felt like an excited schoolboy.

The royal family came in a procession. They were all moving along the line of celebrities, but Prince Philip decided to stop when he got to us, extended his hand to each of us, and said, 'So, you boys are The Walker Brothers. Why are you three boys staying in this rainy country with all that sunshine in California?' Typical of Gary, he said, 'We like the weather!' That made Prince Philip chuckle. I think Scott and I were too nervous to say much, but we managed a little small talk before he moved on. Contrary to what's been written in *A Deep Shade of Blue* about this event, neither Princess Margaret nor any other member of the royal family invited us to a party, so Scott did not have the opportunity supposedly to turn down the invitation!

On 2 December we released an EP called *Solo John, Solo Scott*. Some people inferred from the title that we were getting ready to split up, but that wasn't true. We just wanted to do something different, and so did Philips. It was Philips' idea to come out with the EP, not ours, the first sign of our record company calling the shots where previously we'd been the ones who made the decisions. Although we had never talked about it, I had noticed a shift towards Scott after *Portrait* was recorded. In later years Scott would actually put his foot down once he saw how he was being manipulated.

For this EP, Scott and I got all the support we needed from Reg Guest, our wonderful arranger, and John Franz, the producer, to make what we considered a generally nice effort. I picked out 'Come Rain or Come Shine', a Ray Charles standard, and John Franz chose Bobby Hebb's 'Sunny' for me. Unfortunately, I wasn't really pleased with my rendition of 'Sunny', and would have chosen something different. Bobby had done a brilliant version and I thought it should end there. I wasn't involved with the arrangements or anything, and really just showed up and sang it. The song never seemed right for me. That was a perfect example of what happened when Philips started to dictate more and more what they wanted. I just went along with it.

Reg and I decided on the arrangement of 'Come Rain or Come Shine', and I had a lot of input. I think it's one of the best songs I did.

Scott had more latitude because he now had John Franz's complete support, whereas early on Franz had supported the whole group. Scott chose his two songs, including 'The Gentle Rain' and his own composition, 'Mrs Murphy'. It was quite daring for its time, with a lyric about a married woman having a baby by another man. Maybe Scott was looking to write lyrics that were more true to life and less romantic.

Around this time, Scott visited Quarr Abbey on the Isle of Wight, probably to study Gregorian chant. He always enjoyed learning more about older Western music, and had a vast record library of classical and related recordings. He didn't discuss his trip there with me, but the whole thing turned into a ridiculous media-fest involving photographers and other press, who somehow got wind that he was there. Scott appearing on the cover of prominent music magazines – monk's robe and all – was a publicity dream, whether it was planned or not. Supposedly he was given a key to the abbey, which he wore on his belt. One day I did notice a key, and I asked him what it was for, and he said, 'To make people ask me what it's for.' Typical Scott.

We had been asked to write and perform the theme song for a movie, *Deadlier Than the Male*. Scott and John Franz wrote the song, and we recorded it in December. The film wasn't due out until the next year but, without telling us, Philips released the song immediately as a single, which pissed us off as we were completely left out of the decision-making process. We refused to promote the song because it wasn't meant to be a Walker Brothers' single in the first place, and was in fact just a formulaic song without a lot of pizzazz – also, we'd had our noses bent out of joint. Philips seemed to be determined to squeeze every penny out of any project associated with us at that time.

'Archangel', the B-side, another Scott composition, featured the enormous pipe organ at the Royal Albert Hall, and for that reason the press insisted that it was based on a Bach fugue. Some have claimed that Scott had based it on the theme music from the 1964 epic, *The Fall of the Roman Empire*, but to my knowledge there's no truth in this. 'Archangel' is basically a standard pop song with all the requisite drums, strings and harmony, but the addition of the pipe organ lent more drama and at the time I thought it was quite original and fantastic. Peter Olaff, our sound guy, brilliantly engineered the entire recording and the mixing process for both tracks.

The rumours continued, with the three of us allegedly always at odds among ourselves and with our managers. By now we had become the focus of a lot of needless hysteria and were always trying to stay clear of it all. Scott, Gary and I were the last to know about the dramas in which we were supposed to be involved. Although the three of us did have disagreements and heated discussions, and mouthed off immaturely at times (usually because we had drunk too much), our end goal was ultimately to make good music. Those kinds of things happen with every group, and we worked very closely and spent a lot of time together, so of course there was friction from time to time. But up to this point, we had always managed to sort things out and get on with the business. Little did I know that soon there would be pressure on us as a group to split up – and that things would then unravel at a very quick pace.

We started working on *Images*, our third album, in December 1966. There were 12 tracks, of which I wrote two. One was 'I Wanna Know'. John Franz and Scott wanted a rock'n'roll song with distorted guitar sounds on it, so they asked me if I had one. I wasn't crazy about that song, which I had recently written, and didn't feel that it really belonged on the album, but it was handy and easy to learn. It was intended to be a duet, with me singing lead and Scott harmonising, but that didn't happen. It should also have been recorded with The Quotations, not a studio orchestra. The whole effort wasn't what I really wanted.

I had written 'I Can't Let It Happen To You' in a hotel room during our most recent tour and when I played it for Scott he liked it too. I wasn't given adequate time to work with Reg Guest on the song so, again, the track was quickly recorded and we went on to spend more time on other things. The French dance music artist Kid Loco did a very original cover of 'I Can't Let It Happen To You' around 2001.

I thought that the first track on the album, 'Everything Under the Sun', originally recorded by The Ronettes, should have been a single because it was another Bob Crewe song that I liked (he had written 'The Sun . . .') and, most importantly, it took us out of the big emotional ballad mode. In fact, it was an 'aggressive' style for us at the time, but Philips made the decision not to release it, which surprised me.

Scott contributed 'Experience', 'Orpheus' and 'Genevieve' to the album. I would agree with the many people who think that 'Genevieve' is Scott's finest solo from the Walker Brothers era. That song is definitely one of my favourite Scott tracks. 'Orpheus', like 'Mrs Murphy', deals with the theme of adultery and was explicit for its time. I think that perhaps Scott wanted to be taken more seriously as a songwriter and chose real-life drama themes over 'Moon and June'-type pop songs.

'Experience' is perhaps the strangest and most untypical track on the album. Reg did the arrangements, and I have no idea what input Scott had. The first time I heard 'Experience' was in the studio the day we recorded it. It sounded like a popular German or Italian folk song, and I couldn't figure out why it was on a Walker Brothers album.

'Just Say Goodbye', penned by Tony Hatch and Jackie Trent and previously recorded by Petula Clark, and Ben E King's 'Stand By Me' were both songs we had talked about doing at some point. The remaining tracks comprised a ballad by the Italian composer Iller Pattacini, 'It Makes No Difference Now', Fats Domino's 'Blueberry Hill', which I sang, 'Once Upon a Summertime', by Michel Legrand and Eddie Marnay, and 'I Will Wait for You', both of which Scott performed solo. I think *Portrait* was the best album we made.

It was during this time that I started to feel real tension between us, particularly with Scott and John Franz. Normally, we were very open with each other in the studio, but now it was different. Scott, Gary and I had always discussed every detail of each track we recorded, but now there were subtle and, eventually, quite blatant signs that I was not going to be involved in many decisions to do with this album. With a few exceptions I wasn't even made aware which songs had been chosen, if and when we would be rehearsing, what the arrangements would be. There was one thing after another, which at first left me completely bewildered. Then it dawned on me that something was wrong.

To begin with, I gave everyone the benefit of the doubt, but before long it was made clear to me, by John Franz in particular, that he now wanted to go in a completely new direction. The Walker Brothers were no longer the focus: Scott was.

I didn't have a problem with that. Franz loved the purity of Scott's voice, as did we all, and he was moving towards creating a solo career for him, very much as he had done with Dusty Springfield when he took her out of The Springfields. I would have been the last one to stand in the way of Scott's career, and in fact, have been very happy for him – and the rest of us – that he had the opportunity to develop and promote his extraordinary voice. And I feel the same for Gary, who went on to form The Rain, touring and recording with much success.

But still, at the time, the biggest problem for me was the way Franz handled this decision. I was disappointed and very quickly became quite angry, because I had been equally responsible for the success of our group, and was now suddenly to be left uninformed.

I had been drinking quite a lot before, but it had not been too much of a problem. Now my drinking increased, which only exacerbated the situation. It had become a refuge for me. I didn't realise it at the time but people must have found it difficult to deal with me. Yet things were difficult for me too. I'd walk into the studio each day for the *Images* recording sessions, and only then would I usually find out what I was meant to be singing. With no time allowed for me to give much thought to my parts, I found myself more or less improvising everything I was doing. It wasn't right. It seemed clear to me that John Franz was doing everything he could to diminish my role. Until now he had always been in the recording studio for each track, but he didn't bother to be around for the session when I recorded 'Blueberry Hill', for example.

Things rapidly got more difficult and unsettling for Gary, Scott and me. There was a new underlying hostility between us all that hadn't been there before. What distinguished this recording session from those of the past was the total lack of joy and excitement – at least on my part. Prior to *Images* I had anxiously looked forward to getting started on our tracks, but this time the atmosphere was exceedingly chilly, so I got out as quickly as I could and didn't say anything because I knew that it was costing Philips thousands of pounds per hour to have us all there in the studio. I took everything personally and felt that I had was getting a very cold shoulder from John Franz. I don't think Scott was aware of the unspoken animosity between John and me, and I didn't say anything to him about it. Things got so bad that we wouldn't even do a photo session together for the album – the cover shot of us is actually three photos carefully combined into one, with my hair cropped from the original photo, so that I looked current.

Poor Gary was caught in the middle of a situation that got worse each day. I was resentful, but determined to show up and do the job well. I was also hoping to find out what the hell was going on. After all the crap we had gone through to get to where we were, it was terribly hurtful that everything had changed so much, so quickly, and without warning. Mostly, I was really pissed off that there was no discussion with me about whatever new direction we were taking.

I didn't know what had happened. Not being particularly clued in musically, or involved in the recording process, Capable Management didn't get it – that the group were dissolving right under their noses. John Franz appeared to me to be a large part of the problem. He was left in charge of the music and, without actually having the courage to tell me himself, he chose this time to drive home his opinion that my contributions to The Walker Brothers were never of any importance.

I have no idea how much or how little my managers discussed John Franz's plan – and I certainly never discussed it with them. It's quite possible they just handled business, and let John handle the recordings. I do believe that Barry Clayman would have told me what was going on had he been privy to any information regarding such a bold idea on John's part. It was because of this lack of communication that, within a few months, I would make the decision to leave the group.

We all spent the Christmas holidays in England, Kathy and I at our house at Sanderstead. Things stayed quiet on the home front. I didn't discuss business with her, in fact until I got much older I never shared problems in my life, or any sensitive issues, with anybody. I kept all of that to myself.

I tried to relax, watched the Queen's Speech, overate, drank too much Scotch and smoked too many cigarettes. I also worked on my music, started writing quite a few songs, and played my guitar a lot. Some time later, during my solo career, I ended up recording some of these songs: 'I Cried All the Way Home', 'Little One' and 'I See Love in You'. Another, 'You Don't Understand Me', ended up as the B-side of my first solo single, 'Annabella'.

I'd purchased an open-reel tape deck from Philips that was capable of sound on sound, or overdubbing – quite advanced equipment at the time – and I worked with it, ultimately using it to devise the arrangements for the songs I was writing. I got quite creative with one of my songs, 'I Can't See You Anymore', recording my 12-string guitar at half speed and then playing it back at full speed – giving the effect of a poignant electronic mandolin accompaniment. Later, when Scott was producing my singles, I played the track for him and he really liked it, so we recorded it at Philips' Stanhope Place studio. Unfortunately, it never got released.

On 15 January 1967, The Walker Brothers departed from Heathrow Airport for our tour of Australia and New Zealand with Roy Orbison and The Yardbirds. There were 2,000 fans waiting to give us a rousing send-off from the terminal roof, which was in danger of collapsing. But chaos really erupted as we got out of our car and the fans invaded the terminal, chasing us. We ran for the nearest door, which turned out to be a ladies' room and, without hesitating, we went in, which caused quite a commotion inside. Female voices could be heard yelling, 'There are men in here! There are men in here!' – immediately followed by, 'It's The Walker Brothers! It's The Walker Brothers!' But our first thoughts were of barricading the door, so the three of us leaned hard against it. Within seconds, there was heavy pounding and screaming on the other side. The scratching, clawing and strange screeching was unnerving and quite frightening. We were breathless from having run up a flight of stairs, looking for a place to hide, and were now using every last bit of our combined strength to hold the door closed. Gary apologised to the women who were in there with us, turning to them calmly and saying, 'Sorry for the inconvenience, ladies.'

Finally, after about 20 minutes, the police did come, and managed to get the scary girls away so that we could finally come out. We signed autographs for the patient ladies who had been barricaded in there with us, then hit the duty-free shop.

As if that had not been enough, the three of us were in for a 28-hour flight and, as usual, loaded up with tranquillisers and alcohol. Within a year of arriving in the UK, all three of us had begun regularly using tranquillisers and sleeping pills to deal with the madness we encountered daily. If we stayed medicated, we were able to disregard the unique pressures of our lives, emotionally and mentally. Hash and coke were recreational, but alcohol consumption went from social to excessive with all of us, me in particular. Eventually Scott, Gary and I became extremely jittery and nervous if someone was walking behind us, or we were in a big crowd. I've tasted that adrenalin rush the body produces in threatening situations thousands of times. I'm still quite jumpy if I hear a loud noise or something sudden happens. I just want to hit the roof. It's completely uncontrollable.

Scott always took Valium and I took Serenid-D. Gary usually had his own pills, but for this flight he asked me for one of mine, which I warned him were very strong. He wasn't concerned, took a whole pill, and later went into a state of slow-motion. He couldn't even light a match, trying unsuccessfully for several minutes. We fell asleep for some hours, ate, watched the movie and slept again, which was our plan. I don't know anyone who likes to be stuck on a plane for 28 hours. Some press people wrote that we had to be carried off that plane, but miraculously we didn't: we walked off and took care of business. Youth can do that.

We were to do 14 shows in Australia and New Zealand, opening at Sydney Stadium. We were all surprised that Sydney was so modern. They had four television stations, whereas Britain had only two, or three if you were lucky. They actually served American-style hamburgers and malted milks, the kind I grew up on. Everything in Australia seemed larger than life. When ordering dinner, it was enough for three people. The Australians seemed generally to be statuesque people, even the girls. It was entirely different from England. During the tour, we had to take aeroplane trips from city to city, and found that each place had its own climate. We were passing through different time zones and the weather was the opposite of what we were used to. We had terrible jet lag for the first week.

The members of Roy Orbison's backing band were all from Texas and looked like American football players. They got in all kinds of trouble during the tour. We had all been cautioned about the groupies, and the surprise presents they might leave with us, which we'd have the misfortune of discovering two weeks later. So the band members immediately set out to find one girl each, to take on the entire tour with them – for companionship, and especially to be on the safe side. There were lots of wild parties and 'group activities' in their hotel rooms every night. Someone managed to record one particularly wild session, and the tape was played back – at a loud volume – on the plane the following morning. Gary, Scott and I were rolling in the aisles, especially when we heard a familiar voice on the tape say, 'Hey y'all, why don't we take off all our clothes, and get in a big pile in the middle of the floor.' There were other passengers aboard as well, and the recording left little to the imagination. After several minutes, one of the Texan guys stood up, and looked around very menacingly. The tape stopped suddenly. The band's girls on board were not amused, and in fact some of them split the next day.

Without notifying any of the artists, one of the theatre owners decided to tape a performance of the whole show, something absolutely prohibited in all contracts. We found out only by accident when one of the guys in our band saw the recording equipment being used. We were really pissed off, and made a split-second decision to confiscate the recording. The plan was for one of the guys in our band to get it while everyone was packing up after the show. He managed it, and gave it right away to a crew member, who took it immediately to his friend to erase our bit.

The following morning Gary and I were awakened by loud, insistent knocks on our door. The police were out in the hall, demanding that we let them in. We were even more hung over than usual, because we'd been celebrating the success of our little illicit confiscation. I put on my dressing gown and looked around the messy room littered with liquor bottles and overflowing ashtrays. Gary was sitting in the corner, in the lotus position, with a sheet wrapped around him and a towel over his head, all intended to distract the police. He also had his sunglasses on.

The police were still pounding on the door. I said, 'Beads, are you with us?' He didn't reply, so I lit a cigarette and went over to open the door. The cops bolted in and wanted to know if one of our band members was with us. I said no. The police asked, 'Where's the stolen tape?' I said, 'I don't know.' They asked very loudly again, 'We know you know where it is. Who has the stolen tape?' Then they saw Gary, and froze. After several seconds of stunned silence, they pointed to him, and asked me impatiently, 'What about him? Does he know?' I said, 'He's meditating.' They looked back at me angrily. Finally, Gary broke his silence, and said calmly and quietly, 'Tape? There is no tape,' and went back into his trance. With that, the police left our room. We found out later that the tape mysteriously appeared back at the theatre. It was blank, of course.

The three of us were surprised to find that the audiences in Australia and New Zealand were quite conservative, almost reserved. We had become so used to the screaming and pandemonium back in the UK, and now we could actually hear ourselves. But the concerts were successful, and I loved New Zealand and its spectacular beauty.

After finishing the tour with Orbison we went on to play at the

National Theatre in Singapore. The first thing we noticed when we landed was the unbelievable humidity. Our clothes were damp when we took them out of our suitcases. All the instruments were so wet the players had to use hairdryers to dry them out before the performance.

The covered stage was in an open-air amphitheatre, and the show was sold out. There were thousands of people. Curiously, we could see that everyone came in with a sort of baton – half red, half white. We wondered what these were for. Halfway through the show, there were loud claps of thunder, and sheets of rain suddenly poured down. The batons became miniature umbrellas. We were looking out over a sea of red circles – it was surreal. The weather didn't seem to faze the audience in the least, but the whole experience was new for us. Fortunately, the stage was dry so we carried on as usual.

The authors of *A Deep Shade of Blue* assert that the differences between Scott and me became obvious on this tour, as did growing incompatibility, and that, while Scott was artistic and offended by money, I was 'deeply materialistic'. These assertions, aside from Scott's artistic leanings, are figments of some journalist's imagination, and have sadly fed the press and fans through the years. All three of us considered ourselves to be professional musicians who should be fairly compensated for our work. None of us was offended by making lots of money at any time, and we all enjoyed spending it. Scott's determination to put forth his musical ideas over the years – whether or not they brought commercial success – is highly commendable, and this is what should be emphasised instead of the fairytale 'poet seeks poverty' story.

Basically, as long as John Franz and Maurice King weren't around, the three of us were fine. Barry went on the tour with us, not John or Maurice, and we all just fell back into our usual mode. In fact, we had a great time on that tour, despite the 90-degree heat at Sydney Stadium. We played the big venues, to thousands of people, and were well received each night by the crowds. Orbison knocked everybody's socks off, night after night. For a couple of weeks it was the same routine: do the show, go back to the hotel to have some drinks, get up early to catch the next flight to the next town – and start all over again. Even when we had a few days off we were still confined to the hotel, stealing away just once or twice to see some kangaroos hopping about in Brisbane, and later some ostriches and emus at a park elsewhere.

Our next stop was a short, strictly promotional tour of Japan – no shows yet, but a lot of press – and here's where we got the surprise of our lives. We were the last ones off the plane and, as we started to descend the stairway to the tarmac, we saw an enormous sign – at least two storeys tall and 50 feet wide – that said 'WELCOME WALKER BROTHERS'. Then we saw the crowd – there were at least 10,000 people, we were told – all waiting and cheering for us from the roof of the airport terminal building. We were so stunned we just froze and stared. There were at least two dozen policemen waiting down on the tarmac. They immediately surrounded us and we were whisked quickly through customs. They put us in a lounge, with security everywhere – I had never seen so much security in my life – before we were taken to our limos and driven into Tokyo. Cabs were speeding towards us from all directions, and recklessly pulling up alongside our car with photographers hanging out of the windows and clicking away at us with their big Nikon cameras. The driver said, 'Cab drivers kamikazes!' It was an amazing trip.

Before going to our hotel we were taken to the largest record store in Tokyo to sign autographs. It looked as if there were thousands of people there, all crammed into the huge, cavernous place. Security handled the crowd for as long as they could, but we had to leave shortly after we arrived, having signed only a few autographs, as the crowd was just too large for them to contain. Off we went to the hotel – the New Otani, a super-luxurious modern hotel that was used in the James Bond movie *Quantum of Solace*. The hotel had a revolving restaurant on the roof, so we got a spectacular view of Tokyo. Although the decor was very traditional Japanese, there were Western amenities such as beds and chairs.

After the Japanese promotional tour, Gary and Scott went back to the UK, and I went to Hawaii for a few days. I looked up my old Oasis Club crowd, had drinks and hung out. After that, I flew to LA to see my parents for a few days and then on to the UK. I had been back and forth to America several times since coming to

England, and I'd always checked in with my family. Although they probably would have liked me to stay close to them (though they never mentioned it out loud), they realised that I'd started a new life in England. My parents never came over, but Scott's mother, Mimi, visited frequently.

I returned home late in January 1967, and on 3 February our latest single – 'Stay With Me Baby'/'Turn Out the Moon' – was released; it reached Number 26. I suggested doing 'Stay With Me Baby' after becoming familiar with the Lorraine Ellison version on one of my recent trips to America. It was a big dramatic ballad, perfect for our style at the time, but it was a very difficult song for both Scott and me. Aside from the technical demands, we hadn't worked it out as we used to. Instead, we left all the work to be done on a tight schedule in the studio. Despite this, Gary, Scott and I were very pleased with the track. Scott wrote 'Turn Out the Moon'; it was always a good idea for an artist to contribute an original song.

My intuition told me that The Walker Brothers needed to start moving in a new direction regarding production and material as staleness was beginning to set in, but I didn't have any control over the situation, and Scott and I were moving further away from each other. We were getting restless, musically. I'm sure that we were frustrated because of this, but no one really voiced it out loud. Looking back now, I'm sure this situation contributed to the break-up of the group. Much later, in the seventies, Dick Leahy – the president of GTO Records – got a new producer for us in Nashville, to try to breathe fresh air into our tracks. The same thing needed to happen in 1967 but we weren't given the opportunity to evolve. Outside forces were exerting too much influence and the group's future looked bleak. Philips, and John Franz in particular, wanted us to keep recording the same type of music and if that formula became passé, I think the next plan John Franz had was to focus on Scott and promote him in the Jack Jones/Frank Sinatra style. I don't know that Scott was even consulted about all this, as he was just as tense as we were, not figuring out completely what was going on. Capable Management didn't disagree with Philips, simply because it was in their best interests not to.

Unfortunately, this thinking was not in The Walker Brothers' best interests. Had the three of us still been as tight as we used to be as a group, we would have evolved into what we wanted to be – and the hell with the rest of them. But Scott and I were doing things completely out of our normal character: we were behaving like a couple of asses. We didn't prepare for the recording sessions properly, or consult each other about material, nor did we map out our next move as we had always done right from our Hollywood days. The other problem was that we were very inconsiderate to each other. For example, Gary and I smoked a lot even though Scott constantly complained about it. Scott was always late for everything, with no explanation, which stressed us out. Ultimately we stopped talking to each other. I can't imagine how frustrating it must have been for Gary. After all, he had organised the whole adventure in the first place and had been supportive throughout.

In mid-February, *Images* was released and went to Number 6, but despite the success we'd had the group's days were numbered. By the time *Images* came out we weren't talking to each other.

Capable Management had signed us up for what turned to be our last UK package tour in the late spring of 1967. The inducement for us to do the tour was that we ourselves would be promoting it, or so were told. We left this in Capable's capable hands, and signed on the dotted line that said we owned half of the tour. We were told that instead of the fees going to a promoter, as normally happened, the money would be split between the three of us. However, we were later to feel totally deceived, because when the time came to pay us after the tour, Capable Management claimed that there were 'extremely high expenses', therefore the projected profit was zilch.

Around this time Kathy learned that she was pregnant and told me that she wanted to go home to America to be with her family. I knew why she wanted to go: she wasn't very happy, and I wasn't around a great deal, so I wouldn't have been much help. Therefore she made the decision to return to her parents. Whether I liked the thought of her leaving was another thing that wasn't discussed. I didn't know what her intention was: she may have wanted to remain in America after the birth, but the subject was never discussed.

In March she lost the baby. When she came back to the UK I was staying at Barry Clayman's flat in Maida Vale, so we didn't have our own place to live. I found a flat as soon as I could, but things were becoming even more difficult between us. The same problems were even more evident and, because of the miscarriage, Kathy was more sensitive than ever. I was made to feel that everything that had happened up to that point was somehow my fault. I was angry and very hurt. I was keeping more and more to myself. I didn't talk about how I felt; I didn't see the point in it.

In the spring of 1967 psychedelia started taking over the pop scene. The climate was warm and beautiful – not the typical dreary, rainy English weather – and everyone seemed to be celebrating and happy. Flower power was everywhere; a quiet revolution was taking place. People were smoking a lot of dope, wearing flowers in their hair, and mirroring what was happening in San Francisco. The atmosphere was open, carefree and seemingly innocent. People had money to spend and things were not very expensive. There were protests over the war in Vietnam. Peace signs and the slogan 'Make Love, Not War' became the new symbols of the time. Men wore kaftans, sandals and beads, and grew their hair. Girls were donning bright colours and flowing, soft, flowery fabrics, or exotic prints from India. Guys loved the whole look: no bras, see-through blouses, super miniskirts. Unisex was in – clothes, hair, everything was interchangeable between the sexes and completely acceptable. I loved it, and had a few kaftans of my own, made of tapestry. The new popular pastime was the 'love-in', which was basically a big orgy with everyone passing their partner around and having wild sex. Soon, acid became as popular as dope, with Timothy Leary extolling the virtues of the mind-altering substance. I never tried acid: the chemical part of it didn't appeal to me, so I stuck to booze and hash.

Of course, this cultural revolution affected the music and entertainment industries. New groups and artists such as The Mamas and the Papas, The Fifth Dimension, Scott McKenzie, Donovan, Joni Mitchell, Joan Baez, Bob Dylan, Sonny and Cher, Simon and Garfunkel, Janis Joplin and, of course, Jimi Hendrix and the Experience, were offering up a whole new wave of songs and images. London was where it was all happening and it was wonderful to be at the centre of it all.

Sometime in March, Barry Clayman asked me to go with him to New York City on a business trip. The trip was exploratory: Barry was genuinely trying to find a way for The Walker Brothers to break into America, and I suppose I was asked to go with him because I'd been used to dealing with all the business meetings back in Hollywood, and Barry thought I was more hip to what might be current in America than the others. To begin with I was quite hopeful for some action there. We met a high-powered entertainment attorney and various promoters, but Scott's draft status was still an issue that needed to be resolved if we were to work in America, and by the time we finished up I didn't come away with a feel for any potential business, only the suspicion that the trip would be another huge expense charged to The Walker Brothers. I was right: nothing ever came of it.

When I arrived back at Heathrow Chris Hutchins, my PR guy, who had been hired by Capable Management, appeared with a girl called Jayne Harries, who had recently been chosen as *Disc and Music Echo*'s 'Girl of the Year', and was commissioned by that paper to write up our forthcoming tour. Jane was to gain a reputation in the media as the 'heiress' of wealthy parents, and my association with her started out as a publicity stunt set up by Chris. I hadn't even met the girl until that moment, but Chris was intimating to the press that something was going on between us, and we ended up being photographed together several times.

One nice thing did come out of this episode: I met Mr and Mrs Harries, who were really charming people. They invited me to their townhouse in St James's Park for lunch, and we got along well and became quite good friends. After I had known them for a while, I was asked if I would like to attend the Horse & Hounds Ball at the Grosvenor Hotel. I remember Mrs Harries politely asking me if I had suitable attire for the event. I asked if black tie would do and she was probably a little surprised that a pop star owned a proper tuxedo. At the ball I met a lot of rather interesting society people who were secret Walker Brothers fans, so I had a great time.

Afterwards there were pictures in the society columns of me with Jayne at the ball. One report described her as my girlfriend, another said we had known each other six months. Neither was true, and when I found out what Chris was up to I was extremely pissed off, thinking it was all in very bad taste, and refused to have anything further to do with his plan. I didn't need that kind of press, and had no intention of being associated with it in any way. Also, Jayne's reported age was 17, although she was actually 15 at the time. As far as I was concerned, those reports that she was my girlfriend were really pushing the envelope.

We were the headliners on The Walker Brothers Tour. The other featured artists were Cat Stevens, Engelbert Humperdinck, Nick Jones and the Californians, and The Jimi Hendrix Experience, who were performing in their first major UK tour. Our backing band was The Quotations, as usual. Gary had seen Jimi playing in a London club and he couldn't wait to tell us how amazing he was, and that he should be on the tour. Scott and I both agreed, so Jimi was signed on. Jimi and I became quite good friends. We both came into the theatres a little early to jam, play blues and chat and would keep in touch until he went to America, six months or so later.

I'll never forget being at a Variety Club function shortly after the tour, where Jimi was going to be presented with an award from the organisation. Some of the lesser-known people attending made some very unkind remarks about Jimi's dress and so on, and I was glad I was there because I think I was the only friendly face in the gathering. Jimi's manager wasn't with him, so we sat together and hung out for the evening. I was really offended by the attitude of those people, who were supposed to be professionals.

Jimi worked hard at his craft. He spoke softly and was a very polite and shy man. Reserved in person, he was the opposite on stage, with no inhibitions at all. Once he'd walked on, it was as if a wild genie had popped out of the bottle. He was extraordinary. The worst thing that happened to Jimi was when he got to America and he got lost in the drug scene big time, then all hell broke loose. Even his stage antics went beyond passion, and actually became quite destructive.

It's been written several times that we displayed jealousy of Jimi during the tour, but this was completely untrue. Someone even claimed that I went to his dressing room after a show and reprimanded him for setting his guitar on fire – again, that's nonsense. I did ask him after the first show if he was planning to set his guitar on fire every night, and when he said yes, I said, 'Great – we need to get a fire marshal!' It was a very friendly exchange between us.

The tour lasted about a month. Scott and I were now very much at odds, but the hostility was all unspoken – kind of like a cold war. We shared the dressing room, as usual, and somehow came up with a little conversation while we waited for our turn to go up on stage. As the tour went on, everybody got really moody. Scott began constantly turning up late at the theatre, making Gary and me paranoid that he would finally just stop showing up at all. He was quoted as saying that when he turned up late after attending a christening, I was 'inhuman' and stopped speaking to him at that point, but that's not true. Everything Scott did at that time was last-minute, and he never said a thing to us when he arrived late. There was no apology or any explanation – nothing. I guess that by then he was tired of touring and all its hardships and inconveniences. It was difficult for all of us, but I got really pissed off because his behaviour was creating more undue stress for Gary and me. Even so, none of us said anything to each other. Our goal was just to get through the tour. Once our show started, everything fell into place, and each of us did his job, but it was pure misery backstage.

There was the odd light moment. One night, Cat Stevens came into our dressing room and started playing the piano, doing the 'moody genius' composer thing, looking very serious and deep while playing a very forgettable, quasi-poignant original piece. Scott, who was looking very amused by the whole performance, handed me a note that said, 'Are you getting the genius bit?' We both tried to keep a straight face. I really liked it when the old Scott was back, and I'm sure it worked the other way around, too, but there was so much heavy drinking going on that who knows how we came across to each other? I'm sure Gary and I must have driven Scott crazy with our heavy cigarette smoking – he always complained. Even though the clubs we all went to were smoke-filled, it was different being cooped up in a small, poorly ventilated dressing room. Now that I've not smoked for several years I wouldn't be nearly as tolerant as Scott was.

Engelbert Humperdinck and I were fairly friendly. He struck me as being a big unsure of himself and his success. At the beginning of the tour he asked me what he should wear, telling me he had brought a suit. I told him to wear a jacket with the shirt collar worn over the lapel, not tucked behind it. He took my advice and looked terrific. He went on, of course, to be one of the most enduring stars in Las Vegas, and very popular around the world, but back in 1967 he was just starting out on his first big tour, and his song, 'Release Me' a massive worldwide hit, had just reached Number 1.

Engelbert stopped me backstage early on in the tour, and said confidentially, 'John, I've got to tell you something.' I asked him what was going on. He said, 'I've been with Jayne Mansfield.' I replied, 'Jayne Mansfield?', thinking to myself that she was rather on the older side. He said, 'Yeah, I slept with her last night.' Then he told me how he had gone to a local club after the show the night before, and how a guy came over to him and said that Miss Mansfield was in the club and wanted to meet him. They had a few drinks and she invited him back to her hotel. He went, and I got a brief blow-by-blow account of what followed, and of course a revealing description of her. Engelbert was quite pleased with himself. I just said, 'Cool,' and gave him the thumbs-up.

I'll never forget how impressed he was when all the girls screamed at us when we went out on stage. He couldn't believe it and seemed quite overwhelmed by the whole thing. I think he got some of the spillover action.

Scott, Gary and I had reached an agreement early on that we would stay together as long as it remained fun, but that when the joy was gone we would part ways. It's important to mention that, despite what happened in the end, we'd had a lot of fun and enjoyment during much of our early career, and that we continue to be friends.

Several circumstances contributed to the break-up of The Walker Brothers.

First, my marriage. Once I got married in 1965 the personal dynamics of my relationships with Scott and Gary completely changed. They were single and I was now more homebound, except for work-involved things, so we no longer hung out together as much as we used to. It may have appeared to them – and to everyone – that I was now a 'part-time' member of the group, even though I didn't think I was.

My attitude didn't help. I'm sure that, with our increasing fame, I became more and more arrogant, and probably wasn't an easy person to deal with. Scott and I had always had a high opinion of ourselves as artists, going way back to the Hollywood days, and with the success of The Walker Brothers that may have got blown out of proportion a little bit. So we probably acted like asses on many occasions.

Then there was John Franz. I had begun to feel really uncomfortable during the recording of *Images*, in late 1966, because he was so focused on Scott and made it clear to me that my contributions were unimportant. For the first time, I wasn't involved in the preparations for the sessions, as I had been previously. In the studio John took great pains with anything that Scott was doing, but he didn't show much interest in my tracks, often leaving the studio during my solo sessions. I didn't blame Scott for any of this, and in fact it put him in an awkward position. Instead, I kept everything to myself, not complaining to Capable Management, Scott, Gary – or anybody.

Another factor was my drinking. I drank more and more during the *Images* sessions, which got me through but numbed my judgement, and it didn't help the situation because I gave everybody the impression that I wasn't taking things seriously. It was a vicious circle. It's very likely that Scott felt my behaviour I was letting him down. Yet nobody said anything. I got in and out of the studio as quickly and quietly as possible because I didn't want to cause a scene, which I surely would have done had I stuck around long enough. Recording is a delicate, emotional thing, and I didn't want to upset Scott. Also, I was well aware of studio costs and didn't know how to approach anyone about the situation, even though I was close enough to Barry Clayman to have discussed it with him.

On that last UK tour, Scott's seeming lack of commitment became apparent, and he made it very clear that he didn't like touring. Half the time Gary and I didn't know if he would show up for each show. It was nerve-racking. We weren't even travelling together as we used to: Gary and I were on the bus and having a great time, but Scott was travelling with the bass player in the band. He chose to separate himself from us as much as possible, and we didn't know where he was most of the time. I finally told Barry, 'I've had enough of this,' referring to Scott's seeming uninterest in the tour. Barry just listened. I also told Gary I'd had enough, but he may not have known how serious I was. By the end of the tour, Scott and I weren't speaking to each other. There were no loud arguments, fights or disagreements, none of that stuff, just a lot of drinking, quietly hanging around the dressing room, doing the shows, and Scott going his way, Gary and I going ours. I was no longer having fun, and I doubt Scott was, either.

We weren't any different from other successful groups in that we needed strong guidance and sound advice. Good management overcomes the obstacles a band can encounter, if they want to stay together. Had Capable been more experienced as a management company they would have figured out a way to keep The Walker Brothers going as a group. They really should have ironed out the obstacles that crossed our paths: for example, we never played the US because of Scott's fear of the draft, a problem that could have been resolved had our managers been on the ball. Scott would have played America had the fear not been there. That should have been addressed immediately, but Maurice chose to keep sweeping it under the carpet, which severely limited our careers and also put Scott more and more at risk. I think of managers like Robert Stigwood, Brian Epstein, Peter Grant and Andrew Oldham in the very early days of the Stones: I realised a long time ago that these guys were in it for the long haul, and somehow kept the groups together, regardless of internal strife and problems.

All these factors contributed to my formal decision to leave the group. By the end of the tour, in April, I told Barry that I was leaving The Walker Brothers for good. I never talked to Scott about my decision, although I had mentioned to Gary that I was done during the tour. Barry already knew that I wasn't happy with Scott's apparent lack of interest; he just listened and didn't try to talk me out of my decision. Later, when I met with Maurice, he didn't have anything to say either. They just contacted the press to tell them the news.

On 30 April, we played our last performance as The Walker Brothers at the Tooting Granada Theatre. The show went off without a hitch, as usual. We were just glad that it was finally over, and I felt a lot of relief. We each simply went our own ways – there were no goodbyes – and that's pretty much how the group split up. It was a quiet and undramatic ending, considering all that we had been through together. The split was announced in the papers the next morning.

I was difficult to talk to at that time. I became more and more insular, keeping my thoughts to myself. The Walker Brothers would be a tough act to follow, and I was wondering what I was going to do next, professionally and personally. Kathy and I had drifted further apart but even so we got another flat in Hampstead and lived there for several months before returning to America late that year.

It felt as if a rug had been pulled out from under me as everything in my life had unravelled so quickly. I also faced cold, hard reality in finding out that I had a lot of acquaintances, not friends. Barry was about the only person whom I trusted, even though I didn't confide in him much either. I don't think Barry wanted the group to split up and, had it been up to him alone, I think he would have found a way to sort things out so that everybody would be happy.

At night I would go to different clubs, but mainly to the Bag O' Nails because it was convenient for me to get there from Maida Vale. I'd take taxis because I knew I'd be smashed by the end of the evening. I'd get to the club and find a dark table in the back somewhere, and the owner always took care of me if I wanted something to eat or drink. I also spent a lot of time at the Lotus House on Edgware Road, a really good Chinese restaurant where the owner, Ken, always looked out for me, especially when I'd had way too much to drink. He'd call a cab and make sure I was OK. I loved the spare ribs and sweet-and-sour pork they served there – in fact, that's all I ever ordered. I always felt better after I'd visited the Lotus House.

I wasn't worried about what Scott would do as I'd guessed that, between them, John Franz and Maurice King had mapped out his future. I did have concerns for Gary, even though I'd always considered him to be very resourceful, but I completely lost touch with the two of them, too busy worrying about my own problems to take on board anyone else's.

Two books – *A Deep Shade of Blue* and *Scott Walker: Long About Now* by Ken Brooks – have wrongly asserted that Mette was somehow involved not only in the break-up of The Walker Brothers but also in some kind of royalty-cheque scam between

Scott and me. That's all totally untrue. And, contrary to what has been reported, we did not split up amid a flurry of lawsuits and recriminations. Nobody sued anybody, and there was no legal battle that I know of.

Financially, we didn't come out of it very well, as we didn't know where our money had gone or how much we were owed, and there were lots of other unanswered questions. I suddenly realised that I had no idea how much money I had – not a clue. I blame that on my own lack of vigilance. We had let Capable Management and their accountants take care of everything, never even bothering to ask how much we were making. I am quite certain that none of us were ever fully compensated for all the work that we'd done. Even to this day, I still can't believe how stupid I was about that. It's as if I had left some of my common sense back in Hollywood. Yet I still had faith in Barry Clayman and in fact trusted him with my future career.

I would not say that the circumstances of the split left underlying traces of bitterness: there was never bitterness, but rather disappointment in my own immaturity and the behaviour of other people around us. Looking back after all these years, I feel the same way now as I did then: that The Walker Brothers' break-up was premature, and that we never realised the full potential of the group. That was unfortunate, both for us and for our fans.

CHAPTER 6

ON OUR OWN

'WE LOVE GARY!'
GARY WALKER

As solo artists, we were assigned different managers by Capable Management. Scott and I ended up with Maurice King, while John went with Barry Clayman. I was still thinking of forming my own group and writing my own songs. I discussed it with Scott, and he asked if he could play the bass in my group. That was all he wanted to do, but the management and record company had other plans for him. I would talk to him on the phone now and then as we were both struggling and a little cash would have helped. We had trouble getting our money because the management controlled it, and if you wanted some you had to go through a hassle to get it. There was never any talk about playing or re-forming, which perhaps would have been the right move.

John got on the road with the group he put together, The Techniques, and Sue and Sunny, two great singers. Sunny would later sing on my single, 'Come In, You'll Get Pneumonia'. She had a big voice that drowned all of us out in the studio.

I remember Paul McCartney coming around to the house off Park Lane I shared with Graham Nash and his wife, Rose, one spring night in 1967. Graham and I were experimenting with sounds on three tape recorders at once to see what effects we could

211

get. We were the only pop musicians at the time to own a stroboscope, a device I'd come across it in some scientific magazine. What it did – put at its simplest – was determine speeds of rotation and check for flaws in machinery. We had found that by playing the tape recorders at a slow speed and placing microphones around the room, we could create a two-second delay in reproducing sound. This gave, along with the flashing stroboscope, a very psychedelic effect, completely in tune with the flower-power movement that was then gaining popularity. We also discovered that if we played the same recording on the tape machines at different speeds it would create a sound that none of us had heard before. At the time we didn't know that we were creating the kind of light shows that groups would soon be using on stage.

We showed the setup to Paul and the next night he brought John Lennon round to see and hear what we'd put together. What was so amazing was that this sound Graham and I had created would be used by The Beatles on 'A Day in the Life' on their *Sgt Pepper* album. We were very proud of this, even though we never got any recognition for it.

One night, at the Playboy Club, I met Andree Whittenberg, a tall bunny girl with long blonde hair. I asked her to come back for some drinks but when we got to the flat I discovered that I'd left the door keys on the table and could not get in. We had to call the fire brigade, who promptly came with a ladder and got through an open window high above us. Everybody was looking and staring, and I was embarrassed and starting to think maybe this was not such a good idea because firemen should really be called out only for an emergency, and this really wasn't. The other thing I'd realised was that there were recreational drugs left on the table upstairs. But it was alright, as one of the firemen had recognised me and asked if I would sign autographs for him and the others, which I did with relief and pleasure.

I saw a lot of Andree and would visit her house in St John's Wood, where she was staying with her parents. Later, she and Ann rented a flat over a petrol garage in Maida Vale. Mike Williams and I would spend a lot of time there, because he was going steady with Ann. In one corner of the house we had a ping-pong table, and played all the time, with Scott sometimes joining us. Andree

would always insist on waving goodbye to me from the roof over the garage, and once came out there wearing just a T-shirt and a pair of knickers, in full view of everyone. Guys were whistling and cat-calling, and I got so mad about this that I called her from a phone box on the main road and told her never to do that again. All she did was laugh, and the wilder I got, the more she laughed. I wouldn't see her for a while because of the roof incident, but we did have a lot of fun together. She had a wonderful personality and was extremely funny. She eventually married Dave Munden of The Tremeloes and has a great family.

Later that spring, we moved to 25 Upbrook Mews in Paddington. Allan Clarke and The Hollies came there often to see Graham. He was trying to get The Hollies to go in a different direction, and that year they recorded 'King Midas in Reverse', one of my favourite records (I even did background vocals for it). It went to Number 18 and gave them a lot of cred. I let Tony Hicks use my Marcos sports car in a promo film for one of The Hollies' songs. John and I drove all around England in those Marcos cars. John had had his converted to American specifications, so that he could take it home with him if things went wrong, which later came to pass. My managers eventually took mine because they said I owed them money, which was just not true.

Allan McDougall, our old PR guy who had worked for Brian Sommerville and one of my very closest friends in the sixties, would often visit us. He later went on to become the head of the A&R department at A&M records in Hollywood. At one time, it seemed as if everyone who was anyone was on that label – The Carpenters and The Police were just two of the acts – and we often said if the Walkers could get signed to it we really would get somewhere. Alas, it was not to be.

In May 1967, a girl called Barbara Goodman had joined the fans who marched in protest at The Walker Brothers splitting up; one of the girls had my address in Upbrook Mews, so Barbara was among the large group who came round to my house. I was at a window, dangling Mars Bars on a string for the fans below, and I remember seeing this outstandingly beautiful girl. After she'd gone, I asked some of the others who she was; they thought her name was Barbara.

Barbara and her friend Rita kept showing up outside the flat, and eventually I asked Barbara in briefly and she gave me her phone number. After that, we started seeing each other. To say that she was tongue-tied was an understatement: she was really shy with everybody, and she didn't need to be – she was so attractive. But she was a very down-to-earth girl. As we saw more of each other, I tried to draw her out and get her to talk to me, but with little success. I was several years older, which was probably part of the problem, so after a few months I stopped seeing her.

I was keen to put together my own group so that I could at last record the stuff I had always wanted to do, and I wanted to play live just as I used to with The Standells and The Walker Brothers. In the summer of 1967 I started looking for the right people for my new band. Mike Williams, whose father owned the Bull & Bush, was to be my rhythm guitarist. He was really a hairdresser but he looked like a pop star. Nicky James, a friend of Graham Nash, introduced me to John Lawson, who had played bass guitar for a group called The Universals. He got a good reaction from the girls outside my house, so he was in. Joey Molland from Liverpool would play lead guitar and piano. He had once backed The Merseys and then worked with Andrew Oldham. He was flat broke, and had heard from a girlfriend that I was looking to form a group. I thought he was a dead ringer for Paul McCartney, but much nicer. I hired him at once. I was to play drums.

These guys were really talented, and the only reason we called our group Gary Walker and The Rain was that my name was a powerful draw. I had a huge potential market in Japan, where I had enjoyed more popularity than Scott and John. In fact, as soon as they heard I had formed The Rain, the Japanese record company wanted an album right away.

I was still under contract to Maurice King. Maurice didn't want be involved with the group, and wouldn't help with equipment and money. We couldn't get our hands on anything I was owed from The Walker Brothers because it was tied up, or so we were told, so I contacted Brian Epstein. Brian revealed that he had been to see The Walker Brothers at some of our live shows, which was very flattering, but had never made his presence known. I think he liked Scott. I went with Mike Williams to a meeting with Brian at the NEMS offices in the West End. The Bee Gees' manager, Robert

Stigwood, was also there. I showed them a picture of The Rain and said, 'What about this?'

Stigwood stalled. 'Well, I don't know.' So we gave up but, as we left, Brian followed me out and said, 'It doesn't matter what Stigwood says, I'm going to sign you anyway.'

'Alright,' I said. After that, he came to see us with Brian Sommerville. They knew each other quite well. Brian then instructed his lawyer, David Jacobs, to free me from my management.

One day, during that 'Summer of Love', Epstein called and asked if Graham and I would like to go down to Abbey Road to do a TV show with The Beatles. I didn't quite know what to say, but I thought this opportunity sounded great, or 'fab', as people said back then.

The programme was to be recorded on 25 June, and we had been told to get to the studios around 7pm. When we arrived at Abbey Road we were directed to the Number 1 studio, which was vast enough to take a full orchestra, or even the *QE2* if necessary! It had been divided into two sections, with the orchestra on one side, and on the other The Beatles and a gathering of the 'beautiful people' they'd invited. Among them were Mick Jagger and his girlfriend Marianne Faithfull, Eric Clapton, who was a member of Cream, at the time, the model Patti Boyd, who was married to George Harrison, red-haired Jane Asher, Paul McCartney's girlfriend, Keith Moon from The Who, and many other pop celebrities, including Graham, Rose and me. The Beatles were perched on high chairs, and everyone else just sat wherever they pleased on the floor around them, with us to their right.

Brian Epstein came across to us and I told him I was really looking forward to getting another band going. He revealed that the show was going to be broadcast simultaneously to at least 26 countries via a historic first-ever satellite link, and that The Beatles had written a special song for the UK end of the event, which was to be titled *Our World*. The song was called 'All You Need Is Love'. It perfectly reflected the mood, and the message, of that summer.

For me, the magnitude of the event just didn't register. I was more aware that it was very strange for The Beatles to be performing without any audience at all, which surely contributed to the lack of atmosphere or excitement while everyone was waiting for things to get going. Brian and The Beatles announced that they had invited all their guests to unite to underline the song's message. Everyone had spontaneously come dressed in flower-power gear, in bright colours, with beads. Nobody had been told what to wear – they all somehow just knew what would be appropriate.

The Beatles did a run-through to check the cameras and sound, which was the first time anyone present had heard the song. I loved it instantly, its structure was good, and the message it conveyed appealed to me. As we rehearsed it, what struck me most was that the man leading the orchestra, whose members were all wearing full evening dress, was Mike Hugg of the Manfred Mann group. This just got to me because I wouldn't have expected Hugg, a drummer, like me, to be there doing that. I would have expected somebody like André Previn!

After the rehearsal everyone was milling around for a while, and Graham and I went to talk to Paul McCartney. I knew The Beatles quite well by now, but I always felt edgy in Paul's company because he seemed aloof and always testing you in some way or other. I can't say I didn't get along with him, just that I never could talk to him at length. Maybe it was the Liverpool sense of humour, although I didn't have that problem with the other Beatles. Of course Paul had the looks, and all that fame, and I always felt he was a bit of an intellectual, so maybe that's why I felt awkward when I was with him. It's possible that it wasn't Paul's fault at all, but mine. I got on very well with his family though. In fact the first time I ever had fried bread for breakfast was when I stayed in Paul's bedroom while I was visiting his father James. But that's another story.

I always got along with very well with John Lennon. He had a way about him that would put you at ease. I don't think it mattered at all to him that he was a Beatle. As far as he was concerned he was just another musician like the rest of us, and musicians talk the same language so we got along. John was always very conversational and interested in other people's opinions. He would often ask me what music I was listening to, or what I'd been doing, and he was fun to be with because he always liked to joke around, and had a great sense of humour that I could relate to. I gained the impression that his background had been

quite tough and that had stayed with him through his life. John had a firm grip on what was real, and he carried that into his songwriting. I did hear, though I never saw it myself, that he could get quite aggressive.

I remember also having a chat with George Harrison while we were waiting for the recording. From the first time we met, George and I would always get into these long conversations about right and wrong. Of course, with George you got 'the Cliff Richard', as I call it, because Cliff was always talking about being religious, and George had got like that with his Indian religion and the Maharishi's teachings. I thought that he'd have enjoyed a little more fun, but he was always very serious. Even Ringo would tell him to lighten up every now and then.

Most of the time George Martin was in the control booth, but I chatted with him too. We had met each other back in Hollywood, some years before. He told me he had never forgotten our first meeting there.

Everyone now realised just how big this was going to be, although they had no idea then that it was going to be seen by more than 350 million people all around the world. Even my parents saw it in LA. As the recording progressed, and Paul started singing the chorus, everyone just joined in with him and sang along. The Beatles got just the reaction they wanted when everyone started to scream, yell and clap. Towards the end of the track you can hear Graham and me whistling loudly and clapping our hands. At the end, people were walking around with placards in different languages, just to make sure that audiences in other countries got the peace message.

As it all came to an end, it struck me how strange it was that I had been able to hear everything so clearly. I wasn't used to that because everywhere The Walker Brothers played, even in a TV studio with a small audience, the screams would make it impossible for anybody to hear the music. It struck me deeply how silent it was. Apart from those involved in the performance, there were no other noises, no screaming fans. It was this lack of an audience that made this show unique for me, and it felt even stranger when I remembered that massive audience around the world. I believe it might even have been the first time that anybody was actually able to hear The Beatles singing when they performed

live, because all their other performances would have been drowned out by the screams, just as The Walker Brothers' were.

My dad, Jack, came over to see me to help tie up the deal with Brian Epstein. He wanted to visit the Tower of London, so I took him for a visit. The fans soon recognised me and things got so hot that that they had to shut the part of the Tower we were in. Jack couldn't believe it because he only thought of me as his son, not as a pop star. It was his first real taste of the fan mania.

One Monday, Jack and I were having a meal in the Angus Steak House in Marylebone, one of The Walker Brothers' regular eating places. That was the day Brian was going to sign Gary Walker and The Rain. I wanted my father there because I was still not released from my contract with Maurice King, and I feared the negotiations might be difficult. But while Jack and I were eating, the Steak House got a telephone call from Allan McDougall, who had desperately been trying to locate me. His call was to tell me that Brian Epstein was dead.

I don't think Maurice cared about The Rain; anyone wanting to get involved would have had to put up some big money. After Brian's death we just carried on as before, and Maurice tolerated us as long as we were making some cash.

Mike Williams soon realised he wasn't up to playing in The Rain, so he quit to pursue a film career which was he wanted to do more than anything. He later had the honour to 'marry' Bridget Bardot in a film she was making, and we often gave him a bit of a dig about it. In November, I replaced Mike with Charlie Crane, who had been with Liverpool band The Cryin' Shames. He was a great guitarist, had a good voice and fitted in perfectly. I chose him as my lead singer. Soon, we had a contract with Polydor and our management were paying us each a salary of £10 a week.

We decided that it would be best if we got a place together, so that we could develop ideas, write songs and rehearse. We took a five-storey house in Knightsbridge that was owned by the actor Peter Finch, who charged us £40 a week rent, then we got down to work. The first song we wrote was 'The View', which was about Lee Harvey Oswald. Joey wrote 'The Market Tavern', based on the pub we used to go to in King's Cross, and 'Thoughts of an Old Man'. I was thrilled to discover that all the guys were good at

composing songs. I'd been worried that all we would have in our repertoire were the two solo singles I had recorded in 1966.

First, though, we had to release a single. We chose to cover 'Spooky', which had been a hit in America for Classics IV. Scott produced the single, and we kept pretty close to the original, but I didn't sing on it. For the B-side we recorded 'I Can't Stand to Lose You', which I wrote with Charlie, and which was more typical of The Rain's sound, with strong piano, drum and bass backing. We were among the first to mix the songs in the headphones in 3-D, which is now accepted practice in the movie industry. Get a copy of the album and you will see what I mean.

Before the single was released I had to fulfil a contractual commitment to tour Japan with John and Scott, reuniting as The Walker Brothers only for that purpose. Deep down we were OK about it all and had a good time. Because we were so used to playing together, it didn't take long to get the show together. We were greeted by 2,000 fans at Osaka Airport and performed ten concerts, including important ones at Tokyo (to an audience of 10,000) and Osaka, both of which were broadcast on primetime TV on the same evenings. My single, 'Twinkie Lee', got into the Japanese Top 10, and shot me to mega-stardom.

We had the honour to play at the Budokan Stadium, where The Beatles had done their first show in Japan. The arena was vast: it could accommodate close to 15,000 people, and was one of the biggest at that time. The thing that got me was a Japanese flag suspended above me: it was about the size of the Royal Albert Hall in London, and I had trouble taking my eyes off it, so Scott and John had to keep yelling at me to look straight ahead.

The TV people put us on a half-storey riser 20 feet high, so that everyone could get a good look. The crowd was 25 feet from the stage, which was a good security move by the organisers. The show was in five parts: The Quotations were on first, then we followed to tremendous screams. Scott was on the right side of the stage and John on the left, about 15 feet apart, so neither could hear or see what the other was doing. The Japanese girls would yell their heads off, settle down when the singing started, then go wild when we'd finished the song. We all did our solo slots before coming together again for the finale. I wore a bright yellow coat with flared sleeves that had been given to me by George Harrison and came from The Beatles' Apple Boutique on Baker Street in London. The fans in Japan thought I looked like a butterfly. Scott introduced me as 'the one you've been waiting for, Garwee Reeds', mimicking the way my name was pronounced in Japan. It was a good show, very well received, and it's a shame that the videotape of it was lost.

Once more we were a great success in Japan. The Japanese took to me in particular, and I found myself even more famous than the other two. I did a lot of commercials for products there, and was told that people who did these became overnight stars. A live album of songs from the Osaka concerts was released in Japan, but not in the UK, and has become highly collectable. It was issued on the Bam Caruso label in 1987, and much later on CD.

After the tour, I cut a single with top Japanese band The Carnabeats, with Scott producing. We had to put something together quickly. We tried to write some lyrics in Japanese, but found out that we couldn't: we wanted the song to sound like rock'n'roll Japanese style, but that was harder than we thought it would be. The record did have a weird feel to it. In 1969 I would go to Japan on my own to promote 'Cutie Morning Moon', doing TV and radio shows. It went to Number 10 in the charts, and has since become a collector's item.

After working with The Carnabeats, Scott and I flew to Hawaii for a holiday, then on to California to stay with our parents for a few weeks. When I came home, I re-established contact with Barbara, and we began dating again.

'Spooky' was released in February 1968 amid great publicity. I had taken nearly a year to make a comeback, and people were eager to see what I would do. For our publicity shots, which were given wide distribution, we decided to capitalise on The Walker Brothers' image and go for the mean, moody and magnificent look, in artistic black and white. It seemed we could not fail.

But there was a legal hitch. Just after the record came out, we were due to appear on a TV show, *All Systems Freeman*, but out of the blue this French guy appeared claiming that he was Charlie's manager, and he got an injunction that prevented them from broadcasting our slot, which we had previously recorded. I contacted The Beatles' lawyer, David Jacobs, and tried to take legal

proceedings against the French guy, but it was too late. We were unable to promote 'Spooky', and it made no impact on the UK charts. However, it was a big success internationally.

Undaunted, we set off that April to tour England with The Tremeloes, The Kinks and The Herd. People wondered if we would be up to their standard, having been so recently formed, but we gave a good account of ourselves. Our set consisted of four or five songs, our own as well as 'Morning Dew', 'If I Were a Carpenter' and 'Dance to the Music'; we didn't attempt to play The Walker Brothers' hits. We wore sharp black suits and ties and white shirts. We went down really well, with the girls screaming as in the old days, and had a lot of fun.

In Japan, Philips were pressing us to record an album. Once the tour was over we went into the Philips studios in Marble Arch and got to work. Fritz Fryer, former bass guitarist with The Four Pennies, was brought in to assist us. Although the late sixties were the era of psychedelic music, the studio just had an eight-track machine and no real facilities for special effects. But we played around and experimented, and achieved some quite unique sounds. Within two weeks, we had our album completed. It comprised nine of our own original songs, 'Spooky', The Drifters' 'If You Don't Come Back' and 'Whatever Happened To Happy', written by Bonner and Gordon, songwriters for The Turtles. It has been called 'an exceptional set of psychedelic-tinged pop'.

The recordings were rushed to Japan, where they brought out a single, 'The View'/'Thoughts of an Old Man', an EP and, finally, the LP, which was titled *Album No 1*. Incredibly, none of this material was ever released in the UK. It may be because 'Spooky' hadn't sold well, but we were told at the time that the album would be put out here. It just didn't happen.

We went on playing theatres for a bit, and then came the offer we couldn't refuse: an invitation to tour Japan for three weeks. I warned the other guys to prepare themselves, because it was going to be like Beatlemania. They just told me to shut up. They thought I was having them on.

I was right, though. After a long journey with several stops, we got off the plane at Tokyo to see thousands of screaming fans waiting to greet us. They had banners saying 'We Love Gary' and 'Welcome to The Rain'. It was incredible. The others were totally shocked because they had never had that kind of response, or encountered screaming girls who knew their names and everything about them. Later, we discovered we were in papers and magazines all over Japan.

In Kyoto we stayed in a hotel that looked like it might have been in a James Bond movie. This was a beautiful place and the promoter said that when The Beatles stayed there John Lennon bought some tables costing half a million yen, and charged them to him. No one bothered us and we kept ourselves in order and *watched* the TV rather than throwing it out of the window.

We were taken on a bit of sightseeing to the famous Golden Pavilion, a three-storey building in the grounds of a temple. The top two stories of the pavilion are covered with pure gold leaf. The pond in front of it is called the Mirror Pond, which has many islands and stones on it representing the Buddhist creation stories. I could see how the beauty and the Japanese way of life might make you fall in love with the place. This was a very important time in my life and made me view at things differently. I came to realise the importance of taking a little time to look at the wonders around us and the good things we have.

We did ten shows, in Kyoto, Osaka, Sapporo and other places. Scott was to have joined us on the tour but by then his flying phobia had got to him, so he opted to take trains for most of the way. When he got to Russia they wouldn't let him in, so he had to turn back and never turned up. That meant we had to do two performances each night in big venues. Some people who had booked to see Scott didn't show, so there were a few empty seats, but we weren't too worried about that. There was one night when the power went, and we had to play our whole album acoustically. That was really something. Scott would have loved it.

Coming back to England after that successful tour was a dampening experience. Polydor hadn't bothered to put out a follow-up to 'Spooky', so we were transferred to Philips. Late in 1968 we recorded a single for them, 'Come In, You'll Get Pneumonia', which had earlier been recorded by The Easybeats. None of us liked the song or the single. We thought it sounded awful and knew it wouldn't chart. By Christmas, we had split up. If, by an outside chance, the record had been successful, there's no doubt we would have got back together pronto, but on its release in January 1969 it received unfavourable reviews and bombed. That was the last song we ever recorded together. The Rain was history.

There was some talk later that year of reviving the group, but it went nowhere. Maurice King had never been a fan of our special brand of music and once we'd split up he wouldn't help any of us to get started again, and we never knew if we'd see our next retainer cheques.

Graham Nash's desire to move in another direction eventually led him to leave The Hollies and form the group Crosby, Stills and Nash, who enjoyed enormous success in all over the world. When he was leaving for California in 1968 to launch the venture he asked me to go with him, but it was way too difficult because Maurice King threatened to sue me and said I wouldn't be able to work if I went ahead. He went so far as to take out an injunction that made it impossible for me to work here, there or anywhere else. In the end I would have no choice but to return to America. Joey later joined the group Badfinger, while Charlie went into music publishing before running a pub. Problems with alcohol wrecked his health, and tragically he died, aged 54, in 2000.

Nowadays, records by The Rain are very collectable, and mint original copies of our *Album No 1* fetch over £1,500 when they occasionally surface, and I've read that we are now regarded as one of the foremost psychedelic pop groups of the late sixties.

One night early in 1969, Allan McDougall I were talking when the phone rang. It was an American photographer called Linda Eastman, in the UK to do a shoot. Allan asked her to come around for a chat, and she did. We all got on well and I think Al fancied her. I asked if she liked the UK, and she said it was great and that she admired the old houses and buildings. I asked her what she was doing here, and she said, 'To take a few pictures, and to marry Paul.'

'Paul who?'

'McCartney.'

Well, we thought, she has a good sense of humour. But she did marry Paul, as all the world knows. She had the last laugh.

Allan McDougall went on to do well in Hollywood, and did a lot of work with Graham Nash in LA. When he had a heart attack, around 1987, he moved back to England in the hope of having a transplant, but it never came about and he passed away. He was a very good friend and helped me, like Graham, when I needed a bit of advice with my career. I miss him.

By now, Scott had moved to Amsterdam. On one occasion he wanted to drive there from England because of his ever-worsening fear of flying, and asked me to go with him. As the miles passed, I realised that he was acting strangely.

'Are you alright, Scott?' I kept asking.

'Of course, my boy,' was always the reply. I knew there was something wrong: he seemed a bit anxious, and I noticed we were clipping along at a fair pace, which was not his usual technique. As we approached the border that separated Belgium from the Netherlands, Scott's orange VW Beetle seemed to be gaining speed rather than slowing down. I was tempted to mention to Scott (who on occasions ran out of petrol) that our speed was unacceptable in the circumstances. But as we got ever closer to the border he was becoming itchier in the driver's seat, and he went straight though without stopping! I didn't know if we would be shot at, or what, but nothing happened.

I told Scott to pull over, and asked him what was the matter. He said he hadn't seen the border but he was clearly still on edge. Slowly the truth started to come out, as he told me he had taken some caffeine tablets to keep him awake on the long run. 'How many did you take?' I asked.

'Three.'

'Let me see the box.' This, along with all his other stuff, was in his big khaki canvas shoulder bag, which went wherever he went. It was small wonder that he was over the top, because he had clearly drunk the equivalent of two hundred cups of coffee. Of course, this was the last thing Scott wanted to hear.

Matters were only made worse when Scott took three Valium to help himself calm down. He was like a dog when it gets really excited and shakes all over. He just lost control, so I had to take over the driving. Scott never took those caffeine tablets again, or even drank coffee.

It's been claimed in one book that 'one of the Walker Brothers' was

at Brian Jones's house in Sussex on the night he died in July 1969, and hurriedly left when he realised that something odd was going on. That certainly isn't true. I recently got a phone call from a writer in LA, asking about Brian's death. I call this kind of thing 'the Cynthia Lennon effect': somebody calls you and says, 'Oh, I heard you were sleeping with Cynthia Lennon,' and you deny it. Then in the paper it says, 'GARY WALKER DENIES SLEEPING WITH CYNTHIA LENNON'. It's a trap, and I thought this guy from LA was up to the same thing. He said, 'Did you know Brian?'

'Yeah, I knew him,' I answered.

'What about the person who killed him then?' was his next question. He told me it had been alleged that I was at his house at the time.

'No, I know nothing about that,' I said firmly. 'I've never been to that house or anything.' I didn't even know where it was at that time. Later, I found out it was called Cotchford Farm and was where AA Milne wrote *Winnie the Pooh*.

When I asked this writer where he'd got his information, he said it was just rumours, and apologised. I think journalists are so desperate for a story that they would do almost anything to get one. What bothered me the most was that I had to hear about Brian's death from the media in this way, and even though I didn't know him well it was a big shock. Of course, we all discovered that being famous meant you had to learn to cope with reporters constantly looking for a sensational story all the time, regardless of anyone's personal feelings.

Later in 1969, I returned to America, where I lived until 1975. Barbara and I had continued to see each other, but going back to California put an end to our relationship. It also spelled the end for another relationship I had, with Marianna Lindberg, the daughter of Sir Con and Lady O'Neill. Mike Williams had introduced me to her. She was from Finland, with that blonde, blue-eyed Scandinavian look. She had the greatest sense of humour, which made her a lot of fun to be with, and a strong personality that got her into arguments with her mother; they took no notice of me, and treated me like a family member. Both of us were dating other people at the time – that's the way we played it. When I left for California I didn't think I'd be gone that long, so I didn't tell Marianna I was going, but when she found out she went wild. After I left, she started to go around with Scott, and they got on very well. She was a good friend and it would be nice to see her again.

Back in California I had no money and couldn't get any without suing everyone. At first, I lived with my parents and did some work on cars with my old friend Dean Gerard, until I finally got a job customising cars for a well-known establishment. I also had a sideline in making hand-painted miniature porcelain jewellery discs. There have been rumours that I was employed as a mortician, but the only connection I ever had with that trade was through my grandfather, who once worked in a funeral parlour in LA. This particular story was started by yours truly in a radio interview, when I was in a funny mood.

Another tale had me suffering from some serious illness such as pleurisy. It's easy to see where that one came from. While I was living with my parents in Glendale, I had some blood tests. One day I had gone to see Dean when my father showed up and said I had to go into the hospital right away because I had polycythemea vistra – the opposite of leukaemia. There was panic in the streets! Anyway, I didn't have it, but because I had been in England so long my blood had thickened – all Californians have thin blood because of the hot climate – and, when they checked it, it was sky high in the red count.

There were also tales of my being addicted to heroin, or being confined in a mental home. How they started, or where they came from, is a mystery. In fact, I found myself working and living my life like everyone else in Glendale, and I was also having fun because the pressure of being a Walker Brother wasn't blighting my existence. I became Gary Leeds, another number in the system, seeing my friends, paying for my flat and my food. On occasions Dean and I would go to clubs, and I would sit in with groups that I knew. Because I had never fallen for the star routine I was able to adjust back to normal life and get on with it. I could always be myself, and that's what got me through it all.

After a time, Susan came over to California. Although she was living with some record producer at A&M records, we saw each other on and off over several months, but it didn't go anywhere. She eventually married an American politician in high office, and

brought her parents over to live there with her. I have not heard from her since.

In 1969 I went to a party with Joe Manzeo from Universal Studios in Hollywood, and met a girl called Carol Woods, a blonde who could have been Sharon Tate's double. We got on well right away, and started seeing each other a lot. Carol had two children, Tim and Mike, from a previous marriage. They were good kids and I had a lot of fun playing sports with them.

Things got very serious between us, but there was a lot of static from my parents because of her being divorced and having two children. My mother didn't think it was right, but it didn't matter to me, as I liked Carol a lot. We got a place in Montrose, California, in the apartment block in which my maternal grandmother, Helen, lived, which was another black mark against Carol.

Carol was studying to be a dental hygienist. I was painting and fixing up cars in Glendale. I told her about my musical past and how successful I had been in England. Carol urged me to go back and try to get something going, and said she would pay for my fares, which is how I ended up returning to the UK in 1974.

On 18 December 1973, Scott married Mette Teglbjaerg in Las Vegas. Then they set up home in Copenhagen.

Mette was a pretty girl with nice eyes, very Scandinavian in her humour and outlook. I never really got to know her very well because Scott kept her out of the way – perhaps he was scared I would talk her out of marrying him! But who could have predicted that Scott would do a 'Pearl Harbor' and get married out of the blue? This was along the lines of finding snow on the moon. I would have lost millions at the bookmakers had I bet on it never happening. I think Scott was almost embarrassed that he'd got married – I don't think he was the marrying kind. He offered me a job in the Copenhagen company run by one of Mette's uncles, who had asked him to work for them too. Needless to say, neither one of us took the job.

When I returned to Britain I stayed in Sunbury-on-Thames with Brian Slater, a very dear friend who had been the road manager for The Rain. One night we were playing some records, and he said I should record a cover of The Easybeats' 'Hello, How Are You', which I loved.

I was lucky to know Martin Davies, who had been PJ Proby's manager and was now the head of United Artists records. We had become good friends after I helped him to deal with the problems that arose from PJ's heavy drinking. I played Martin 'Hello, How Are You' and he liked it, and gave me the go-ahead to record it, with 'Fran' as the B-side. I cut it at Studio 2 at Abbey Road Studios, where The Beatles had made their classic records. Allan Clarke of The Hollies produced the single, with both him and Brian doing the harmonies. To my joy the single was featured on a TV show honouring great stars. My choice had to be Humphrey Bogart, and, of all people, they picked him. I was stunned, not least because of all my past connections with him. They even did a drawing for the record sleeve, making me look like Bogey with a ciggy hanging out of my mouth. My dad would have loved it, and HB too, I think.

In England, to begin with, things were tough financially. I found out that one of the girls in Maurice King's office had forged our signatures on contracts and royalty cheques; apparently, one cheque we got for The Rain from Japan had been for £60,000. Unfortunately, when I heard about that, it was too late to do anything about it, and anyway it would have been difficult to prove it.

I was not getting any help from the record company, and because Carol had just started out in her new job she couldn't keep sending me money all the time. She did come over to see me, and we got along well, but not as well as we had in California. I could tell she felt insecure because she was trying to make me jealous all the time she was here. In the end, she got mad at me and we drifted apart. I owe her a lot, however: she helped me to go forward. Carol is more than likely married to some lucky man, and I don't suppose she would ever want to speak to me again. All I can say is that I am sorry things didn't work out.

After breaking with Carol, I got back with Barbara. Having lost her number, I wrote to her. I wanted to see her, and, as soon as she got the letter, she knew she wanted to see me too. We've been together ever since – it was just meant to be.

'Hello, How Are You' gave me a Number 1 hit in Italy, and in

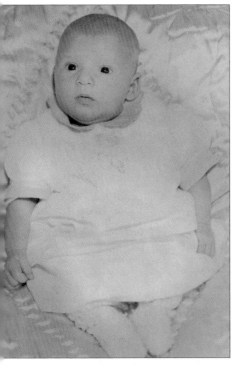

THE STANDELLS

ove left: Baby Gary.

ove right: Young Gary.

ow left: The Standells.

ow right: Gary and mother at Amy's house.

Top: Barbara and Gary.

Middle left: Barbara – still as pretty.

Middle right: Gary.

Bottom: The way they really looked.

*: One of the only pics leaving LA
*o to the UK.

ow: Caught on Keith Moon's
*m kit.

ht: At LA Airport with, far left,
*e Missing Walker Brother.

Above left: A bit moody here.

Above right: Gary – the happiest day of my life.

Below: One of the first publicity pictures, taken in Soho, London.

●: Not bad.

ldle: 'Don't you tell anyone that I have a sense of humour…'

tom: …yes, he does have a sense of humour.

Top: With The Beatles doing the live 'All You Need is Love' – no need to hide on the left.

© *Rex Feat*

Middle: Jimi Hendrix – one of the nices people Gary ever met. The tour of tours There has never been anything like it.

© *Rex Feat*

Bottom: This is what your face looks lik after a very long flight (38 hours – that' a story in itself).

フン・クラブと交歓会

バシの使い方も慣れました

Wonderful Days In Japan

8月にスコットとまたくるよ！

「8月が来るのが待ちどおしいなあ！」と言いながら日本を去ったゲイリー。
滞在中の忙しいスケジュールの合い間をぬってのレジャーの一時です。

Playing in Japan.

あなた出番です！！

テレビ、ラジオとプロモーションに余念のないゲイリー。

楽屋では見るもの全てが珍しくて一つ一つ手に取ったり、裏返して見たり、あげくの果ては侍のかつらをかぶって大笑い。

そんな彼を目でおって行くと、まれに見せる淋しそうで厳しい表情には前途多難な将来に、一生けん命ぶつかっていく意気込みが秘められていました。

カーナビーツのアイ高野クンと

ＴＶ番組「あなた出番です」てのゲイリー

ジャズ喫茶「ACB」に飛び入り出演

三味線って難しいね

Above left: Playing in Japan.

Above right: Everyone had more hair then.

Below: Gary – the second-happiest day of my life (when Michael was born!).

January 1975 it made the BBC playlist. But Martin had underestimated the sales (the record entered the lower part of the Top 30) and didn't press enough copies to boost its further progress. By the time we tried to get it back up the charts it was too late because there weren't any copies in the shops to buy.

Then I got a call from Scott.

BETWEEN A ROCK AND A HARD PLACE
JOHN WALKER

Immediately after the split it was decided that Barry Clayman would look after me and Maurice King would look after Scott. Shortly after the last tour Capable Management renegotiated my contract with Philips. I was to record one album and two singles the first year, and receive an advance on royalties. The contract extended for the next five years, with Philips having the option to renew or decline its renewal each year. But signing it turned out to be a bad career move on my part, given that John Franz was still going to produce my records. Barry was under the impression that, since I was now a solo artist, Scott and I would now receive equal promotion and support from Philips. Unfortunately, that proved not to be the case.

Philips released the last Walker Brothers single – 'Walking in the Rain', which previously had been recorded by The Ronettes – on 12 May 1967. It reached Number 26 without our promoting it. Later that year, Philips would cash in on The Walker Brothers' success with their release of a double compilation album called *The Walker Brothers' Story*, which reached Number 9 in the album charts, proving how popular the group still were.

The fans blamed me for the split and marched in protest. First they came to Barry's flat in Maida Vale in northwest London, because they had found out that I was staying there (before the tour started, I had moved out of my house in Sanderstead). Hundreds of them surged up the street to Barry's front door with a petition for me, insisting that The Walker Brothers should not split up. Barry went down and got the petition, and the police arrived to stop the ensuing chaos, as the girls were screaming, wailing and crying. The whole event was touching, but there was nothing I could do, even if I had wanted to. Then, on the following Sunday, the fans filled the streets around Capable Management's London offices. I was told they were carrying banners, signs, petitions and pictures. The press covered the whole protest, and there were photos of it in the national papers. I was already overwhelmed with the situation, and these protests just made the situation seem more shocking and dramatic. It seemed that every aspect of my life was falling apart, while the future was still unclear. I reacted by going 'underground', emerging only when necessary, and, thankfully, folks were very nice wherever I went. I wasn't yet 24, so the whole series of events leading up to the break-up of the group, and my marriage, was more than I was ready for.

Very quickly, though, I got into pragmatic mode and put together a plan, although, with hindsight, I still hadn't thought things through well enough. I knew that I wanted to work and had to put a band together. Barry made some calls for me, and I ended up using John 'Johnny B Great' Goodison as my bandleader; he was now without work as The Quotations had primarily backed The Walker Brothers. We assembled a new four-man band, The Techniques, plus a duo called Sue and Sunny, who John knew. The girls were experienced session and backup singers, and when they auditioned with the band they were terrific. Sue and Sunny were sisters of Anglo-Indian ancestry from Camberley, Surrey; of the two, Sunny was the leader and the more extroverted, while Sue was quiet. In 1968, they sang the backing vocals on Joe Cocker's hit 'With A Little Help From My Friends' and, with John Goodison, they went on to become part of The Brotherhood Of Man, who had a big hit with 'United We Stand' in 1970. I would later call on Sue and Sunny to do some work on an album of mine that Bill Wyman would produce. All the guys in the band sang too, except for the drummer, so I had a lot of background support if I wanted it. Bobby Hamilton was retained as my roadie.

Barry lined up my first solo shows: on 1 June I was to make my debut at the French Pop Festival at Le Palais des Sports in Paris, and on 4 June I would appear at the Paris Olympia. I was not ready for it. Bobby made the trip with me, and I was backed by a band booked by the venue. I was very apprehensive about going on stage, and used to doing shows that coincided with a record release, but this was not the case here. My crutch was my guitar,

and wearing cool clothes also made me feel more comfortable and confident; I donned a green felt military-style jacket with brass buttons and long tails down the back, with grey trousers, all made at the trendy Lord John boutique in Carnaby Street. To my relief, the show turned out to be a success.

One name that immediately conjures up the phrase 'child of the sixties' has to be Marianne Faithfull. She had the perfect image for that period. She looked like an angel, and sang like one too. Marianne had it all, and always attracted a great deal of attention from the media and the public. I met her in Paris when we were on the same TV show. The name of the TV show escapes me, but the events of those days' haven't.

A guy called Dominic was a PA assigned to ensure that we all had everything we needed: food, drink, wardrobe, pretty much anything. This also included sightseeing, if we had time for it. When Dominic introduced me to Marianne, I couldn't take my eyes off of her. I finally managed to say hello and somehow we started talking about how great it was to be in Paris. Just small talk, but we did spend a lot of time looking at each other. I was really taken with her: she was soft-spoken and confident, but had an underlying vulnerability about her that made her even more appealing.

We were going to have a rather long break in the day's shooting, so Dominic asked if we wanted him to take us to a quiet place for lunch. I guess Dominic had figured out that something might be going on, and that we'd like to be alone together. We said yes, but we never did get to the restaurant. A few minutes after we got in the car, Marianne had this smouldering look in her eyes and the next thing I knew, she was in my arms. Her lips were sweet and passionate, we kissed for what seemed like an eternity, and then we stopped as quickly as we had begun. For a moment we had forgotten about Dominic, who was in the front seat, trying to be very discreet. I remember that 'I Feel Free' by Cream was out at the time, and Dominic had a record player in his car. He played that song over and over while Marianne and I held hands and looked into each other's eyes, thoroughly enjoying our drive around Paris.

We spent as much time as we could together while doing the TV show. We even managed to get away and go to a café for a while. We knew we wouldn't have another opportunity to spend any more time alone together in Paris after the show was finished, because we both had commitments back in London. Marianne gave me her address and phone number so we could meet again when we got into town.

I called her a few days later and arranged to meet her at her flat later that evening. She answered the door and just smiled. I wanted to make love to her right then, but I managed to contain my feelings. We thought about going out to a club or maybe somewhere to eat, but we didn't do either of those things. Instead, I got up and went over to her, drew her up from the chair, pulled her close to me and began kissing her. It was like a dream sequence in a movie, as if we were floating in space and holding onto each other. Suddenly we were in her bedroom, and she was lying back on this enormous mass of pillows like great white clouds. I kissed her gently, and slowly began to undress her. She was truly lovely, and I was barely able to control myself: the desire to take her immediately was so overwhelming I almost lost my senses. I had never experienced anything like that before; it was like some strange of mixture of pleasure and pain.

But then, in less than a heartbeat, everything changed. Marianne looked at me and said, 'We can't do this, it can't go anywhere, we just can't.' We both knew very well that one night wouldn't be enough but, considering our circumstances, even that couldn't happen. I certainly wasn't free, and she was about to become very involved with Mick Jagger. There was no way forward for us. She was right of course, but that didn't make leaving her alone that night any easier.

On 30 June 1967, my first solo single, 'Annabella', written by Graham Nash, Nicky James and Kirk Duncan, was released; it reached Number 24. Nicky was a friend, a really good singer and talented songwriter who used to hang around Capable Management, and was well known within musical circles. I had met Graham Nash through Gary; Graham consequently gave me his song, 'Annabella', to record.

I'd written the B-side of the single, 'You Don't Understand Me', during the Christmas holidays of the previous year. I chose both songs myself, and recorded them at the Philips Studio in Stanhope Place, London. John Franz presided as the producer, sitting in his

usual chair, and never offering any comments or getting in any way involved. Reg Guest was my arranger, and we worked out the parts together, particularly for 'You Don't Understand Me'. For the first time in ages I was having fun again in the recording studio, despite the deep frustrations I'd had with Franz only six months before. I was really happy – and so was Graham – with the arrangement of 'Annabella', particularly the rhythmic cello accompaniment.

I embarked on my first UK solo tour in July 1967, starting at The Princess Theatre in Torquay. I was very nervous. I don't remember a thing about the first few shows, but do recall – again – what I wore: a black three-piece tuxedo. I didn't play guitar in the show – it didn't suit the act, and I wanted the freedom to move around and use the hand mike. One date – Bournemouth – always stands out in my head. I started my act with 'Same Old Song', a great upbeat Motown number made popular by The Four Tops. We normally followed that with two or three more energetic pieces to get the audience in a party mood, then we would slow things down and do a variety of material. Much to my surprise that night, the audience was all OAPs and I had to think quickly about my choice of material, as I knew it wasn't appropriate for this group. Before the first song was over, I had attracted Johnny B Great's attention, and told him that we would be going straight into 'All in the Game', a nice quiet ballad. I said I would let him know what the rest of the act would be as the show went on. Fortunately, we had a large repertoire, and the audience really warmed to us. I closed the show with 'Swing Low, Sweet Chariot', and by the time we'd finished, the people were clapping and dancing in the aisles.

During the tour I did quite a lot of press, radio and television. I appeared on Simon Dee's popular TV show, *Dee Time*, and many others too. The BBC had a lunchtime show, *The Radio One Club*, on which I sang two or three songs live with the BBC orchestra. One of the songs was 'I Just Don't Know What To Do With Myself', a Dusty Springfield hit, and one of the songs I was doing in my show. Everything was going along fine until I got to the second verse and suddenly forgot the words. My knee-jerk reaction was to announce, 'My God, I've forgotten the words!' The orchestra had continued playing, so I just jumped in when I remembered what I was supposed to be singing. Nobody picked up the comment on air, but when I heard the tape a few days later, there it was – as clear as day. I was shocked by the whole thing. It's a good thing I didn't use my standard expletive!

The odd thing about my live shows was that I never performed any of the material I recorded – neither my solo singles nor any of my solo recordings as a Walker Brother. I don't know why it didn't occur to me. It was as if I had reverted to my pre-Walker Brothers Hollywood shows, where I did the Top 40 stuff that everyone knew well. It seemed obvious to me at the time that it would be out of the question to sing The Walker Brothers' hits, which people strongly identified with the group, so I didn't even think to include those in the show.

Somebody got in touch with Barry, enquiring if I would be interested in writing some music for Franco Zeffirelli's upcoming cinema production of *Romeo and Juliet*, and I met with Franco to discuss what he wanted. He described the opening chorus in the actual play, and was thinking about setting it to music. I got started on some ideas, but then he decided to have the chorus spoken, and that was as far as it went. Subsequently, I met Leonard Whiting and Olivia Hussey, the stars of the film. Leonard and I have remained long-distance friends over the years, getting together from time to time in California or London.

In the meantime, Scott and Gary were pursuing their own careers. Scott's first solo single, 'Jackie', aired on the radio only for a short time before it was pulled because he referred to 'queers and phoney virgins' and said 'stupid ass' at the end of each verse. The BBC thought it was too risqué at the time. I liked the song, and didn't think it was as outrageous as some others did. The album *Scott* was released in September, but I was so busy with my own life that I didn't have time to listen to it. I also didn't realise that Scott had made his solo debut at the Fiesta Club in Stockton, appeared on *The Billy Cotton Band Show* and, in December 1967, had an appendicitis scare. The first time I remember speaking to Scott after the break-up was on a Japanese tour in early 1968. I'd heard through the grapevine that Gary was forming a band called The Rain, but I didn't see him until Japan either.

In September, I was featured in a five-page spread in *Penthouse* magazine modelling trendy designer clothes. I launched own my cabaret debut that month at the Tito Club in Stockton, where I had

played with The Walker Brothers. It was a resounding success, which is why Barry wanted me to stay in cabaret afterwards. I played six nights in a row to packed houses. I had the band wear matching suits, and the girls glamorous gowns; I still wore my tuxedo. Generally, the set list remained the same as in the first shows, except I took out some rock'n'roll songs and replaced them with more sophisticated material. But, well as the shows went, they still didn't fit into a proper overall career plan. I was now a club act, not a recording act, which wasn't a good career move. I was working, but going nowhere. I hadn't defined myself. Now, more than ever, I needed someone to guide me.

In October 1967, my second single, 'If I Promise'/'I See Love in You', was released. The A-side was written by Jerry Reed, an excellent country guitarist, and I had some good players backing me: Alan Parker, Vic Flick and Big Jim Sullivan. Unfortunately, the single didn't do as well in the UK as it did in Holland, where it was a hit. I went there for promotion and appeared on a television pop show, and met up with David Bowie, who I hadn't seen in a few years.

I had met Bowie in 1965, when I first came over to the UK, in Arthur Howes's office in London. He was 'Davy Jones' then. At the time he was like a lot of other hopefuls, trying to break into the music business and have a long career. It struck me that David was an incredibly good-looking young man – very androgynous. The next time we met was in 1967 on the television show in Amsterdam. We hung out in the same dressing room, and had a long conversation. David was still waiting to be discovered, so he was very interested in how The Walker Brothers had achieved success. My advice to him, which seemed so obvious, was to capitalise on his unique look, which was potentially more theatrical than that of any other artist I could think of. I also found out that David was an extremely accomplished mime artist, a talent he ultimately incorporated into his music, with great success.

David was very quiet and extremely mannerly, and also very focused on improving his craft – not just making hit records. He listened to every word I said without interrupting, just taking it all in. I could tell he was very artistic – much more so than most pop singers – and I knew that if he became successful, it would

be in a very unique way. Not too long after our meeting, David created the character Major Tom for his first big hit record, 'Space Oddity', which was a very original and theatrical concept for its time.

In *A Deep Shade of Blue*, it is asserted that I met my second wife, Julie Parker-Cann, Simon Dee's PA, in November 1967 when I appeared on *Dee Time* as his guest. Not true. I certainly did the show, to promote my first album, but I didn't meet Julie until several months later.

Philips released that album, the only solo one I recorded for them, in December 1967. The title track – 'If You Go Away' – has been one of my favourite songs for many years, and the whole album was in keeping with the theme of poignant love songs. Unlike those of many other artists, my personal life has rarely had any influence on my lyrics and music. None of my earlier songs were about any particular person or situation in my life. My ideas came from a variety of sources: a line I liked would suddenly pop into my head, or I'd pay heed to what was happening around me. It is only recently that I've begun writing more autobiographical songs.

'The Right to Cry' – the first track on the album – was written by Gerry Goffin and Carol King, and is about not having the right to feel bad about losing love you hadn't deserved. 'Guess I'll Hang My Tears Out to Dry', written by Sammy Cahn and Jules Styne, is about being abandoned by love. The third and fourth tracks – 'Reaching for the Sun' and 'Good Day', both written by Kirk Duncan, Graham Nash and Nicky James – are the only feel-good tracks on the LP. 'An Exception to the Rule', with its lively, brass band accompaniment, was OK, but nothing special. 'So Goes Love', another Goffin and King song, is about unrequited love, while 'It's All in the Game' had been recorded by an American guy named Tommy Edwards, and was a song I had wanted to record for many years. 'Nancy (With the Laughing Face)' was recorded by Frank Sinatra, and is very romantic. I included an uptempo number, 'It's A Hang-Up, Baby', which had been recorded by Jerry Lee Lewis – and have no idea why I did this song, because I never really did like it much. John Franz suggested I do 'Pennies from Heaven', which offered some nice light relief from the other tracks.

I wrote the last track, 'I Don't Want to Know About You', another uptempo piece, in late 1967.

Although it turned out OK the album, in general, wasn't really well thought out by me or anyone else. Again, except for 'All in the Game', I didn't feature any of the songs in my live shows, which was really stupid. The whole point of live shows is to promote current recordings. I don't know where my head was. I completely lacked direction, and desperately needed professional guidance, but nobody sat me down and pointed out the obvious. I was an emotional artist adrift.

I had some unfinished business with Capable Management. I felt that it was time to be released from my contract with them as I wasn't getting the career help I needed. I told them that we needed to part company, it wasn't going well, my career was stagnant, and I wanted new management. I also informed them that I was going to America for a while to think about everything.

While Barry was understanding, Maurice wasn't having it. He wouldn't release me. We went round and round, him repeating that he had a legal, binding contract, and me arguing that I wasn't happy with the way my career was going and wanted out. After getting nowhere, I finally resorted to a form of blackmail: I threatened to not go on the Japanese tour that The Walker Brothers were scheduled to do the following year to fulfil a contractual commitment. Maurice didn't believe me.

I left the office and waited for a reply from Capable Management. After a few days with no news, I called up Maurice and told him I had a telegram that I would send to the Japanese promoter if he didn't release me from my contract within 24 hours. Maurice didn't think I would send it, and when I called him after 24 hours he still wouldn't let me go, so I sent the telegram. Two days later, I got my release from Capable Management – provided I would do the Japanese tour. The irony is that I actually wanted to do the tour, and also that none of us had actually signed the contract for it at that point.

In December 1967 the press announced that I was going back to America for good; someone had leaked out that I had shipped my Marcos sports car and my dogs back to the US. At that point I was so bummed out with everything that I was drinking way too much, and made a few irrational decisions – like the one to return to

California. It was my way of protesting to the UK, I suppose. But I knew for sure that I wasn't going to be staying in America very long. However, it was pointless to carry on doing dates in the UK and not straighten out more pressing problems, such as the lack of direction in my career. I wanted to get out of England for a while and figure out what to do. Although the last six months had not been disastrous – in fact I had enjoyed success with the various shows and recordings – I still didn't feel that I was on the right solo-career track. I wasn't getting proper promotion from Philips, and they'd formulated no plan for me. John Franz was still at the helm but showing very little interest in me, and I was still considered by the music industry and the public to be a former Walker Brother – not John Walker, solo artist.

I had no idea what I was going to do back in California. I was disillusioned with my management, my record company, my career and my life. It seemed to me that, if there was a mistake to make, I would make it, and if I didn't do it on my own I would somehow manage to get help in screwing things up. The only thing I knew for sure was that I would be going on the tour of Japan with Scott and Gary.

In early January 1968, I flew from Los Angeles to Osaka to join Scott and Gary for our last Japanese tour. We all met up at Osaka Airport, where we were greeted by thousands of fans. Barry had flown in, too, and I was happy to see him; I had never had a problem with him.

There was no drama. We all did the 'hey, man' wave, and everything was back to normal, the way it had been in the days before things went wrong in the group. Scott, Gary and I immediately fell into our old mode of getting along, taking care of business and having lots of fun along the way. Our biggest concern was putting on a terrific performance each night. There was no mention of past events, it was just 'on with the show'. We were all very relaxed and happy to be working together.

I'd really looked forward to this tour because I had missed performing with the guys. I knew it was going to be a nice experience because there wasn't any pressure on us, and it was hard to do anything wrong over there because the fans just adored us. We were more popular in Japan then we ever were in the UK, or anywhere else

in the world. We all did our solo bits on stage and, of course, Walker Brothers material – so the fans got the whole shootin' match. Gary performed his newest hit in Japan – 'Twinkie Lee' – and 'Dizzy Miss Lizzie', with Scott on drums and me playing my Telecaster.

We did ten shows, with the ones in Osaka and Tokyo televised, but unfortunately the films have been wiped, although the soundtracks survive. We played the Budokan in Tokyo, easily one of the largest stadiums in the world at the time, with 10,000 seats, and it was sold out. The lighting box at the back was so far away from the stage that they had to use laser beams to find us. On stage, the bright lights focused on us blocked out much of the crowd as we looked out. Even though we were on a very high stage, we felt as if we were at the bottom of a huge bowl, with people everywhere – it was surreal.

We had an entourage of 19 people taking care of us, all supplied by the promoter, including several very pretty girls and – since they didn't know what our preferences were – pretty boys as well, just to be on the safe side. Whenever the three of us needed anything – a Coke, a whisky, breakfast, a burger, a cigarette, anything – there was a designated person for the job. We rode the bullet train, which went at 200mph from Tokyo to Nagasaki. It was an incredibly smooth ride, but everything was just a blur when we looked out of the window. We also saw Mount Fuji – an awesome sight – and went to various temples.

We ended up doing a chocolate commercial, even though we weren't sure whether we should. But we just went where we were told. We did almost everything together, surrounded by our entourage at all times. We had separate rooms in all the hotels, with an entire floor completely reserved for us. The last concert was at Shizouka, where fans rushed the stage, presenting us with gifts and huge bouquets. I found out later that, as soon as Barry Clayman returned to Britain, he and Maurice King parted company. I was happy to hear it, for Barry and Maurice did not have a lot in common.

I flew to Hawaii for a holiday and just hung out by myself before going back to LA at the end of January 1968. I had a lot on my mind at that time. Things were not good with Kathy. Financially I was alright, with a fair amount of cash in hand, but I still had no idea what I was going to do next.

I stayed in America for only a few weeks, but during that time I recorded two demos, 'Bluebirds Over the Mountain' and my own song, 'Teardrops', with Kathy and my sister Judy singing background harmony. I had no intention of presenting a new act, just the type of material I wanted to do. It never crossed my mind to include Kathy or Judy in anything other than the demo. We did the recording at Goldstar with drums, bass and acoustic guitar. I sent John Franz the demos to show him the direction I thought my music should go.

Coincidentally, he called me up out of the blue around this time and told me he had found a song he wanted me to record – Bob Dylan's 'I'll Be Your Baby Tonight' – and that I should come back to London to do it. I asked him about recording in the US, but he wasn't going for that, so I realised I had to go back to the UK if I wanted to continue with my recording career. I took the call as a good omen that maybe things were changing at Philips, and with him. Also, I was desperate to return to England, and welcomed the invitation.

A lot was going on in my personal life. Matters between Kathy and me had not improved. I had thought they might if I tried to put down some roots in California, but I was wrong about that. I even bought a house, but I didn't spend one night there. I bought it because I knew that Kathy and I would not be together much longer, and I set things up for her so I could have a clean break without a guilty conscience. I guess there was just too much baggage being carried around by both of us. I wasn't as pure as the driven snow by any means, and I believe that knowing that was too much for Kathy. My on/off affair had ended, but I am sure that Kathy never found out about that, as I had tried very hard to be discreet. I was drinking quite a lot, which didn't help. I could accept the fact that I wasn't Kathy's first lover, but I couldn't deal with the nagging suspicion that I wasn't the only man in her life. I couldn't help that. After all the things that had happened, there was way too much distance between us. It sounds very unkind, but I was relieved when John Franz wanted me back to England. I really needed to leave, and I guess that call made the decision for me.

A few days later, I was back on the plane to London. Scotch and Brandy, our dogs, stayed with Kathy in America. She and I had not

yet finally decided to call it a day, but I knew it was only a matter of time.

I felt extremely alone on the flight to England, and even more alone when I arrived. I had left all my money in America with Kathy when I split, so I was flat broke – I probably had just £400 in my pocket. I didn't have a car, as I had shipped my Marcos to America. I had no manager, no agent, and a recording contract that wouldn't do me any good. I felt as if I was in a trap. I had to find a place to live, and ended up at back at Ormonde Terrace near Regents Park, in the building in which I had lived when I was first married. They had one tiny flat to let, and I figured that if I was real careful with money I could make it for another few months. After that, I didn't know what would happen. I had absolutely no prospects at the time. and felt like jumping off the roof.

Initially, things got better. I met with John Franz to set up the recording dates and sorted out the music. I had a deal with Philips, and was to receive a recording advance in a couple of months so I didn't need to be too concerned about money. I waited to see what would happen next.

I had started to grow a beard when I was in the US, so I looked a lot different when I came back to England. I met up with the music journalist Keith Altham in a pub, and no one recognised me. I liked that.

Before I recorded 'I'll Be Your Baby Tonight', backed with another Dylan song, 'Open the Door, Homer', I had Franz listen to the demos and told him I wanted to go in this direction. He said, 'Well, the first problem is – I don't think either song would be a hit.' But within six months 'Bluebirds Over the Mountain' was released by The Beach Boys and was a massive success. I felt that Franz had shown an appalling lack of judgement and that he was no longer taking anything I suggested seriously.

I did have a good time doing the Dylan stuff, at least, and I liked the material a lot. But I got relatively little airplay and only one TV show, and to make matters worse the single wasn't available in many popular record stores, which impacted on sales. Miraculously, it did well on the continent.

The option on my contract with Philips was up for renewal in February 1968. I went into the office to ask John Franz if they were picking it up, and he said yes, so I asked when I could expect to receive my advance. He informed me that recording and promotional costs had gobbled it up. It was a blatant slap in the face. Then he said I was welcome to continue to record singles. I threw up my hands and walked out of the office, not knowing what to do. Philips was no different from other record companies regarding an artist's royalties: all expenses were deducted from sales first, then, after everybody else had been paid their 'fee' and all other expenses were paid out, finally the artist got his percentage of the total sales. In standard contracts, artists usually got anywhere from 1 to 4 per cent of total sales; an artist who got 6 per cent was very fortunate.

I started hanging out at the Playboy Club in Park Lane. Occasionally Scott and I would meet there, have a few drinks and a chat about what was going on in the music business. He knew I was recording again, so we talked about the latest techniques and material. There were a lot of girls from all over the world working at the club and, naturally, I started to date quite a few of them. I became involved with one girl in particular after a really bad night of drinking to excess. I remember that she decided to take me home as I was in no condition to make it there alone. Then we started seeing each other regularly. Her name was Angie. She was from Holland and was quite a woman. I believe that she was the only naturally equipped Playboy Bunny in the whole club – she didn't need any padding, anywhere! She would come over to my flat after work around three in the morning. I would be pretty loaded by then, and we'd have sex until dawn. I still don't know where she or I got all that energy from, but we both seemed to have a lot.

I really don't know how I survived all the drinking, smoking, drugs and sex. It was a never-ending cycle. Nothing seemed to be very important then. I was living a life that had little to do with reality. Sometimes I would think, You're killing yourself; you're still married with a wife in America; what are you doing? But I was carrying on as if there were no tomorrow, and I continued to see Angie for several more months.

Then I really got crazy. I remember one night when I met up with some friends at the Scotch of St James and we got together with some girls who were up for a good time. We all went back to my flat, where the party raged on until all hours in a rather uninhibited fashion, with naked bodies, empty bottles and overflowing ashtrays everywhere – what a scene! Later that morning, I found a girl I didn't even remember in my bathtub. Things like this – the wild parties, sexual encounters, drugs, booze and excessive lifestyle – were taking over my life. I started going out to different clubs every night, getting well loaded and ending up becoming involved with one woman or another. There were always a lot of pretty girls around, and I had a very healthy appetite. I never seemed to go home alone. Somehow I survived it all, and in the middle of all this madness I met the woman who would become my next wife – but not just yet.

In the spring of 1968 Scott and I were each offered £10,000 to do a show in South Africa before a segregated audience, but we both turned it down without a second thought. We had previously agreed that we would never play under those circumstances.

Scott had been recording his second album, *Scott 2*, and another single, 'Joanna', reached Number 2 in April. Scott was told it was going to be used as the theme in a movie with the same name, produced by Mike Sarne. He didn't know it was going to be released as a single. 'Joanna' was not really in keeping with what he wanted to do musically – he just recorded the song for this project, but it was never used in the movie, so Scott was not very happy.

That spring, I had my last recording session with John Franz, recording my fourth single, 'Kentucky Woman'/'I Cried All the Way Home'. I didn't care for the arrangement of 'Kentucky Woman'. John Franz and I couldn't agree on tempos – he thought mine was too slow – or anything else. The objective for him, I think, was to get the song done within three minutes, but you can't always do that. The original vinyl version on the single sounds awful. Aside from other flaws it was mastered poorly. (Fortunately, there is a decent remaster on the recent *If You Go Away* compilation CD.) The same was true for my self-penned B-side, 'I Cried All the Way Home' – the recording sounds quite different from the song I actually wrote. But it wasn't worth wasting costly studio time arguing about it as I knew they would deduct the money from my royalties, and I knew I wouldn't get anywhere.

I complained to Maurice King. Regardless of the fact that we had fallen out, Maurice was still interested in making a buck and, truthfully, I had no other options at the time. When there's money to be made, the past can be easily overlooked, with caution to the future. I then called Scott and told him what was going on, and we came up with a plan that he would produce my records in the future, which was something we knew Philips wouldn't refuse, as he had *carte blanche* to do as he wanted at the time. So we got rid of John Franz; certainly this was the beginning of the end between Scott and Franz and Philips. He'd figured out that either he did what they wanted, or nothing he recorded would get promoted. I don't know the exact time when Scott himself finally parted from Franz.

In the fall of 1968, Scott produced several tracks for me, of which 'Woman', which I wrote, was one of my favourites. Working in the studio together again was a joy for us both; all we wanted was to make good music. Unfortunately, when 'Woman', backed with 'A Dream', was released in November 1968, Philips again proved that they were not going to spend any money on promoting me. Even Maurice, out of character for him, was sure we had a hit and actually pulled people into his office to listen to it. But Philips didn't line up one bit of promotion: no radio, no press, no television – nothing. I knew I had to break with them. Promotion translates into public awareness, and ultimately sales, so Scott and I were disappointed that Philips didn't get behind us when we handed them a good product.

I met Julie Parker-Cann in the Aretusa Club in the King's Road, Chelsea, in the early summer of 1968. I had just emerged from my destructive lifestyle when we met. Julie had been involved in show business for quite some time, working for Brian Epstein and now as Simon Dee's PA. She had short blonde hair and was a typical sixties girl in velvet and lace, flamboyant and cheeky, and always up for a good time. I asked her if she wanted to dance, then we started talking and had a few drinks. We got along very well; she had a lively personality and was very knowledgeable about the music business, which I thought was cool. I asked her if she'd like to go out for dinner one night, she agreed, and we began dating regularly. By coincidence Julie had a flat in Stewart Towers in

Maida Vale, London, and Scott had just moved into the same building. I still had my little flat in Ormonde Terrace.

In the summer of 1968, Kathy returned to London to see if we could sort things out. I met with her but I'd been down that road before. I wasn't angry about things, but I was not prepared to go through it all again. We divorced later that year.

I also ran into Gordon Waller again around the same time. He and I had become quite good friends over the past few years, but I hadn't seen him in several months. He'd used to come around after some of The Walker Brothers' shows and, before long, we'd begun hanging out a lot. He too was just embarking on his own solo career, for he and Peter Asher had parted ways. I'd kept on drinking way too much over the past months, and when I met up with Gordon we would go out and manage to get into a lot trouble. He knew about some afternoon drinking clubs, so we would disappear into one and not come out until closing time.

Other times we'd hang out in Gordon's very cool mews cottage just off of Baker Street, playing songs. It wasn't far from the offices of EMI, to whom he was still signed. One day we went up to see his recording manager, and ran into Little Richard in the lobby. I'd never met him, but Gordon had and introduced me. Little Richard looked quite a character: apart from the 'off-the-shoulder' satin top he was wearing, he had foundation makeup on, eyeliner, mascara and eyebrow pencil; even the little moustache was pencilled in, and of course he had on his full wavy black wig. The thing that topped it all was the black eye! It seems he had a disagreement with his boyfriend and the boyfriend had popped Richard. Oh dear, poor Little Richard!

I was really at a loss in this period of my life. I was so broke I never knew where the next penny would come from. I didn't have a band or the money it would take to put one together, so there was no prospect of work, and very little help from Capable Management. I was screwed. I certainly wasn't doing myself any favours with my bad habits, but I didn't really care. As long as I had a place to stay, plenty of booze, some good drugs and a woman, I would get by. I didn't even have a guitar then, so I wasn't playing or writing music. I think that was the worst part of it. I could always find something in music, but it wasn't happening now.

I managed to get some money from somewhere – it may have

royalties, I don't really remember – but it enabled me to get a guitar, a 12-string acoustic. As far as I was concerned it was the best thing possible. In my continuing efforts to straighten myself out, I wrote a few songs and generally started to get back on track.

Julie and I had been going out for several weeks when she told me she had booked a holiday in Ibiza and would soon be taking off. Gordon was going out with Norma Heyman, a movie producer. He asked me, 'Why don't you come to Malta with us? I've got a deal there and it won't cost you any money.' It turned out that we were going to play in a dinner club in Malta every night. So off we went. I left all my cares behind and managed to get my life straightened out. Even though we weren't getting paid, at least it didn't cost me anything, and I was playing music. It was just Gordon and myself on acoustic guitars. We played a lot of old Buddy Holly songs, and others by Jim Webb, Glen Campbell and The Beatles. The crowd loved us, and we had a great time. Even the local radio station came in to broadcast the show live. I also came to like Malta. It was warm and there were ancient ruins dotted about. It was so different from anything I'd known.

I left Malta when I got a call to guest on *The Sandie Shaw Supplement*, a TV series starring the popular girl singer who had won the Eurovision Song Contest the year before. I remember doing that show very well. The producer wanted me to sing a duet with Sandie on 'Homeward Bound', a hit for Simon and Garfunkel. The first problem was that I had to learn the song on the day of the show; the second problem occurred when I found out that doing a duet with someone you have never sung with is hard enough when you are singing side by side, but almost impossible when you are at opposite ends of the studio. I couldn't see Sandie, so I couldn't match her phrasing. It wasn't working out at all. In the end I asked the director if they could set up a monitor where I could actually see her singing, which solved the problem. I ended up singing to the monitor but, on the TV screen, it looked as though we were singing together.

Julie and I met up again when we both got back to London. We started getting serious, and I met a lot of her friends and eventually her family. We were now virtually living together in my flat or hers, and life for me settled down for quite a while.

Maurice King called me up out of the blue in the summer of 1968

and enquired how I was doing. He'd heard I was back in town and wanted me to come down to his office for a chat. He more or less apologised for all the stuff that had happened in the past, turning on the charm, which he was very good at. I told him about my frustrations with Philips, and he offered to help me out. I was in such a desperate position that I went along with him – he was the only person in the industry who seemed interested in me. He asked me what I wanted to do, and I told him I needed to put a band together, and rehearsal space – all stuff that costs money. He offered to sort all that out, and got in touch with a group called Flaming Youth. Phil Collins was the drummer. Maurice arranged for us to rehearse at the Colony Club – a kind of villain's club where George Raft used to hang out when he was in town. So we started putting a show together.

Maurice booked us to play in some clubs up in the North – pretty rough ones, and a far cry from Tito's, but at least I was playing. However, the venues got worse and worse, and it was soul-destroying. Maurice was up to his old tricks, I guessed. I can't prove it, but I had a suspicion that the deals he quoted me were less than what were actually offered – which meant he was skimming off the top, but at least he was getting me work. He had confidence in my determination to make the shows successful and hoped that some way or another there would be financial gain in it for him. However, we all gave it up after a few months, when it looked like Flaming Youth would get a recording contract. They did, and it resulted in the release of their album, *Ark 2*, to good critical success although, sadly, it didn't pan out commercially. Phil was the only one who became successful, as the drummer and then singer with Genesis when Peter Gabriel left the band. He was an excellent drummer and had a great commercial voice.

Scott had produced my final single for Philips, which I was committed to record. Philips had not renewed the option on my contract, formally or legally, but I took advantage of whatever they did offer us because I wanted to keep recording. I didn't receive an advance, but Philips picked up all the studio and recording costs. The single was called 'Yesterday's Sunshine', backed with 'Little One' – both written by me – and was released in 1969. As I expected, there was no promotion, and the single didn't chart. The songs were actually album material anyway, but

I had fulfilled my contract. It was over with Philips, and my heart wasn't in this particular project anyway.

I never received a royalty from Philips for any of my solo work until October 2008, and that came only after a long and determined enquiry led by my present manager, David Oddie, my attorney, James Collins, and other patient and determined folk. By the time the first cheque arrived, it was practically impossible to account for nearly 40 years of solo sales. Also, I had never been made aware, during those many years, that my singles had been released outside the UK, all over the Continent and in places as far-flung as Japan and Brazil.

After my split from Philips, I saw more of Scott because he lived in Stewart Towers. Between my twice-yearly royalties from Philips, and a bank overdraft, I was able to manage quite well. I once more parted ways with Maurice. This time it was just an amicable goodbye, as no contract was involved, but unfortunately Maurice and I would soon meet again – in a long, drawn-out, gruelling legal battle over a certain royalty cheque that arrived in his office around August 1968. It was a nasty episode that finally alerted Scott to Maurice's ways.

Scott and I had always received our royalties every six months. Capable Management had always deposited them into their accounts, before sending us our payments, but now the cheques required both Scott's signature and mine. One day I received a call from Scott, who asked me if I knew that we had just received a royalty cheque at the office. I told him no. He disclosed to me that Maurice's plan was to deposit the cheque and split it with him, hoping I wouldn't find out. Scott had called to make sure I knew what was going on; he was just beginning to realise that Maurice was not the best manager to be around.

I called Maurice right away, and told him I wanted my share of the royalties. He said flatly, 'That money was owed to the office in back commissions.' Without hesitation, I told him, 'You'd better be able to prove that because I'm going to sue you.' And he calmly said, 'Alright.' End of conversation. I guess he thought I wouldn't do it, but I did. I found a solicitor who agreed to take on my case, and we started proceedings.

It took about six months before my case was eventually heard in

London at the High Court in the Royal Courts of Justice in the Strand. There were three judges wearing full wigs and robes, and two barristers in attendance – Maurice's and mine. Maurice presented his own deposition, which was read over a period of three days, with him rambling on and on, describing what a despicable character I was, referring to my drinking and general behaviour, and throwing in plenty of lies along the way.

John Goodison had been paid by Maurice to submit a false deposition about my character, which was read in evidence against me. Shortly after the case was over, I ran into John at a pub. I just looked at him when I spotted him in there. He came over and apologised, saying he was sorry about the deposition: he had been completely broke at the time and Maurice had something on him that he wouldn't tell me about. Johnny said he'd been paid £250 to do the deed. I knew how Maurice could manipulate people and hold things over them so I actually felt sorry for Johnny, but it really hurt when I heard what he submitted to the court as he'd been a good friend. We lost touch after that, but I never really harboured any anger towards him.

In the end, the judge ruled in my favour, saying to Maurice, 'I've heard three days of testimony regarding Mr Walker's character. What does that have to do with the money he is due?' Of course, Maurice had no answer. Despite winning the case, I had to wait for ever to get my money, and Maurice sent only a portion of what was due to me. I wasn't, however, about to go back to court as the whole thing had been completely draining and maddening.

Meanwhile, I had met a man named Cyril Smith, who was married to one of The Beverly Sisters, who now became my agent and manager. He was a very experienced, knowledgeable professional who knew a lot of people in the biz, and he exuded confidence in his new project with me, which made me feel good about it. Cyril made a deal with Mervyn Conn, who owned his own independent label, Carnaby Records, and also had been involved in publishing, managing and promotion – you name it, he'd done it. He was an entrepreneur in his mid- to late 30s, a very smooth talker with a lot of self-confidence. But he was also the great baffler. Sometimes he pulled everything off, and sometimes he left people like me holding the bag after putting their trust in him. Really, his last name surely suited him.

My Carnaby contract appeared to be a standard deal for one album and two singles per year, with a reasonable advance each year, but I would find out much later that I was the victim of a typical small record company scam: the record company would sign an artist to a worldwide deal, pay a small advance, make an album and lease the album rights to independent record companies throughout the world and get an advance on sales from each. The original record company would make a large profit for a small outlay, and little risk. The artist was never given an accounting of any sales, anywhere.

In 1969, Carnaby released my album, *This Is John Walker*, and a single – 'Everywhere Under the Sun'/'Traces of Tomorrow'. All the material was by other composers, not me, and it was chosen by Cyril, Mervyn and – chiefly – the arranger, Ken Woodman. At that point, I did whatever they wanted without question because it seemed that whatever I had tried in the past year or so had backfired, and I'd run out of ideas. So I left things in their hands this time around. I liked their choice of material and was curious to see how they would present me. Although the recordings didn't seem very commercial, I was quite pleased with most of them, and thought highly of Ken Woodman's arrangements and work ethic. He really liked my voice, we got along well and I thoroughly enjoyed the sessions. Had Mervyn played straight with me, I would have stayed with him, but after a while he just got too greedy and didn't treat me fairly.

I toured Germany and Holland to promote the single, and the record company assigned a very pleasant guy to accompany me. We showed up on time for all the radio, TV and press promotions, drank at perhaps every beer garden en route, and were well behaved – until we got to Hamburg. The Reeperbahn was calling, with all its sinful clubs and goings on. We just had to make a special trip there on the side. We drank and drank and drank. We were on the road about two weeks, in the beautiful German summer sunshine. It was a delightful trip.

The album charted in Spain, so I went over for about a week to do television, radio and press. A few months later, I was offered a two-week tour of Spain. We generally played big clubs in the major cities, but one beautiful, warm night we played in an amusement park. The stage was set up for an outdoor festival and the park

jam-packed with thousands of people. I dreaded the walk through this crowd, even though people were with me. There was no security at all. However, we got to our destination without a problem, the show started, and everything went along as usual. But during my set, the crowd started getting hysterical, just like at The Walker Brothers' concerts. When I was ready to leave countless fans were pushing up against the dressing-room door. I knew it was a dangerous situation, and said, 'I'm not going out there, it's not safe.' I was assured that the crowd posed no threat, so I opened the door. The crowd went berserk. We slammed the door shut. It took over an hour for sufficient Spanish police officers to assemble, calm things down and make a path for me through the crowd. When the time came, we ran like hell. I had to jump over the turnstile because so many people were chasing after me. The cab driver started pulling away – before we got to him – when he saw the crowd coming. Fortunately, someone made him stop so we could scramble in. He was screaming and yelling in Spanish because his cab was being attacked by the fans. Everyone was completely out of breath, but we made it back to the hotel.

I recorded 'Traces of Tomorrow' and 'Sun Comes Up' in Spanish for Ekipo Records during the tour. Both were written out for me in phonetic speech, and the company had the backing tape sent over from Carnaby. I have no idea how well it did. By the end of the tour, I had been voted 'Spain's Most Popular Foreign Artist' and was presented with a medal and a couple of cases of champagne. I had thoroughly enjoyed the tour, and discovered lot of cool things about Spain. I liked the Spanish lifestyle: they got up early in the morning, took care of their business, had the afternoon siesta and started business again late into the night. I also loved the fresh seafood restaurants in Barcelona, and the great nightlife.

I was still signed to Carnaby and due to make another single, but they released a track off the album, which was daft. It was called 'True Grit', the theme tune from the John Wayne movie of the same name that had just come out in the UK. Glen Campbell sang the song in the movie, so the public ignored my single. I tried my best to stop its release, as I actually didn't like the song and hadn't wanted to do it, although I did like 'Sun Comes Up', another track from the album used as the B-side.

Through Cyril Smith I hooked up with an Australian record

producer named David McKay. David was familiar with my stage arrangement of 'Cottonfields', a standard from the American South, which I did in a big gospel style, with the middle section turning uptempo before ending with a fast rhythmic double time. I felt that the arrangement of the song worked really well when I performed it on stage, in a show, but I didn't think it would work for recording. David loved the arrangement, though, so we decided to do it, and Carnaby agreed. Because of the eight-track, we were able to turn a few backup singers into a full choir. The B-side, which I wrote, was titled 'Jamie', and it's pure coincidence that this is also the name of my son.

Only two weeks before the scheduled release date of 'Cottonfields', The Beach Boys released their version! It was just ironic – first they had had a hit with 'Bluebirds Over the Mountain', the song I had badly wanted to do with Philips until John Franz put the kibosh on it, and now they were doing 'Cottonfields'. It was weird, and very unfortunate. EMI launched a massive promotion for The Beach Boys, whose single did well, so by the time mine came out any promotion for me would have been anticlimactic, so Mervyn didn't even bother.

In October 1969, I recorded a pilot television show for a series called *Lift Off*, which co-starred a female singer from India named Ayshea Brough. Muriel Young was the producer, and she, her husband and I became good friends. Muriel had come up with the idea: Ayshea and I would host the half-hour pop show, and we would feature guest artists. At the time, the BBC had *Top of the Pops*, a straight Top 20 show. ITV's *Ready Steady Go!* had followed a straight out-and-out pop format. The difference with *Lift Off* was that it would have Ayshea and me as the hosts, with lesser-known artists appearing. Unfortunately, the idea didn't sell.

On the trip to New York in 1967 I had met a high-powered attorney named Richard (Dick) Steinhouse. Dick was now in London and got my number from Maurice King; he ended up staying at my flat in the Water Gardens for a few days. The American Selective Service had been in touch with Capable Management and were getting more and more aggressive about enlisting Scott, and that finally something had to be done about it. So Scott had to make a trip to the US and present himself to the draft board. He and Maurice had taken the ocean liner SS *France* to New York. Scott took all of the mandatory tests and, in the end, the army decided that based on his psychological test results he was unfit to serve. He was given a 4F status, meaning that he was officially unacceptable for service. And that's all there was to the story. Scott confirmed everything with me later, when we met in a pub.

The authors of *A Deep Shade of Blue* spouted blatant untruths about Scott and the draft – for example, the assertion that Maurice supposedly paid a Harley Street doctor to certify that Scott was gay is outrageous. Another lie was that Bobby supposedly staged a car accident involving Scott. Maurice was untrustworthy, greedy, and many other things – but even *he* had more class than the authors of that book. He never subjected Scott to anything that would in any way cast doubts about his sexuality – which was definitely heterosexual – or Scott's image.

When I told Scott what had happened between me and Carnaby, he confided to me that he was leaving Capable Management for good. He and Maurice split up over money and God knows what else.

Scott had appeared on a *Dee Time* show, and there had met Esther and Abi Ofarim, who'd had a hit called 'Cinderella Rockafella' in 1968. Scott got involved with Esther before finally getting serious with Mette. Ironically, my then girlfriend, Julie, had been dating Esther's husband, Abi, before she and I got together. The Ofarims' husband-and-wife image did not appear to be exclusive. Scott also met Ady Semel – the Ofarims' manager – who would now become his own manager.

Mette and Scott moved into a flat near Castle Acre, directly across the green from the Water Gardens. We would go out from time to time for dinner, usually at the Lotus House or the Greek joint across the street. Scott's mother, Mimi, came over from America several times and would hang out with the girls, go shopping and do girl stuff. Leonard Whiting came over for dinner quite often, and one night brought over the actress Jean Simmons. Miss Simmons was very classy – exactly as she was in the movies. She was quite curious about what it had been like to deal with the fans. She also told us that making films was so much easier now than 'in the old days' because of technological advances. She and Leonard were working on a movie called *Say Hello to Yesterday*.

In November 1970 I got another German shepherd dog, Shannon. She was already ten months old when she arrived at my flat, and was quite nasty and mean, but an amazing-looking animal all the same, large with extremely long black-and-tan fur and beautiful eyes and eyebrows, just like a woman's. The breeder had told me that Shannon's former owner had mistreated her; even the breeder himself was a little afraid of her. Within two days she and I were good friends, and she became extremely protective. However, Shannon rarely warmed to other people and could become quite intimidating, so I had to put her in another room when company came to the flat.

I took Shannon for walks in Hyde Park every day. One day when I was leaving the building I saw a line of limousines with Arabs milling about. One of the men, tall and slender, decked out in full robes, asked if he could pet Shannon, but I told him that she wasn't very friendly towards strangers, and tactfully tried to discourage him. But he was very calm and serenely confident that Shannon would like him. He bent down and put his hand in front of her face; she sniffed it – and he began petting her coat. I could feel Shannon relaxing. During all of this, he and I chatted about her: we both agreed that she was the most glamorous German shepherd we'd ever seen. After the man had left in his limo the doorman came out, all excited, and told me that I had been talking to King Faisal of Saudi Arabia. I found out then that he had a penthouse in the Water Gardens.

My final recording on the Carnaby label was made in 1970, a single I wrote myself. I had a dispute with my publisher at the time so we put the credits in Julie's name – the same thing I had done with my mother's name in regard to my early Hollywood recordings, hoping to guarantee that we would eventually see some publishing money. This single was called 'Over and Over Again', with 'Sun Comes Up' from my album again used for a B-side. With the A-side I tried an experiment: I had no orchestra, just Mike Moran (who later gained fame as a session musician and songwriter) on keyboards, his bass player, myself on guitar, and some percussion – no drummer. The sound was quite different from the usual sweeping orchestral background. I liked the end result, but the single made no impact, which was disappointing, as

it was the start of a new direction for me that probably would have worked out very well.

Now it was year two with Carnaby, and time to pick up the advance. But Mervyn said, 'I'll give you an advance as soon as we do the next album.' That's when the penny dropped, and I knew for sure I couldn't trust him. I had fulfilled my first year's obligations, so I was done with Carnaby, Mervyn and Cyril.

Joey Paige – one of my bass players from my old Hollywood days – was in London and he called me up. He wanted to get in touch with The Rolling Stones. Bill Wyman, Brian Jones and Keith Richards had sometimes come in to see Scott and me playing in Gazarri's, so Joey thought I could help him contact them. My publicist got hold of the number of the Stones' publicist, with whom I left my number, asking if Bill would call me.

Bill and Astrid starting coming over to visit me in the Water Gardens. When I told him I had just left Carnaby, late in 1970, Bill said he wanted to produce an album for me. We went to Bill's house for Christmas, which actually was a working day for us because we spent most of the time going over material for the new album. Bill lived at Gedding Hall, a medieval manor house near Bury St Edmunds – a huge country estate with a moat and all the grand trappings.

On Christmas Day morning, Bill and I went around delivering his presents to the gatekeeper, groundskeeper and a neighbouring family. He told me that the Stones were going to move out of England to the South of France because of the tax situation in the UK, and that I would probably have to go down there and stay at his place to record the album. So, in the spring of 1971, I notified the estate agents, let go of the flat in the Water Gardens, and headed with Julie down to Bill's villa in France in my Alfa Romeo Spyder, bought from a friend of mine. It was an easy move because I just sold everything that was in the flat, including some furniture I had made, but even so the poor little Alfa was jammed with clothes and a steam trunk.

I had decided to drive straight to Bill's place with no break, but didn't realise it would take so long to get there. I knew I was in the general vicinity when I realised I was looking at the Mediterranean – there was the beach, and directly in front of me a café called Les

Chevelles Sur Mer. To my delight, the café was open, so I ordered a double whisky and Coke. I got the drink, went outside, and gazed at the sea. Then it was off to Bill's villa in Grasse.

It was May 1971, and Bill had been working with a band called Tucky Buzzard. We used some members of the band to rehearse the tracks for my new album, which never did get a proper title. After we rehearsed everything, we chose the players we needed for recording: Bill played bass and I played a little guitar, although most of the guitar work was done by John Uribi, an American guy who was staying with Keith Richards. We wanted Nicky Hopkins on keyboard, but he was very ill, so I suggested Mike Moran. Tucky Buzzard's drummer played on the album. We also got Sue and Sunny as backup singers.

At first, everybody stayed at Bill's place. Then Bill got the studio, the Château d'Herouville in Pontoise, near Paris. It would become famous as Elton John's 'Honky Château'. We took it over and lived there; food was served to us, there was horseback riding, a swimming pool and, of course, the studio. We cut the basic tracks in about two weeks, then I went back to Bill's villa.

I felt very intimidated during the recording of the tracks. I was out of practice and there were great players all around me. The sound engineer had a really rough time getting my vocal to sound right – it always came out weak and thin on the tracks, even though Bill and I agreed that I sounded fine in the studio. We were getting really frustrated, and only resolved the problem when we went down to Keith's house during June and July, and used the Stones' mobile studio. They had a much better selection of microphones, and a really great engineer, plus state-of-the-art equipment.

My new album was ten tracks of country rock. We had decided on the material a few months back, up at Bill's place in England. I'd played a lot of my songs for Bill, of which he chose six for the album: 'Midnight Morning', which later became the A-side of a single, with 'Good Days' as the B-side and one of the album tracks; 'Won't You Tell Me Children'; 'Woman', on which Keith Richards played guitar (this was not the song I had recorded as a single); 'Things You Said To Me'; and 'I Have Found My Time In You', all songs I had written in the last year or so. The other tracks were 'Hands of the Clock', which I think had been recorded by Tucky Buzzard; 'Lipstick Traces', previously done by Ringo Star, and Joe

Jones's 'You Talk Too Much', two old-style songs that showcased Jim Price and Bobby Keyes, the Stones' horn players, on brass; and 'Here Today', featuring John Uribi on guitar. Nothing was written down, so we had to really rehearse the songs before recording them, then it was a free-for-all for any players who contributed.

At the time the Stones were writing and recording *Exile on Main Street* at Keith's house, Villa Nellcote in Cap-Ferrat, using their mobile studio. All the equipment was in a big semi-truck, but the recording room was way down in the basement. We kept in touch by video between the two locations. A woman associated with the Stones came into the studio while I was recording. She started slinking around while I was doing my vocal, and was actually crawling around my feet, really loaded. Then she crawled up my legs, doing some weird dance thing, clawing me like a cat. Unknown to her she was on video, and all the guys in the truck were cracking up as they watched. It was a really embarrassing episode.

Although we were on a work schedule almost every day, there was an abundance of opportunities to get into trouble, with drinking, drugs and various other activities, and people were coming and going at all hours of the day and night.

After we had recorded everything, Bill decided that we needed to take a cruise, just to get away for a bit. There were six of us on the yacht he hired, which was called *My Firebird*. We cruised down the French Riviera and then through the Italian Riviera. Bill had many interests, and was quite disciplined and passionate about them. His morning ritual began with drinking his cup of tea while smoking a joint, and writing in his journal. I usually joined him with either a Scotch or a glass of wine. He was getting into astronomy at the time, and educated me on the subject, using the two huge telescopes that were off the balcony of the master bedroom. We used to play a lot of badminton, and Bill and I were always surprised by the seemingly hundreds of butterflies that always appeared during a game and chased the shuttlecock around. They were everywhere.

Mick and Bianca got married that spring – May 1971 – and there was a lot of secrecy surrounding the wedding. No one got an invitation until the day of the event. I attended the reception, which was in a huge hall. There was an area off to the side of it

with all the equipment and gear set up, in case anybody wanted to play. The crowd included the rich, the famous and a long list of who's who in the music industry, plus the usual wannabes and hangers on. Of course, there were endless photographers clicking away. The Stones assembled and played 'Tumbling Dice'; it was the first time I ever realised just how good Bill and Charlie were together. Then Mick and Keith did their thing – it was quite phenomenal: they were an awesomely strong, tight band.

I divided my time between the UK and Bill's villa at Grasse for the rest of 1971. Julie and I got married in July that year in Norwich. We didn't have a very settled lifestyle. At first, we rented a little house near Julie's family in the village of Mulbarton, near Norwich. In January 1972 we went back to America and rented an apartment in Hollywood. There, in February, I met up again with Bill; The Rolling Stones were in town finishing up *Exile on Main Street* at Sunset Sound studios. Mick had some leftover studio time, and offered it to Bill and me so that we could redo a couple of things on my album tracks.

In the spring of 1972, Julie and I moved back to Mulbarton in the UK for several months, and I got Shannon out of the kennels. Just like the previous year, I split my time between living in the UK and travelling down to Bill's newly rented villa in St-Paul de Vence in Provence, perched in the mountains between Nice and Cannes. It was another old French house and had a lovely large colonnade with vines growing all over it. There was an annex attached to the villa where cloistered nuns had once lived, and that is where I stayed. The beautiful garden had a pond in it, and there were flowers everywhere. It was a very relaxing atmosphere to continue working on my album.

Bill and I are both Scorpios, and that year he had a nice birthday bash for us, taking us out to eat at a very cool nearby restaurant. I wanted to get Bill a really great Christmas gift and looked up an art collector friend in Gloucestershire for assistance, as Bill had everything. I couldn't choose between a sailing scene and a country scene, so took both. I showed Bill both pictures, and he decided on the seascape. It was important to me to present him with something special after all he had done for me. He knew that I didn't have a lot of money during the time we were working on the album, and he'd more or less taken care of everything. I

appreciated him taking care never to put me in an awkward position, which would have been easy; he was a very gracious host, and sensitive to my situation. I was really happy to see him so pleased with my gift.

After spending Christmas 1972 in the UK, Julie and I again moved back to America. Aside from the album, there wasn't a lot else going on in my life. I had a flat on Gardner Street now, eventually moving into a big house in the Hollywood Hills that we shared with a musician duo from Columbia and their girlfriends. Like Bill, I was anxious to get the album released, and he had given me copies of the masters to see if I could get something going in America. Originally, I was to be slotted on the Stones' label, but that fell through, so I approached the William Morris Agency in Beverly Hills and discussed trying to get a deal with an American label. Although they were very enthusiastic, nothing happened. Then I met Charlie Green, of Green Mountain records, who was really excited about the prospect of releasing a single from the album.

Once signed to the Green Mountain label in 1973, I recorded several tracks in Hollywood: 'Dixie Sunshine', 'Ha, Ha!', 'Remember Me', 'Woman, You Chain Me' and 'First Day', all self-penned. On these tracks, I sang and played guitar and piano, Tiny Schneider, my former drummer from early Walker Brothers days, was on drums, and Sammy McCue played lead guitar; he, like Tiny, had toured with The Everly Brothers. I recently became aware that these tracks and others are circulating as bootlegs, and that people are under the mistaken impression that they come from the album I recorded with Bill Wyman, but they are just unfinished basic backing tracks with only a 'guide' vocal. Guide vocals are done on any microphone so that all the musicians playing can stay together, so these particular tracks are light years from being finished and I have no idea how they got into the public domain. The other tracks in question are 'You' (not the title song of my 2000 CD), recorded in London in 1973–74, 'How Long Can the Road Be' and 'Lovin' on the Run', but I can't remember where or when I made those last two demo tapes.

Because I was getting so desperate for some action I did a very stupid thing: I agreed to give Charlie the publishing rights to two of the songs – 'Midnight Morning' and 'Good Days' – as part of a deal to release them as a single. Later, when I told Bill what I had done, he was rightly angry about it. He had, after all, produced everything, and spent a lot of his own money getting the album done, and if anyone deserved the publishing rights it was him. It was one of those awful decisions that I still really regret. The terrible tragedy in all this was that Charlie never told me that his company was completely broke; because of this, the single was never properly released. At least he didn't get the other eight tracks.

It was now the spring of 1973, and my last royalty cheque was almost completely used up, with nothing else in view. John Francis, an agent formerly with Capable Management, called me up from the UK – another timely call completely out of the blue – and told me of an idea he had to form a group called The New Walkers. John was a typical wheeler-dealer who always had a lot of irons in the fire. He had already booked a lot of club dates, was organising a band, and had lined up a singer named Jimmy Wilson who sounded exactly like Scott. John sent me the airfare, and off I went, back to Britain. Arthur Howarth was taken on as our roadie. Our backing band was Mike Keeley on bass, Jim Gilbert on drums, 'Big' Dave from Ipswich on guitar, and a Scotsman named John – nicknamed 'Haggis' by the band – on a Hammond B3 organ.

We started doing gigs in late spring 1973. Even though the pay was really good the tour posed its share of financial problems for me. When I got paid each week I first paid the band members. Then, thanks to travel expenses and paying for two homes – one in Hollywood and one in the West End of London for when Julie wanted to come over and stay a while – I had very little money left. But The New Walkers were quite successful, even though my overheads were higher than I would have liked. We played some good clubs, made lots of money and had great audiences; but after several months of the same thing I got restless musically. After a few more months we disbanded.

In the summer of 1974, Julie and I moved back to America and found an apartment in Brentwood, LA. I remember it was extremely hot and that I built a sunshade over the balcony. Through a friend of Julie's we met up with a guy we knew from England – Mike Basset – who was now residing in Hollywood.

Mike had lived upstairs in the Water Gardens, and over time I had discovered that he made a lot of money running a couple of porn shops in Soho and a call-girl service. He drove around in a new E-type Jaguar and had an expensive girl on each arm – the whole works. He was a very questionable character – Shannon used to growl when he was around. Now Mike was going to live in a cottage in the grounds of a wealthy 'client' in Bel Air; he claimed to be a born-again Christian – he was very convincing – and had set up a ministry to preach to the rich. Once the entire story was revealed to me, I asked him, 'Why not minister to the poor?' and he remarked, 'The poor find their own way to God.' I didn't have a problem with ministries, or being a born-again, but Mike was up to his old tricks – this time in America. I found out he had just posed for a nude picture spread in *Playgirl*, and now he was telling everyone he knew to buy up all the magazines because he was a born-again and didn't want anyone to see him naked. I had never heard such a load of crap.

In the meantime, I was trying to get a recording deal going. I located Bob Crewe, who had written 'The Sun Ain't Gonna Shine Anymore', and discussed doing more work with him, but he was interested in more than just music. I stayed at his place on La Cienega one night, crashing after having too much to drink, and that's when I had to make it clear to him that I was interested only in music – nothing else. Once we got that straightened out, he played some songs for me that he had written, which would become future hits; 'Lady Marmalade' was among them. Bob also played me an amazing demo track of a song written by Allen Toussaint that sounded like a finished product – a great piece. Unfortunately for me, the deals for these songs were already made with other artists. He was trying to get something together for me, but said that he was in kind of a lull himself at the time.

During the summer of 1974, I was watching television, and on came the film *Deadlier Than the Male* – the movie for which The Walker Brothers had sung the title song. As I heard it again, it struck me that we sounded really good, and I decided to call Scott and talk about re-forming. We had kept loosely in touch in the intervening years. I reached him at his home in Amsterdam, and he too thought it was a good idea, so we planned to meet up in

London within a few weeks. In the meantime, he said he would get in touch with Gary.

I called John Francis and told him to line up some gigs and find a band for me in the UK as soon as possible, so that I would have the means to sustain myself while we negotiated reforming The Walker Brothers. Of course I didn't tell John Francis about the idea to re-form. I wouldn't know who would actually end up representing Gary, Scott and me until the three of us met and talked about it, and we were keeping that under wraps. John got to work right away lining up a few jobs in England and Scotland, and getting a band organised. I borrowed my airfare from a friend of one of the agents at William Morris, promising to pay it back once I got my next royalty cheque, which was due soon.

Now that Scott and I were talking about re-forming The Walker Brothers, I focused on pursuing that, and left my album in Bill Wyman's hands; he still has the masters, as far as I know. The Green Mountain episode was my last attempt at releasing any of the tracks.

Around September 1974, Julie announced to me that she had met some born-again Christian ladies and that she was starting a ministry. Suddenly she was a 'born-again' too, in a very big way, and I had no means of dealing with that. Mike Bassett had had something to do with this, but I don't know what. Julie was then about four months pregnant, but she chose to stay with the ministry rather than go back to England with me, so that was it between us. There have been stories that have appeared in print about our break-up, but they are all untrue. I simply told Julie that, when the royalty cheque arrived, she should pay back the money that I owed for my fare, and keep the rest for herself.

I left for England within a few weeks and got in touch with a friend, Mike Williams, whose parents – Fred and Eve – ran the Bull & Bush, a popular pub in Hampstead. Mike had been a long-time friend of Scott and Gary also: he'd been Scott's road manager and was also involved with Gary's group, The Rain. I had stayed at this pub in the past, in one of the little bedrooms that had been converted from the former stables on the property. I needed a base near London, where the band would be

rehearsing, and the Bull & Bush was convenient. It was while I was staying there, in late February 1975, that I got a call from my father informing me that my son had been born, and that Julie had named him Jamie.

Scott and I were in touch often, making phone calls between London and Amsterdam. He had to make a lot of arrangements to get over to London. We needed to find a place to stay and work. He was still signed to CBS records, and he and his manager Ady Semel were in the process of dissolving his contract. It was imperative that CBS didn't find out that we were thinking about re-forming because they wouldn't have let Scott go, and Gary and I would have been forced to sign with CBS, whether we wanted to or not.

I was pretty much on my own again at this time – never a good idea. Every bad habit reappeared as if nothing had changed. Mike and I started going out to the clubs and as usual I met a lot of girls. Mike didn't drink or do drugs, so he spent most of the time trying to keep me from doing either. He did introduce me to a lot of the girls he knew, probably hoping that I would stay out of trouble if I was seeing someone regularly. It almost worked. But I got a call from my agent friend, John Francis; he'd got a band and some dates organised, so I was off again.

I played a few uneventful shows in the North of England, then headed up to Scotland. I was due to stay up there for a fortnight, but it turned out to be several months. Initially, I played about five shows there before John told me that he didn't have anything else booked, and sort of disappeared. I couldn't reach him anywhere. Thankfully, I was collecting my fees.

I talked to Henry Spurway, the promoter who had booked the shows with John Francis, and had him book a few more dates for us. My sister Judy had come to visit, and did some backup singing; we played a few shows in small Scottish venues. When that ended, the band went back to England and Judy went back to the US, while I stayed in Scotland for about three more months before returning to the Bull & Bush.

Henry Spurway was good friends with a man named Tom Gillespie, who owned the Meadowhead Hotel, a cool place out in the country in West Calder. While I was working for Henry I stayed at the hotel, and became very friendly with Tom. I'd always signed autographs and met the fans after the shows, so I met quite a few people every night. One particularly attractive girl had come to the last four or five shows. She would watch me when I was signing autographs and chatting to the crowd, but she never asked me for anything, she just stood there and looked at me. Her name was Avril, and I found her intriguing. She had a sort of Latin look about her, dark and sultry.

I finally went up to her and said, 'I've seen you several times, but you never say anything to me. What do you want?' She smiled and said, with a lovely Scots accent, 'I want to take you home with me.' She was rather intense, and I thought I could get into some real trouble here. I suggested that she come back to my hotel for a drink and a chat. I didn't know how this was going to turn out, so I thought a little prudence was not a bad idea. We talked for quite a while but she never really told me much about herself. It was just light conversation.

We got to that moment when it's time to make a decision, and I asked her to stay with me. She wasn't the one-night-stand type, even though she made it clear that she wanted to make love to me. For a long time, it had seemed that the women I attracted were very physical and into the moment, so I rarely saw any of them more than once or twice. Not this time.

When we got upstairs, I got the feeling that she didn't make a habit of sleeping with anyone who came along. Our lovemaking was not the usual frenzied desire for instant gratification; it wasn't going to be like that with this girl. I think she wanted something more like a long-term relationship. I didn't know what I wanted then, but I knew that I didn't want to be completely alone. I really liked Avril a lot, and got along well with her children, so we became quite an item for several months. I felt really comfortable up there in Scotland, and light up whenever I think about it.

Julie came back to England with Jamie when he was a few months old, to visit with her parents, so I went to see them. That was the first time I saw Jamie. I spent just a few days there before returning to the Bull & Bush. Julie was determined to stay with the ministry in America, and I made it clear that I wanted nothing to do with that sort of thing. So we parted ways at that time, and she went back to the States. We didn't encounter each other again until

we met up at Heathrow Airport about four years later, and that was just for a few brief minutes in passing. I didn't see Jamie for years after that because I did not feel that it was good for him to have a part-time father.

CHAPTER 7

THE REUNION AND AFTER

WELCOME BACK!

G A R Y   W A L K E R

In the late summer of 1974, Scott called and asked if I was interested in re-forming The Walker Bothers. By that time, all wounds were healed and hopefully we'd learned some lessons. I thought about all the good times we'd had and realised I'd always known that we still had plenty of ideas and lots of good music in us. So I said yes. I was really happy about it.

We all met up at the Blue Hotel overlooking Hyde Park. It was as if we had never been apart. We knew we had to get some good songs together and secure a record deal. Scott's manager, Ady Semel, agreed to manage us as The Walker Brothers. I really liked Ady, and still do. He was an intellectual who could speak five languages, resembled an exceptionally good-looking Herbert Lom and had a very commanding presence.

Dick Leahy and Maurice Myers had formed a label called GTO Records, and had three or four artists, including Billy Ocean and Gloria Gaynor. Pub and wine-bar gossip suggested to them that The Walker Brothers were re-forming and looking for a record deal. Dick contacted Ady with a proposal, we had a few meetings and signed.

We were all living in separate flats, and realised that we needed to get a flat together in order to write songs and practise. GTO were paying us a salary and agreed to fund a flat in the King's Road in Fulham, hoping to recoup the money later from record sales. They had a lot of faith in us. The flat was over Newton's restaurant.

We met Marc Bolan in the restaurant, and found out to our surprise that he was living just around the corner. We became good friends and were invited to his house to play some music. Marc had turned his living room into a studio with various instruments, and he suggested we jam together. We started to do a blues number with me on drums, Scott on bass and John and Marc on guitars. After about 20 seconds, Marc stopped playing. He just couldn't believe how well we played our instruments. It had never occurred to him that we could play. If only we had recorded what we did that day!

I think Marc's girlfriend Gloria had a twinkle in the eye for Scott, and I even suspected that Marc might have had an even brighter twinkle. Gloria would come on to Scott, who didn't fancy her but, being the perfect gentleman, and reinforcing in the process the 'Walker Sisters' legend, did not respond.

Jimmy Connors had just enjoyed great success at Wimbledon, and Scott was really into tennis. He wanted a racquet, so we went to Harrods to get one. We waited and we waited to get served. Fifteen minutes soon became thirty minutes, and we were moving into injury time. I approached an assistant at another desk and asked if he would come over and help us, but he told me he couldn't, as it was not his department. I said, 'It's ten feet away!'

'Sorry,' came the reply. I went back to Scott. By now we were getting really pissed off. This was Harrods, for God's sake! By now we had worked ourselves into a frenzy and there was no turning back. I asked the assistant if he had a phone, telling him I was going to call Capital Radio and announce on air that Scott and I were in Harrods, the top store, that we couldn't get served, and that we were going to get a couple of cricket bats and smash the fucking place up. Needless to say, this finally got a reaction, but I had to restrain Scott, who was all ready for a fight. The sales assistants called their security people, and the police, but when they arrested us, and we told them what had happened, they agreed with us that Harrods was out of order and ended up asking us to sign autographs for their kids, before letting us go.

We bought lots of LPs in our search for material for the coming single and album. I chose 'Hold an Old Friend's Hand' for John and Janis Ian's 'Lover's Lullaby'. That song came closest to what we wanted to do, which was Schumann's 'Pretty Fly', the children's lullaby from *Night of the Hunter*, the film starring Robert Mitchum. I was responsible for the crashing guitar solo on the track that became our first GTO single, 'No Regrets'. A session musician had originally recorded this solo, and Scott asked what I thought. I said, 'It's fine, but turn it up.' He did, and I said, 'More!' When it went the highest we could get it, everybody absolutely loved it. Contrary to what has appeared in print, I certainly did contribute to this album, and the other two we would record. I played drums, shakers and maracas on various tracks, and gave a lot of constructive advice.

We wanted Cecil Beaton, the society photographer who had photographed us in the sixties, to do the cover shoot for the album, but he was too ill so we opted for Michael Joseph. I can be seen on the album sleeve wearing the pendant that Michael was to give his bride on their wedding day, which was the day after the shoot. We didn't want a moody sixties-style Walker Brothers cover – we wanted something bright and happy, and that's what the cover conveys. It's untrue that Scott had to be carried out on a stretcher, as has been rumoured, but he did get pretty tipsy.

In November 1975, amid much publicity, we released our single 'No Regrets'/'Remember Me', and our album, also called *No Regrets*. The single was promoted through several TV appearances, and at *The Vera Lynn Show*, at Christmas 1975, we received an outstanding ovation. They had clapped after 'No Regrets', but when we'd finished 'Lover's Lullaby' they just didn't stop applauding, and were clearly glad to have us back. That really shook us, and we got very emotional on stage: this was the first time that any of us had experienced that one magic moment when we knew we had done something really special. Dame Vera said, 'Sounds like someone's been missing you. Welcome back.'

In February 1976, the single reached Number 3. For us, it was some achievement because we had been concerned about its six-minute length. It was great to be in the charts again and we were really glad we had got back together.

We promoted the single abroad and we appeared on *Top of the*

Pops three times, although I couldn't play on one show because I didn't have my union card with me. Instead I introduced Scott and John, wearing a bandage on my arm. Where most artists at that time mimed to their records, Scott and John, with their great vocal capabilities, were almost forced to sing live, thus giving the BBC Orchestra a reason to justify its existence. Scott was always nervous about singing live because the sound was usually below par, and that could lead to unfair criticism.

We all gave interviews, and GTO arranged a publicity tour for us – no shows, just media. We opted to travel by train and were accompanied by Michael Peyton, head of publicity at GTO. Coming back from Scotland to Newcastle, we lost John. He'd gone off to see some friends without telling us where he was going. We had a TV or radio interview that night, and we got rather agitated. When we finally got hold of him, he said, 'Hey, man, I'll be there, I'm gonna hire a plane.' It cost him £600. The weather was dreadful – as on the night Buddy Holly's plane, the same type, had crashed. We were all a bit worried, and Scott was ready to have a heart attack, but John made it ten minutes before transmission.

Scott was going through a divorce at the time. He had been spending an increasing amount of time apart from Mette, in London, and she had long been extremely envious of all the fan attention. When Scott did his shows, and she attended, she would accuse him of looking at different girls in the audience. He said to me, 'Of course I'm looking at different girls! That's my job, to entertain them.' Otherwise he'd have been facing the other way. Mette's jealousy would extend to girls in the street, leading to horrendous arguments. Eventually, Scott just couldn't carry on. The divorce was amicable and simple – I went with him to the Danish embassy, he just signed a few papers and, when we came out, Lulu happened to be driving by. She waved and I could not help but wish that Mette had been there to see it! After that, Scott never referred to the divorce, nor did he ever display any emotion. He continued to visit his daughter Lee regularly and ensured he played a major role in her upbringing.

After the divorce he became friendly with Denise Simpson, Dick Leahy's PA, but it didn't last very long. He told me he'd realised she wasn't his type. He then met a lady called Libby, who used to come to the flat in the King's Road. They were together for at least ten years.

In 1976, we recorded a second album, *Lines*. John was drinking again, which caused problems. After several takes he still couldn't sing, 'There have been times I've found myself thinking of committing some dreadful crime' (from 'Many Rivers to Cross'), and when it got late in the day and the cleaning lady was coming in, Scott and I felt as if we might commit a dreadful crime! Somehow it got finished, and in late summer the album, and a single from it, 'Lines'/'First Day', was released. 'Lines', which is said to be about cocaine addiction, was Scott's favourite Walker Brothers song.

A second single was put out later that year with two more tracks from the album, 'We're All Alone' and 'Have You Seen My Baby'. Scott and I had been saying that no one reveals a sense of humour in music, and that people took it too seriously, so at the end of this last track, which John sang, I did my impression of an elephant. Scott liked it so much he left it on.

We'd cut 'We're All Alone', one of my favourites. Somehow I obtained the key to the studio and smuggled Barbara in that night, when it was deserted, to play it for her. She thought it was absolutely brilliant. We might have had the field to ourselves, but after a mysterious phone call to Dick Leahy, Rita Coolidge's version suddenly appeared on the airwaves, and ours was sidelined. We were bigger in England than Rita was, so it seems that someone was pulling out all the stops to build her up.

Late that year Dick Leahy paid for John and Scott to go to Nashville. They were only going to record one song, so it wasn't worth my while going. Then we disappeared for a year to work on our third album.

Nite Flights is my favourite Walker Brothers album. We got a new feel and sound that proved we could be quite original – so much so that when we presented it to the record company they didn't know how to categorise it. It wasn't rock, blues, country or anything they had ever heard before, so they had no idea what to do with it. But it was to influence some big names, among them

David Bowie (who covered the title track), and would inspire some famous albums.

We decided we would each do four tracks. We worked in three separate rooms, and no one knew what the others were doing. I wasn't as quick as Scott and John at writing songs, so I ended up with only two tracks. Originally the album was going to have the title of one of my tracks, 'Death of Romance', which I still feel would have been highly appropriate because it marked a departure from romantic ballads. That song is based on experiences I had in Amsterdam, and the lyrics shook Scott to the ground: he absolutely loved it.

'Den Haague' is about Monique van Cleef, a dominatrix who operated in the Dutch capital after being thrown out of America. I went to her chateau with a friend who was going to write a book about her. The song describes exactly what happened. In Monique's room, there was a big statue of Christ, and I did hang my coat on it. One of her dogs was slobbering, hence the reference to a vet. I kept hearing a moaning noise and finally asked Monique if the dogs were alright. She replied, 'Oh, my God!' and ran down the hall. There, in a closet, was a gentleman trussed up and gagged with his own underpants – in the excitement of my visit, she had forgotten he was in there!

She insisted we all went to dinner later that night. We were accompanied by a senior member of the Dutch police who had a thing about dead bodies, a disgraced airline hostess who had been fired because she'd constantly been playing with herself in the toilets and, last but not least, a millionaire businessman who was accompanied by the two dogs wearing spiked collars – he was made to pay for the meal as a punishment for breathing too loudly. Monique also had a spiked collar above her leather dress, and had her 'slave' with her. She got the best table in the restaurant and placed me at the end against the wall, with her blocking my exit. She insisted on ordering spicy food, and warned me, 'If you don't eat it, I'm going to give you a two-litre enema!' I did, however, get the strong impression that she liked me because I wasn't into all the kinky stuff.

Big Jim Sullivan, a session guitarist who has played for The Walker Brothers and other famous people, became good friends with us and played guitar for us when we were recording *Nite*

Flights at Scorpio Sound Studios in London. The sessions went well, and when we were finished, it came to me strongly that the only previous time I'd heard an album that represented such a radical change of direction was when I'd first played The Beatles' *Sgt Pepper*.

Storm Thorgerson, the acclaimed graphic designer, and his company Hipgnosis specialised in album covers. We met up with him to discuss ideas and told him what we thought would make a good cover, but when Scott disagreed with some of the ideas that Storm put forward, Storm walked out. It was resolved only by Scott's giving way, but he was definitely pleased with the finished cover, a gatefold that features fragmented black-and-white images of us that relate to the musical themes. I personally called, on behalf of the three of us, to thank Storm for one of the best sleeves we'd ever had, and he said, 'You're the first group that's ever called me and said that.' We became friends from then on.

In July 1978, we released *Nite Flights*, which proved to be the last album we ever recorded as a group. A single, 'The Electrician'/'Den Haague' (released in August) and an EP, *Shutout*, featuring Scott's four tracks, were taken from the album. The big shame was that we didn't get to carry on and develop this new style; Scott would build on it for his next album, although that would not appear for another six years. Another thing I liked about the album was that it reflected our three personalities.

Nite Flights was critically acclaimed, but didn't sell well. At the time, it was our worst-selling album. To begin with, it defied definition, and no one knew how to promote it. Also, it was such a departure that it put all our fans in shock.

Instead of touring we did cabaret dates arranged by our new manager, David Apps, who took over when Ady Semel returned to Israel after learning that his mother was ill. Scott had been complaining to me, late at night, how John kept hounding him to go on tour, and he was adamant he couldn't take the chance because of John's drink problem. John, in turn, was constantly saying that Scott's nerves were shot and that he was afraid to go on stage. What Scott was really nervous about was John's inability to perform.

There was some truth in what John said, and it may well be that it was at this time that Scott developed what has since been

described as a 'total phobia' about live performances. He and I were now very dependent on Valium, taking the highest-permitted dose. Everything was fine until that tablet started wearing off and then we became very, very edgy. This distorted our judgement, and Scott's built-in perfectionism made him near-obsessive. As in the sixties, he was terrified of the Valium wearing off on stage, and had panic attacks while performing. I wasn't as bad, and I certainly wasn't jittery on stage or a nervous person generally, whereas Scott was not the sociable type and liked keeping to himself, giving him more space to nurture his fears. My theory is that these factors put Scott off performing. The only way to resolve the problem was to take more Valium or give up playing live. The thing was, Scott and I would never admit to being addicted to Valium, or that it was Valium that was causing the intense anxiety.

Eventually, though, Scott agreed to tour. Those cabaret dates in 1978 were our last appearances as a group. We all wanted the shows to be good, and I felt they would give me a chance to use different percussive effects on stage, which added to the sound. I did a drum solo at every show and got overwhelming responses from audiences. What Scott enjoyed about the tour was our getting to play tennis every day with the band, who hated it, as they wanted to sleep off their hangovers. I think maybe John did sing more than Scott on this tour. There are a lot of untrue stories circulating about these cabaret dates, yet there was one funny incident: a girl was calling out to John, and he jumped off the stage, ran over and gave her a big kiss; when he came back, someone told him he'd kissed the wrong girl, to everyone's great amusement.

We made a big mistake in deciding not to include The Walker Brothers' classics. It wasn't so much that Scott was reluctant to perform them, or his own solo hits, but that we wanted to give our fans some new material, when in fact the hits were what they wanted to hear. The album hadn't sold, and things weren't looking good. Above all, Scott didn't want to tour again after the last shows we had done. In the end, we just drifted apart. There would not be another reunion. There were a couple of times over the years when we got close to it, and needed to make some money, but it never happened.

After the split, I remained in England. I didn't want to leave Barbara, so her family invited me to stay at their house in east London. I was short of money – if we'd wanted any cash from The Walker Brothers' reunion, we'd have had to sue for it.

Barbara and I married in 1979. I'd been determined all along that I would never get married until I found the right girl. Because my mother had been divorced twice I was adamant that, when I myself tied the knot, it would be once – and once only.

After our marriage, we lived in east London, near Barbara's family. By 1980 my Valium dependence was out of control and I resolved to stop taking them. It took me six months to get just about back to normal. I would often hyperventilate and had to breathe through a paper bag; one morning, when I was lying in bed having an attack the doctor told Barbara to throw a bucket of cold water over me, but she was hesitant because the electric blanket was on.

In the end I got through it, and started a business making reproductions of famous castles out of sand, but when the eighties recession kicked in the business wasn't bringing in enough to live on, so I worked as a motorcycle courier for about three years. By coincidence, I once had to deliver a royalty cheque to Scott, but missed seeing him as he wasn't there when I arrived.

Scott was now signed to Virgin Records. I remember going into Virgin to see if they would take all three of us, but they wanted only Scott. He was so excited about being with a record company that would allow him to do what he wanted, and he thought he would really move forward at last.

One day, when I went on my bike to visit Scott in Stamford Brook, where he had a flat, he was just leaving to do TV promotion in Amsterdam for his single, 'Track 3', taken from his 1984 album *Climate of Hunter*. He was very impressed with my motorbike. I talked to him on the phone and visited him on several occasions after that, and he told me he'd had to sell his classical record collection to raise some money to live on. The problem was that Virgin was not as supportive as Scott had at first thought, and there had been problems with the marketing of his album, which sadly turned out to be one of Virgin's worst-selling records. There would be no follow-up for 11 years. Instead, Scott completed a three-year course at the Byam Shaw art college in London. In 1987 he appeared in a TV ad for Britvic orange juice, with other sixties stars, as he needed the money. For all that he was becoming an iconic cult figure, he and I were both broke, and anything that came along was worth considering. Scott was as elusive and publicity shy as ever.

In 1986, my son Michael was born. Soon after his birth, we went to stay with Scott's mother in California – she had looked after my stepfather, Jack Leeds, in his final weeks – and she gave us some of Scott's baby clothes for Michael. I was always to regret not having Michael sooner, but I had thought myself too insecure and had worried about never knowing how I stood financially. I also travelled a lot, which I felt would not have been fair on Barbara. However, I was to find out that none of this mattered: the only important thing was that we all had each other, and that was never truer than when things got worse financially. We had to sell our house to pay our debts, and move in with Barbara's sister. This was in 1991. A couple of months later, Barbara was diagnosed with breast cancer, but fortunately it was caught early and cured. That was a very stressful and worrying period for us.

Just after that, we moved into our present home in Essex, and I started a new business making life sculptures, bronze casts of hands and feet, which I still carry on today.

Throughout these years my musical interests had taken a back seat, although I was still writing songs. In 1989 I made a rare TV appearance in the quiz show *Tell the Truth*. Jill Gascoine was on the panel and, after the recording, she expressed shock that one of The Walker Brothers would do a show like this. In fact, it was one of my favourite shows and I did it because I wanted to. I also met the well-known soap star Shirley Stelfox, and it turned out that she was a big Walker Brothers fan.

I didn't have much contact with Scott and John in this period. We had always had a good relationship, and some very good times together, but now we were all living very different lives, in different places. When I did see Scott, it was as if the intervening years had never been – indeed, where did they go? We just picked up where we'd left off. All this time, John was in LA and we didn't know what he was doing. We could have called him, but we wondered if he would still want to talk to us. Later, when John told me what a hard time he'd had in California, and that he had

almost died on one occasion, I wished I had contacted him, or that someone had let me know of his troubles.

CONSTANTLY LOOKING FOR SOMETHING
JOHN WALKER

During the summer of 1975, the Bull & Bush was my base. Scott and I were meeting at different pubs in London to talk about our ideas for re-forming, and what to do next. Neither one of us was doing much at the time. Then Scott finally located Gary and told him about our plan. Gary was all for it so the three of us had a meeting. Although Gary and I had never met Ady Semel, we agreed that we wanted him to be our new manager, as he was already managing Scott. We would continue The Walker Brothers where we left off – just eight years further down the road. Scott and I also decided to go back to Freddie Winrose, Scott's vocal coach in the sixties, and get back in shape.

Ady had managed to get Scott released from his CBS contract, then he and Dick Leahy – who owned GTO Records – struck a deal. Dick had been a music publisher before starting his own label. He'd heard we were re-forming and wanted to sign us. It was the usual contract, but stipulated that Scott would be the producer, and we got a reasonable advance. The press announced that we had re-formed, and got very excited at the prospect. For me this was great fun. We were all getting on so well, and it was great to be back in the UK and performing with the group again.

Scott got a flat in Kensington and moved in, leaving Mette and his young daughter, Lee, in their home in Amsterdam. He was always shuttling back and forth between the two places to see them.

We went out and bought a couple of Martin acoustic guitars at a music store in Shaftsbury Avenue. Scott bought a D28, and I got a D35 – two really great instruments. Neither of us had brought any gear to London, so we were starting from scratch. Later that year I bought a blond Stratocaster because it looked so cool, and played really well.

In choosing material to record, Gary, Scott and I listened to everything we could, trying out different pieces in Scott's flat. Dick Leahy also contributed, and ultimately presented us with 'No

Regrets'. We listened to Tom Rush's version, which he sang solo with female backing singers, and really liked the idea of covering it. We were once again calling the shots, as we had done in our early recording days, discussing ideas for each track and working them out ourselves. It was a really good, creative time, and all of us were working hard, even though we were still sometimes drinking more than we should.

Initially we decided that, because of its six-minute length, 'No Regrets' would be an album track, not a single, and that Scott would be the soloist with a female session singer adding some background. I didn't sing at all on our original version. When Dick heard the recording he said, 'I don't hear John.' When we told him I wasn't on it, he replied, 'This is going to be your single, so John, you'd better put your voice on it.' Despite our adamant protests and concerns about the track's length, which was twice that of the average single, we went ahead and laid down the final version within an hour or so, which is what it took to work out my harmonies and match Scott's phrasing. So much for calling our own shots. The song didn't lend itself as easily to harmony as other songs, but somehow it all worked out and proved to be very successful.

Scott asked me if I had anything for the B-side. I told him I had written a country-type song called 'Remember Me'. When I played it for him, he said, 'Let's do it.' It was that simple, and we threw it together rather quickly: I played rhythm and slide guitar and sang lead, Scott played bass and sang harmony, and Gary played the guitar case, shaker and tambourine – an unusual, spur-of-the-moment percussive idea. Talk about getting back to basics! I was still signed to Miracle Songs publishing, and didn't want them to get a penny, so the songwriter's credit went to 'A Dayam', Ady Semel's *nom de plume*. In later years, I finally had to fess up to Miracle Songs that it was my song, so they got their money after all.

We were working on the album – also called *No Regrets* – during this time. Choosing the ten tracks was an ever-evolving process, with everyone bringing lots of ideas to the table. After it was decided that 'No Regrets' would be the single, we knew that many of the other tracks should follow suit with a country-rock theme. 'Boulder to Birmingham', originally recorded by Emmylou Harris, and 'Hold an Old Friend's Hand', which had been done by

Rita Coolidge, were perfect for the album. 'Everything That Touches You', by Michael Kamen, had a little country feel to it. We also included a Jerry Butler song – 'He'll Break Your Heart' – which we treated in a reggae style. That song would become very popular in Germany, and we performed it on the German TV show *Beat Club*, in Hamburg. 'Lover's Lullaby', written by Janis Ian, was too beautiful not to include. Kris Kristofferson wrote 'I've Got to Have You'. I sang a song called 'Lovers', written by Mickey Newbury, which moved away from country, and was a standard love song. 'Burn Our Bridges' was another track that wasn't in keeping with the country theme. We also did a blues number called 'Walkin' in the Sun', written by Jeff Barry.

No Regrets was released in November 1975, along with the single. By February 1976 the single had reached Number 3 in the charts and the album went to Number 49.

Ady, Dick and the GTO team lined up massive promotion for *No Regrets*, and we starting doing a lot of television – especially after the single charted in February 1976 – as well as radio and press. It was great. One of the first TV appearances was at Christmas 1975, on *The Vera Lynn Show*. We performed 'No Regrets' and then 'Lover's Lullaby', which really seemed to captivate the live audience – you could have heard a pin drop. When we finished 'Lover's Lullaby', the audience leapt to their feet and gave us an enormous standing ovation – they loved it. I later heard that, for some reason, the second song wasn't aired, which was a pity.

We were really nervous about doing this show because it was the first time we'd appeared on TV together in nearly nine years, and it was important to our future. We didn't want to mess up on Dame Vera's show. She was totally professional, making us feel comfortable and at ease, and was just as gracious off camera. A lot of television people immediately transform back into assholes when the cameras stop rolling – they're total fakes. But not Dame Vera – she was really genuine.

We did promotional films shot in Copenhagen, appeared on *Top of the Pops* three times, *Supersonic* – from which our live segment was also broadcast on Twiggy's US TV show – *Musik Laden* in Germany, and some Dutch TV. People have asked why Scott and I always grinned at each other when we sang the lines, 'We'd only cry again, say goodbye again.' It was because I had to look at him while singing the lines so that I could get the phrasing, and every time I looked at him, it made me laugh which started him off. We were always just shy of cracking up. Performing the song required a bit of drama on our parts, and we could only manage a straight face up to that point.

In February 1976 I appeared on Page 3 of the *Sun* newspaper with a topless Nina Carter for a special Valentine's edition. This was set up by our publicity people. It was different! I was there for the girls, and she was there for the guys.

We were taking trains, first class, all over England, Scotland and Wales to do a two-week promotional tour; the train was much more comfortable than a car. GTO wanted the public to see that we were alive and well, and back together. When we got to Scotland I wanted to visit my friends in West Calder, so I stayed overnight – counting on taking the train the following day back to Newcastle for a promo appearance. My mistake: there was no train, so I hired a private plane to fly me down, and got there in time to do the interview. When we were in Manchester, we'd hook up with an old friend, George Best the footballer, who had a club there, Slack Alice's. We'd get together, have a night out and get loaded. I liked him: he had a good personality and he certainly was one hell of a football player.

Even though Julie and I had called it quits, I was still very good friends with her sister Sue and her family, so I stayed at their house in Berkshire while the business side of re-forming of The Walker Brothers was being sorted out. Sue's husband, Patrick, and I went out to the local pub one night and, yes, there was a very attractive girl working at the bar. She was tall and fair, and really well put together. Towards the end of the evening, and after plenty of 'Dutch' courage, I decided that I should go up and order a drink. I managed to get her attention and she asked me what I'd like, so I smiled and said, 'A large Scotch and Coke, and your phone number.' She came back with the drink, looked at me for a few seconds, and then handed me her number. Her name was Jen.

I couldn't call her for a couple of days because I had to be in town for meetings, so I thought it best to go back to the pub to see her again. That night we went to her place. She had a cool little terrace house in a town nearby. It was almost dark in the lounge and there was one of those electric coal-effect fires that give off a nice glow. We didn't spend a lot of time talking: she was very, very sensual, and I really wanted her. We didn't even make it upstairs – there was a large, white sheepskin rug on the floor that became the setting for some torrid lovemaking until dawn. We didn't move until late the next day, and then we started over again.

I was still staying at Julie's sister's house, but, after about a week or two, I moved in with Jen for a while. We had a lot of good times together, even though I was always busy with The Walker Brothers. We actually stayed together for over two years, right up to the time I was recording *Nite Flights*. In the end things just didn't work out.

Eventually Scott, Gary and I moved into one big flat in the New King's Road, which made it easier to discuss recording and material. There was never any talk about the past, just the present. We were more adult in the way we handled ourselves and things in general, or at least I like to think so. We had made a sort of unspoken pact to stick together, and to do what it took to achieve success this time around. There was no 'five-year plan' so to speak, just talk of day-to-day stuff.

Our flat on the New King's Road was very cool. It was directly above Newton's restaurant and near the Chelsea football grounds. The only challenge we had to work out was that there were only two bedrooms, and three of us. Scott wanted the small bedroom upstairs, in the back. I, of course, had to have the master bedroom and poor Gary had to fend for himself. He was very resourceful, though: he turned the dining room into a tent, and had a day bed inside. He was able to close off the tent so he had some privacy. I thought it was very cool. Whenever we answered the phone, and the call was for Gary, we'd say, 'Hold on, Gary's in the tent!'

Scott still had his orange VW. When he drove down the street, Gary would do his typical under-the-breath voice, rubbing his chin, and looking sideways, saying, 'There goes Scott in the orange peel.' Somewhere along the line, the aerial got broken, so Scott stuck a coat hanger there. Gary would then say, 'Never trust a guy with a coat hanger on his car.' Scott did a lot of funny things without even realising it. It was hilarious.

Gary and I did all the cooking, and the cleaning up too. But one night Gary made a great roast and we told Scott that he had to clean up. We soaked the dishes, but the next morning they were still there. We got on at Scott to get started, but he said, 'I'm not going to put my hands in that dirty water.' He was helpless. So Gary and I got to work.

Through Mike Williams, Scott and I met a couple of young ladies who shared a house not far from our flat. One was English, the other Swedish. Scott took a liking to the Swedish girl, and I fancied the English girl. We'd go over to their house and then out to the clubs or dinner. Some of the time we'd go off on our own as couples, but for the most part we'd all go somewhere together. When we got back to their house we would always disappear into their respective bedrooms, later to emerge the worse for wear, and creep unsteadily back to our flat.

Another cool thing about our flat was that you could get up on the roof to sunbathe naked. Gary never went up, though: he had more important activities in his tent. The summers during the mid-1970s were exceptionally hot, and Scott and I were up there every day taking advantage of the roof and getting a good tan, and there were many times when, just to brighten up the day a little more, we'd have some female company. It's a good thing the paparazzi with their zoom lenses were not around in those days.

I still hadn't settled down. I was constantly looking for something and I just never seemed to find it. I wasn't even sure of what I was looking for but I knew I'd know when the time came.

After *No Regrets* we decided to start working on the next album. Somebody had given us a song called 'Lines', written by Jerry Fuller, which really appealed to Scott, who thought it was one of the best songs he'd ever heard. Interestingly, the lyrics are clearly about cocaine addiction. We decided to name the album after the song, which turned out to be our next single. The B-side was 'First Day', a number I had written some years before, which was also included on the *Lines* album. The single was released in the summer of 1976 while we were working on the album.

Dick Leahy came up with two more songs for us. The first was called 'Everything Must Change', and after we had made the backing tracks for that Scott started to put his vocal on the song. He did about four or five takes, then suddenly dropped everything, walked into the control room, and said he just couldn't sing the song because 'the lyrics are too inane'. The original version we'd heard was done by a really classy black jazz guy, but Scott just couldn't get into the lyric. So that was the end of that song.

Dick then presented us with the second song – 'To All the Girls I've Loved Before', which later became a massive hit for Willy Nelson and Julio Iglesias. But it was a case of *déjà vu* for Scott. We again made the backing track, he started singing, came back into the control room and pointed to me, saying, 'John, get out there, you're singing this one.' He couldn't get into this song either, and refused to go any further with it. So I did the song and we played it for Dick, who was disappointed that it wasn't a joint effort, and we noted a little hostility from him from that point onwards. GTO got back at us with our next single though.

Lines was released in late summer 1976 along with a second single taken from it, 'We're All Alone', by Boz Scaggs. Rita Coolidge had had a hit with this in the US, and her version was already on the English airwaves, so by the time GTO got around to releasing the single the hit was hers, not ours. We figured out that was our payback for not going along with Dick's ideas for the earlier tracks. The B-side, which also came from the album, was 'Have You Seen My Baby', written by Randy Newman. This was an afterthought about which I wasn't really crazy. It was Gary who added some interesting sounds at the end of it – his imitation of an elephant, which Scott found amusing, so he left it on. Looking back, I realise that in the seventies we didn't make the best choices for our uptempo songs on the *No Regrets* and *Lines* albums. Aside from 'He'll Break Your Heart' and 'First Day', the other uptempo numbers were mediocre at best.

The other tracks on the album were Tom Snow's 'Taking It All In Stride', Tom Jarvis's 'Inside of You', 'Many Rivers to Cross' by Jimmy Cliff, 'Brand New Tennessee Waltz' by Jesse Winchester, 'Hard to be Friends' by Larry Murray – which I sang – and 'Dreaming as One' by David Palmer and William Smith.

With the release of our *Lines* album things seemed to be smoothed out between Dick and us. He called us into his office one day for a meeting and strongly suggested that we try working with a co-producer, somebody he had in mind named 'Papa' Don Schroeder. Schroeder worked out of Nashville, Tennessee, and had produced several hits with a black duo, James and Bobby Purify, who had had a hit with 'I'm Your Puppet'. So off we went – Scott and I – to Nashville.

We arrived in Nashville in the winter of 1976–77. There was a blizzard and it was freezing. As soon as we got to our hotel apartment, we grabbed a cab and headed for the famous Music Row – Nashville's Tin Pan Alley. We hit ten or 15 clubs and it was the same story – fantastic players everywhere. The next day we went to the recording studio. We watched as the session musicians arrived and chatted among themselves, then Papa Don handed them the charts for 'People Get Ready'. Suddenly the guys got serious and played their asses off in one take – they were real pros, and could obviously read anything. Our jaws dropped: we were super-impressed.

After laying down the basic backing track, the band members left Papa Don to work on the vocal with us. But things turned out a lot different from what we could ever have planned. Scott and I had recorded the song in 1966 and were very familiar with it, so he went into the studio while I stayed in the control room. He did four or five takes until he got what he wanted, and when he took his headphones off I knew he was done. Then it was time to listen. After we'd played it back a few times, Papa Don said, 'OK, now let's get out there and do it for real.' Scott shot me the 'I'm in total shock' look; as far as we were concerned, he had sung his ass off, so Papa Don's remark went down like a lead balloon. We didn't know what we were dealing with.

Scott obediently went back into the studio. The track played, and he sang the opening two lines, but before he got any further Papa Don suddenly stopped the tape. Scott looked up. I looked too. Papa Don asked me what I thought. I said, 'It was fine. Why did you stop the tape?' He replied, 'Because I want to review it.' Scott was asking, 'What's going on?' from the studio, and I told him through the control-room microphone, 'There was a question about something. Just carry on.'

'Should I sing the first line again?' he queried. Without consulting Papa Don, I took it upon myself to answer, 'No, we'll drop you in from where you left off.' The tape rolled, Scott starting singing the next phrase – and Papa Don suddenly stopped the tape again. I asked him why he'd done that, and he said he was concerned about the way Scott sang the word 'don't'. In the meantime, Scott was out in the studio, looking at me in bewilderment. I asked Papa Don if he always stopped the tape, to which he replied, 'Yes – I drop in every phrase. I did the same thing for James and Bobby Purify.' At that point, I said, 'Hold it, we've got to talk about this.' And I motioned to Scott to come back to the control room. We both explained to Papa Don that we were used to singing the entire song in one take, with adjustments being made if necessary after that. He answered that he strongly disagreed with that method of recording.

Scott and I were pretty much worn down from all the proceedings, and weren't really getting anything done, so we politely excused ourselves and told Papa Don we'd be fresher the next day. We talked about what we were going to do and decided that the situation would only get worse. We knew there was no way we would be at our best with a cut-and-paste type method: it would sound too contrived. So I called Dick the next morning and explained what was going on. I knew our venture was costing him a lot of money, but insisted there was no way that Scott or I could make a decent track in this manner. We left a few days later, after Dick made new arrangements. Scott went back to London and I went to California for a few days before returning to England. I think Papa Don came over to London later on because he really wanted to record us, but nothing came of it.

Back in London, back in the old flat, we started working on our next album, which became *Nite Flights*. I was really disappointed with the outcome of everything we had done after *No Regrets*; I'd had a lot of confidence in the *Lines* album, and thought it was really good, but without promotion it hadn't made any impact.

We all decided that we would write our own material for *Nite Flights*. We told Dick, and got started, disappearing for most of 1977. The musical experiment was a lot of fun: we didn't discuss what we were doing individually, and each of us didn't have a clue what the others were writing. The end result sounded like three different albums, as each group of songs had no relation to the other – there was no continuity. I still consider *Nite Flights* to be sort of a musical unanswered question. I also think this album was the beginning of Scott's embarking on a whole new type for material for himself – not so much commercial, but more and more experimental. I liked the tracks he wrote for the album; they were a challenge to record and well received. It was his first venture into avant-garde music, and it signalled the direction in which he was going in the future.

For the first and only time in my writing career I wasn't writing songs about love. I wrote four songs for the album – 'Rhythms of Vision', 'Disciples of Death', 'Fury and the Fire' and 'Child of Flames' – about bizarre science-fiction stuff. Perhaps I was influenced by my choice of reading material at the time: Frank Herbert's *Dune*, Isaac Asimov novels and a lot of Dennis Wheatley's books, which were very entertaining. I've been asked if any of those songs were about the occult, and if I was involved in that, to which the answer is no. Back in the sixties, I did the ouija-board thing with a bunch of people sitting around a table with a glass on top that moved from one letter to another, but I didn't take any of that seriously.

Early in 1977 I decided to go cold turkey and quit drinking because it was again causing too many problems. I also stopped smoking for many months. I wanted to see if I could actually give up both habits and what life would be like without them, and I didn't want anything to get in the way of our new opportunity. During the whole *Nite Flights* recording period I was completely sober. I lived like a monk for about a year – and it felt like ten. I didn't like being sober and smoke-free. I missed all of it and finally succumbed once more to Scotch and cigarettes. Being sober didn't really change the way I managed my life, or the way others handled my life.

We dumped Ady Semel as our manager, too. The three of us had become increasingly disenchanted with him as he just wasn't doing anything for us, and I really resented giving him a percentage of our action. Dick lined up a meeting with John Reid – Elton John's manager – but he was too busy with Elton by then. We didn't know who should look after us. Then Gary came up with David Apps's name; he had managed Allan Clarke from The Hollies. So David became our interim manager for a short time.

I realised, around 1978, that we needed to get back out on the road and do some live shows again. Ady had let us down by not capitalising on the success we'd had with 'No Regrets' nearly two years earlier: there had been no tour or concerts, only promo stuff, and the fans should have had more. The only way artists can really ensure continued success is by doing live shows. It's not just about making a living playing music: we owe it to our fans to make the effort. It's that simple.

We discussed tours, concerts and cabaret, and decided to go with cabaret shows in the UK, mainly because it would have taken a year to get a big tour together. I was ready to go back on the road right away, and so was Gary, but Scott was reluctant to do anything live. Nevertheless, Gary and I coerced him into doing some dates, which unfortunately backfired on us. Scott didn't want to do The Walker Brothers' hits, of which we had to include at least a few, and refused to do any of his solo hits. These were all the bread and butter of our show and, whether he liked it or not, the public wanted to hear all the songs they associated with us.

The cabaret dates turned out to be a disaster. Scott was obviously uninterested, on stage and off, which had a negative effect on the audience. Consequently, I felt way too much pressure, as if I were carrying the bulk of the show. Each night on stage I cursed myself for talking Scott into doing this. At least the band was good, thank God. I can't remember if David Apps was present or not but I wish he had ground the shows to a halt long before we were done. We really harmed our reputation by presenting ourselves the way we did: we looked unprofessional. Interestingly, Scott and I weren't at odds this time around, as we had been back in the sixties. I just went along with everything. Contrary to popular belief, Scott didn't have any stage fright: he just detested the hassle of travelling and putting up with all the live work, so there was no point in pushing it any further.

I realised that even if *Nite Flights*, or any other album, charted we wouldn't be travelling and playing to audiences, which is what I really loved to do. I wanted to be on stage again and perform the stuff we were recording. There's an uplifting thrill like no other for musicians who love to play live: that's why people like The Rolling Stones, Paul McCartney, Rod Stewart and so many others, who could have retired years ago, still get out there and play. I knew that Scott was content just with producing, writing and recording, and was not up for live shows, and it was because of this that The Walker Brothers would split again in 1978. There was just no way to make any money and keep the three of us afloat without playing live. It was that simple. Living on royalties alone was too much of a roller-coaster ride.

In July 1978, *Nite Flights* was released; the single from the album, 'The Electrician'/'Den Haague' – with Gary singing his self-penned B-side – came out in August. There was also an EP called *Shutout*, featuring the four songs that Scott wrote and he and I sang.

We'd wanted something really unique and different for the album cover, and the company Hipgnosis, famous for its sleeve designs, suggested the idea of using an anamorphic lens to shoot close-ups of us, instead of the standard fish-eye format for which the lens was normally used. The three of us thought it was cool, and GTO went along with it. Later, we heard that our Walker Brothers fans were a bit shocked by the cover, especially seeing Scott smoking a cigarette. Of course, that was just a prop. Scott never, ever smoked.

The album was a commercial failure; our royalties didn't compare to our successful albums, and GTO probably lost money on the venture. There was, however, a small, exclusive audience that really liked the material, particularly Scott's compositions. Had the album become mainstream it might never have achieved this cult status I think the three of us knew that GTO wasn't particularly happy with it, although nobody from the company said anything. We didn't know at the time that GTO was being taken over by CBS, which wasn't good news for Scott, as not too long ago he'd gone to a lot of trouble to get out of a contract with them. We were still dependent financially on GTO, who paid for our flat, but we now needed to generate some other income. The fact that our latest album wasn't commercially successful, and that we weren't going to play live shows, didn't leave David Apps much to work with. After several months went by, with no positive activity or plans for the future, I told Scott and Gary that I was going back to America, and off I went. There was no discussion about breaking up the group, we just drifted apart.

I met my future third wife, Brandy Neilsen, around the time we completed the *Nite Flights* album. She was of English and Greek heritage, and had black hair and blue eyes, which was a striking combination. She looked a lot like the actress Barbara Parkinson.

She had a fiery temper, which I didn't really care for, but it didn't bother me in the early days. She was quite outspoken with a great sense of humour, not always easily understood, but still very funny at times. Brandy and I went to America and lived in Ventura for the next three years, making just one visit back to England.

I decided to devote my time and energy to learning about the record-engineering process, and purchased a four-track TEAC tape machine while still in the UK – my first step towards building my own professional studio.

Brandy dreamed of being a recording artist and song writer. She was a prolific lyricist, and could write something on almost any subject. Much of what I was planning included her. When we had first met, it had been decided that I was to be her producer. Her ex-husband, Claus Neilsen, a Danish businessman, and his new wife, the actress Sally Thomsett, started a record company – Spectra – and wanted us on the label, with the idea of releasing our material in the UK. Claus funded the recordings we did in a Santa Monica studio, with The Rolling Stones' former manager Andrew Oldham producing and overseeing everything. We did two self-penned tracks, 'Dark Angel' and a new version of 'Remember Me'. Claus wanted John Schroeder, one of the great A&R men, to do the mastering but John also wanted the publishing rights and he had been cited for dealing unfairly with songwriters in a series of famous court cases in England. For me, therefore, the publishing was where I drew the line. I'd been burned once with Miracle Songs, so I put my foot down and told Claus and John I wanted 50 per cent of the worldwide publishing, and 100 per cent of the songwriting rights. Nobody budged, so the deal was off. Claus still released the single, from what I've heard, but I lost touch with him after I wouldn't cooperate over the publishing.

Brandy and I married in America in 1980. Our daughter, Nickoletta (Nickole), was born in April 1981 and we returned to England soon afterwards because we missed living there. It had become more of a home to me than California. Brighton was one of my favourite places outside London, so we moved there. The fact that it was on the coast and had an artistic atmosphere really energised me; I'd always liked living close to water. While there, I met a guy named Bill Viviers who had an antique restoration shop in Kemptown; I learned a lot from him and spent much time in his shop.

Scott and I were in touch quite a bit. He was still living in west London, with a woman named Libby. I had made demo cassettes featuring Brandy and me singing some original material that he really liked, so I asked him if he would produce an album if I got a record deal. He said he would. Instead of going to major labels, I found an independent company called Rough Trade. Geoff Travis, the owner, was also keen on the idea of an album. I figured out production costs with Scott and presented the package to Geoff who gave us the go-ahead, and we started work in 1982. Rough Trade paid for all recording costs and, in lieu of an advance, we had a very high royalty rate. Geoff also formed a record label called Blue Guitar, which would exclusively handle our product.

The downside of this project was that Scott and I went way over budget, which led Rough Trade to start negotiations with Warner Brothers to take over the label. Finally, Geoff made a deal with an executive named Tarquin Gotche, who soon afterwards was fired from Warner Brothers. Our deal went with him so, essentially, we had three tracks – completed to our satisfaction – but no place to go with them. From what I understood, Rough Trade couldn't carry the promotional costs. Now I found myself with three completed masters, a publishing deal, but no record deal, manager or agent. That was typical of the music business. I contacted everyone I knew to locate a label. My old friend, Dave Dee, he said he would make some calls. Alan Parker, who had played guitar on all three tracks, offered us more time in his studio in Kent and gave the masters to his promotional people to get something going.

After waiting a few months, I finally heard back from Alan. He had ominous news. All the labels liked the tracks, and the songs, but unanimously thought that I should have been the lead singer, not Brandy. I told Brandy, as diplomatically as possible, what Alan had said, but she completely overreacted and decided from that moment on that she was through with anything or anyone in the music business. That caused a lot of problems that wouldn't go away. It was total grief at home and never got better. She wouldn't allow music to be played on the radio, in the car or in the house. Music shows were forbidden. It was a total boycotting of anything to do with music, and really irrational behaviour, but I gave up my ambitions to record or write for a long time. It just wasn't worth the drama.

Scott and I would talk on the phone, and we'd keep each other up to date on what we were doing. Now signed to Virgin and managed by Charles Negus Fancy, he was in the process of recording his new album, *Climate of Hunter*, which was released in 1984.

Early in 1986 I got back in touch with Dave Dee, who hooked me up with a promoter who was organising a UK tour for *The Monster Rock'N'Roll Show*. This tour had been around for a long time, with the artists varying. I was taken on as one of the stars and Chris Black and his band – The Black Cats – became my backing group. They had once backed Brian Poole, and were seasoned musicians. Also on the bill were older artists who had had hits in the late fifties and early sixties, including Billie Davis and Screaming Lord Sutch. I was the newcomer: my hits were only 20 years old. I performed a shortened medley of Walker Brothers hits – 'Make it Easy on Yourself', 'The Sun Ain't Gonna Shine Anymore' and 'First Love Never Dies', 'No Regrets' and other oldies that the band knew, such as 'California Sun', 'Way Down Yonder in New Orleans' and 'Reach Out, I'll Be There'. I did a lot of shows, mostly in theatres, clubs and ballrooms in the South of England, but my memory of the whole thing is very vague; I was getting really loaded, as often as possible, during this period of time in my life.

Chris and his band were supportive, and quite protective of me. There were many nights when I slept on Chris's couch, with his wife and family checking on me to see if I was OK. Chris is a real character and a great guitarist, still going strong after many years; his *Come On Everybody* show continually tours England. Sue Walton, a fan of The Walker Brothers, followed a lot of the Monster shows, and ended up collecting my fees. I really needed a lot of looking after back then and I owe Chris and Sue a debt of gratitude.

In 1986, when the tour ended, Brandy and I moved back to America – this time to San Diego, where Brandy had friends. She had wanted to leave England ever since the record deal collapsed. I had no music prospects in San Diego, but made a secret promise to myself that one day I would build a studio, record, continue writing songs and perform again – regardless of Brandy's sour attitude to it all.

In the meantime, I had a family to support, and considered several alternative careers. I was in my mid-40s and had really never had a 'regular' job. I had some engineering skills from my school days, so I took an electronics course as I was going to build a studio. Then I was hired by a firm and eventually became a technical consultant to large manufacturing companies, enjoying a successful career in this sphere while I was my building my studio and developing my musical interests.

I had appeased Brandy by moving out of England and getting a job that had nothing to do with the music business. Now it was time for me to get back to my studio work, having put it on hold for the past few years. I had purchased a house and started setting up my equipment in a spare bedroom. The old bug was back, and I became obsessed once more with everything I could read or hear on the subject of recording.

Around this time, Scott came to visit his mother and Aunt 'Seal', and we met up in San Diego. The two of us hung out for the day at Seaport Village, reminiscing about funny stuff from the early days, but the conversation always came back to music and recording.

In 1992, Fontana released a compilation album, *No Regrets: The Best of Scott Walker and the Walker Brothers*. I was telephoned for interviews by press people, with camera crews even coming to the house, which seemed strange, as that life now seemed so far in the past. The album did very well in the charts, reaching Number 4, and had lots of promotion from Fontana. It inspired me to carry on with my studio work and try to capture that great big warm sound that we'd had in the sixties. Brandy didn't want to know.

Two years later, Scott was working on his album, *Tilt*, and we were in touch regularly. He was trying to decide whether or not to go with the new digital technology or stick with analogue. We had many discussions about the pros and cons of each but, in the end, he chose analogue because of the big sound he'd decided he wanted to achieve. He knew that I was well informed about the latest equipment, so I told him about specific machines and possibilities. It never occurred to me that Scott should have his own studio, and in fact he never did. He simply recorded everything – playing guitar and singing – on an old-fashioned cassette player and then worked things out with the arrangers, who would ultimately write everything out. He liked to work with particular arrangers like Wally Stott, who were more avant-garde and able to interpret his ideas into music. Scott never disclosed the material he was preparing to record as a solo artist until he was in the studio, or with his arranger, so everything was kept under wraps until recording time.

Tilt was released in 1995 to mixed reviews: it was definitely a departure from anything he'd done previously. The memory of critics waiting to shoot Scott down in the sixties may account for his feeling more comfortable making unconventional music these days. I think he has reverted to the kind of musical innovations that Pierre Schaeffer was doing with his *musique concrète*, with experimentation. There is no way to discredit what he does because there is nothing to compare it with.

Gary and I lost touch for several years, mainly because I was in America a lot and he was somewhere in England. I'd heard he had married Barbara, his steady girlfriend throughout the seventies and the Walker Brothers reunion, so that came as no surprise. It would not be until 2004 that Gary and I would meet again in person.

In the winter of 1995–96, I purchased a much bigger house, with an enormous garage that had been completely renovated into one large room. It was attached to the house and a perfect place in which to build my studio. I'd go out of my front door, walk several yards to the studio door, walk in, shut it, and be in my own world. It became a refuge. From time to time I acted as a consultant to young bands and artists who looked me up. They were mostly club and punk bands trying to break in to the music business. That was a real departure for me, but fun. I also started buying CDs again, thousands of them, everything from country to hip-hop. I not only enjoyed the music but was listening to the recordings very carefully to see what I could learn.

I started writing songs again, mostly to use in recording experiments. I was becoming more and more proficient, I thought, with my studio abilities. I had met several people, particularly Geoff Daking, who designs signal processors and had been the drummer in The Blues Magoos; Tim Kauffman – from Rolltop

Studios in San Diego, Kenleigh – who designs speaker systems; Jeff Forrest, the drummer on Blink-182's first album; and Ron Pedersen, who has his own studio, and who shared a lot of information with me about mixing, speaker systems, different methods of signal processing, types of equipment – generally everything to do with recording that would create a more professional, as opposed to demo, track.

When I'd left England in 1986 I left all my guitars behind, never knowing when or if I would be playing again. Now I was looking to rebuild my collection and wanted a variety of guitar tones. I met 'Big' Steve Barker, a real guitar aficionado who deals in vintage guitars, and knows how to find anything related to guitars or amps. Through Steve, I bought a 1970 Gibson 335, and a 1956 three-pickup Les Paul reissue – but I couldn't find a Stratocaster I liked. Steve finally suggested that I buy the parts and make one myself. He got all the stuff for me, and I assembled a guitar that I still use.

I got in touch with Seymour Duncan, a man who had a reputation for making the best custom-guitar pickups. Seymour told me that he had known who I was since 1966, because he actually owned a guitar that I had sold to Jeff Beck, a late-fifties Fender Esquire that I had purchased out of the boot of some guy's car in 1964, the body of which I had customised to feel like a Stratocaster. It was never refinished; I just left it as it was. That was the guitar I used in our first Walker Brothers shows, until we stopped playing our instruments and The Quotations became our backing band. I'd heard that Jeff was looking for a Fender guitar, so I told him he could have my Fender for £75, which is what I paid for it. Jeff made that guitar famous, and had a bunch of hits using it with The Yardbirds and on his solo records. Seymour told me that, way back then, that particular guitar inspired him to make custom pickups for guitars. I was totally flabbergasted.

I also bought a synthesiser keyboard, drum machine, bass guitar and lots of percussive instruments. By 1997 I was making professional-sounding recordings, so I decided single-handedly to make a CD. I wrote, arranged and performed everything on the tracks. Using my synthesiser, I worked out my own orchestral arrangements; I added drums on the drum machine, and percussion, and I sang lead and harmony parts. It was virtually a

one-man show, and the more I worked, the more the ideas kept coming. It was the first time in years that I felt as if my creative juices were flowing again.

It wasn't until I wrote the songs for my *YOU* CD in the late 1990s that for the first time I indulged in my own intimate views of how I wanted love to be. Ever since I can remember I've been almost obsessed with love in its many complex forms, and continue to explore the endless possibilities in my music. Some of my favourite lines in my songs are, 'You're never too far from that dream', 'Lock me in your heart, hold me in your eyes', and 'I'd take more than a chance for you'. I guess I'll always be a hopeless romantic.

At first the CD was intended to be just another recording experiment, but it was going so well that, with the encouragement of my friends, I decided to take it to the next level, hiring Jeff Forrest to play drums, Tim Kauffman to add bass, and some singers to augment my harmonies. It turned out to be a monumental task, but one that I thoroughly enjoyed. Geoff Daking mixed the CD and I had it mastered at Bernie Grunman's famous mastering lab in Hollywood.

I released *YOU* in 2000. I was very pleased to get the critical acclaim I received for this work; it was a real labour of love that had kept me busy for three years.

CHAPTER 8

STANDING OVATIONS

MAKING POP HISTORY
GARY WALKER

In July 2005, when John came over to England to perform at a private gathering for fans in Hastings, Sussex, he suggested that I join him. This would be the first time in 27 years that we had been on stage together. The event was organised by Sue Walton, who ran John's fan club and Yahoo! Group.

At last I fully understood why Scott had been nervous about singing on stage. Before I made my appearance at that hotel in Hastings, I felt like committing suicide. But, being a trouper and knowing that the show must go on, I pushed myself through the door of hell. Before me was a sea of expectant faces and bright smiles. I sang my two songs, 'Twinkie Lee' and 'Dizzy Miss Lizzie', and then, to my total amazement, the audience leapt to their feet as one and applauded and applauded. I was not only embarrassed but close to tears; it got to me so much that I was unable to return to the stage to join John in the final song, 'What'd I Say'.

Afterwards, I did come back and thank the fans, and then I spent a very enjoyable hour meeting everyone and signing autographs. The following day, there was a garden party at Sue Walton's house for all those who had helped to organise the show, and there I met the author Alison Weir and her parents, Doreen and Jim, with whom I have since become great friends. Sadly, Jim passed away in 2006.

That summer, Sue Walton took over the running of my fan club and built me a website. She has always been a good friend and immensely supportive. I'd also like to mention Sue Hadley, who has assisted Sue throughout and looks after my mail.

In December 2005, due to popular demand, I returned to Hastings to perform for the fans, backed by Chris Black and his band. For the first time ever I performed my two songs from the *Nite Flights* album, as well as The New Radicals' song 'You Get What You Give'.

Since then I have been doing some shows with my friend, Mike Powell, making appearances at venues around the country, meeting fans and entertaining them with music and my own brand of after-dinner speaking. Mike is a very good singer, absolutely awesome, and sounds a lot like Scott; he sings all The Walker Brothers' hits, as well as 'Lines' and 'Stay With Me Baby', and he also covers Matt Monroe songs. He can sing straight off, without any music, and deserved the standing ovation he got at these shows.

Two thousand and six was a big year for Walker Brothers fans – and there are evidently still a great many, plus new converts. Scott finally released his long-awaited album, *The Drift*, and gave several interviews. Universal put out a CD compilation of the Walker Brothers' greatest hits entitled *The Sun Ain't Gonna Shine Anymore*. I did a lot of radio shows to promote this, and the release that followed it, the much-publicised and brilliantly reviewed five-CD boxed set retrospective of The Walker Brothers' entire back catalogue, *Everything Under the Sun*. Included in this were 14 unreleased tracks from the sixties, among them the original version of *The Sun Ain't Gonna Shine Anymore*. Another unreleased recording of the song had just appeared on a 2006 Scott Walker compilation, *Classics and Collectibles*.

Two thousand and nine sees the rerelease in Britain of The Rain's *Album No 1* on Universal's Eclipse label, digitally remastered in 3-D, and yet another Walker Brothers compilation album, *My Ship is Coming In*. Joey, John and I have had discussions about re-forming The Rain, and are all agreed that we

would love to do that. We want to record the second album that we never got to do, and include the four existing tracks that were not released in the sixties.

I am now writing some music that is similar to pieces that John Williams has written for films, and hope to be able to release these soon. There are other projects under discussion, but I can't say too much about them now!

As I look back on my life and career, it strikes me how lucky I have been to have helped make pop history and to have been a member of one of the biggest groups in the world. I am endlessly grateful to my fans because, without them, that would never have happened. I am to blame for everything – because it was me who suggested that John and Scott come to England – and I have no regrets. I have had the good fortune to enjoy the company of some of the most famous people, and to have total support from my wife Barbara and son Michael: without them I would never have made it. They are the only thing that really counts.

WHAT DOESN'T KILL YOU WILL MAKE YOU STRONGER
JOHN WALKER

Around 1999–2000, when I knew I was going to release *YOU*, I formed my own publishing company – Arena Artists Association – and my own recording label, Arena Records. I wanted total control over all my product, and to own everything.

I knew a guy named Ray Hall who lived in the San Diego area and played guitar, and we often got together with other people at his house to have jam sessions. Nobody knew that I had been with The Walker Brothers, as I'd decided to keep that quiet when I moved back to America several years before. Once Ray discovered that I had my own studio and was working on a CD, he wanted to become involved in the business end of things. He was new to, and curious about, the record business. I described all the pitfalls, in great detail, to him, explaining that it's very easy to get taken in by trusting the wrong people.

Although we didn't have a written contract, just an oral agreement, Ray wanted to provide financing in return for a percentage of the profits. I was reluctant to have a partner, but

Ray's input and enthusiasm was always energising and motivated me to keep going. Outside of a handful of friends, I didn't get any other support on my project. In fact, I got just the opposite on the home front, for Brandy was still harbouring a nasty attitude towards me and my music, so it was easy sometimes to get off course and let her negativity distract me. To stay focused, I completely stopped drinking for the entire time I was working on *YOU*, and relied on my friends for support.

Everything was going well with the CD: there was plenty of the right publicity being set up over in the UK, which was where I wanted to release it, and I was very happy with the CD itself. Ray and I had spent quite a lot of money getting everything ready for distribution, including shipping the product to the UK. We had a contract with an independent distributor in England who was recommended to us by the guy handling my publicity and PR work – someone I had met in California who also represented Barry White and other artists. I planned my promotional trip to the UK, which involved lots of radio and press, and plenty of airplay of the CD tracks. David Wigg – an icon in the music business – interviewed me for Chatshow.com. It was all terrific, and I felt really positive about stepping back into the business.

The promo trip was my first visit back to the UK since I had moved away in the mid-eighties. It was April 2000, and England looked glorious: the sun was shining, the weather was beautiful, the air was fresh; in short, it was everything good I remembered about it. The PR guy had lined up my hotel, by odd coincidence it was adjacent to the mews where I had purchased my Marcos in 1966.

In among my rather hectic promotional schedule, I managed to hook up with some old friends, including Dave Dee and Mike Williams. Scott was on holiday, and I didn't have Gary's contact details, so I didn't see either of them. Dave put the pressure on me to come over and tour, as he had been doing regularly since I left England. He was so encouraging, and offered to set it all up; all I had to do was say yes. But I told him I didn't have enough confidence to tour as a solo artist at the time.

Lynn Goodall, the devoted editor of the *Walkerpeople* newsletter – which she co-founded way back in 1980 – showed up at the BBC radio studios after my interviews. She filled me in on

all the latest Walker gossip; she seemed to know everything. I had been away from Walker Brothers territory for so long that I found it very touching that there was still such a loyal fan base. By the end of my trip, I would have been quite happy to stay in the UK, but I had to think of my daughter, whose birthday was that month, and other commitments.

Unfortunately, there was a huge fly in the ointment: distribution was poor and my CD never made it to the stores. I still have no idea where all of those boxes of CDs went. It took a few months after I returned from my promo trip before we worked out what had gone wrong – and I was royally pissed off. Ray was too. I emailed and phoned the distributor for updates on sales and so forth, and he had an answer for everything, but we weren't seeing anything in writing. I called friends in England to check things out, and they all reported back to me that the CD wasn't available. Eventually, the distributor lost touch with me; we just stopped communicating. This hadn't been the original plan. Despite our wariness, Ray and I had fallen into one of the pits I had warned him about early on. After this tough lesson, Ray became understandably disenchanted with the whole music scene and we dissolved out partnership. I decided that that was the last time I would have a partner: it's heartbreaking enough when something like this happens to me, but even worse when it happens to someone I feel responsible for.

In 2002, Sony – who had bought out CBS – decided to release a compilation album of unfinished and unreleased Walker Brothers tracks called *If You Could Hear Me Now*. The songs on the album, which had been recorded for GTO in the seventies, never made it past basic track material, which is a long way from a finished product. Scott and I were really annoyed. To add insult to injury, one of the songs included was my rough version of my song 'The Ballad', but Sony called it 'The Ballad of Ty and Jerome', and gave songwriting credits to two Jamaican dudes. It's taken the dedication of my manager, David Oddie, and an entertainment attorney to straighten out that mess.

In the summer of 2001, I had moved up to Washington State. Brandy and I were having a lot of problems and she thought it would be a good idea to start over somewhere new. I bought a house, built a studio, and started work on some new material. Even though my heart was not into moving, Washington was a beautiful place to live. The house overlooked the Puget Sound, a lovely little island, and there was a forest all around us. Visiting the nearest town was like being in a time warp and going back over 30 years, but I needed more action. We left our two cats with friends in California. Only Sam, our little Maltese dog, moved with us. Sam loved the forest and all the woodland creatures, and in a few days he acted as if it were all his territory, defending it against seeming predators such as the raccoons that were twice his size. He was absolutely unflinching. I loved watching him doing this.

In October 2002 I parted with Brandy and moved back to California. I left her the house, my belongings, two cars and lots of money in the bank. The hardest part was saying goodbye, for the time being, to Nickole, but I had to leave. Things were not working out at all. I wasn't ready to hang up my guitar, quit the music business, and quietly drift off into the sunset. At least, not yet! For wheels, I still had a 1967 Pontiac in California, where I was having it restored. I rented a van and all I took with me was my studio equipment, instruments, clothes and a little cash.

I really have to question my reasoning over what happened in the next weeks. Kathy and I had been in touch again. I guess I'd always felt that everything that had happened all those years ago had been somehow my fault. We talked about it and how things change, and that maybe being young and not very experienced had led us to make some rash decisions. So we decided to try it again. That was a mistake. Before I knew it, we were at odds, I'd started drinking again, and that was enough of that. Kathy went her way and I went mine.

At the end of November 2002, I was living in Gordon Waller's house in California until I figured out what I would do next. There, I received an email from Dave Dee. He was insisting, yet again, that I tour. This time I gave in and agreed to join the big annual Solid Silver Sixties tour in 2004. It was such a long way off that I didn't think it would actually happen.

I got back in touch with Tiny Schneider and told him I wanted to start playing again: just clubs, nothing too big. We started meeting and jamming, playing an odd date here and there – but only once with me actually leading his band. I was quite content

just to be the guitar guy for the time being, and let someone else carry the show. I had lost a lot of ground after so many years of not performing live, and had a long way to go. Playing in the studio was a lot different from playing in front of an audience.

I think that one of the contributing factors to my continuing on-again/off-again drinking episodes may have been my seeming inability to find a relationship that lasted more than a few years and actually grew into something worth having. I'm not saying that the right relationship earlier in my life would have saved me from the 'demon drink', but it might have helped. Another big factor would be my tendency to self-destruct, which has something to do with my creative drive. I have to live on the edge. I've been known to have what appears to be 'it all', and then throw it away.

Little did I know that I was soon to encounter someone who would become a positive influence in my life. In March 2003, my sister Judy called me to tell me that she had met a terrific girl called Cynthia. I had just straightened myself out once more and wasn't really looking to meet anyone. I was trying to figure out what I was going to do with my life – again!

When Judy asked me why I hadn't yet gone to meet this girl I didn't have an answer, so I decided right then that I would go ahead and do it. It was the best decision I have ever made.

Cynthia is tall, elegant, poised and very beautiful. I had some misgivings about approaching her. I wasn't sure how she would react to some strange guy walking up and saying hello. Fortunately for me, she remembered her conversation with my sister, so that broke the ice. She was very friendly and agreed to go out for coffee and a chat in a café nearby. I had made plans to go out with Tiny to a club to see a band later that night, but Cynthia and I were getting along really well, so I called him and said I wasn't going to make it.

Cynthia was a delight. We talked for hours, then I asked her if she would like to have dinner one night, to which she agreed. She chose an Italian restaurant, a very quiet place, and she looked gorgeous that night.

We started seeing each other quite often, but there were still some issues to be sorted out. I hadn't yet filed for divorce from Brandy, and still had no idea what I was going to do professionally. As yet, Cynthia knew very little about me, and she wasn't in a hurry to get involved with anyone. So we kept it light. We usually met up with Tiny and his lady friend, Bonnie, for a night out. We went to dinner and the clubs around town to see different bands play. Cynthia seemed to know a lot about music, and I soon found out why. She is a classically trained pianist, and has been playing and teaching for several years. The first time I heard her play I couldn't believe it; I was really impressed, as she was playing classical pieces from memory. I'd never met anyone who could do that, or play like that. Then I thought to myself, I'm never going play any of my music around her! She was way too good, and in a different world compared with what I'd been doing. I was just amazed.

In July of that year, 2003, I had a happy and successful reunion with my son, Jamie Anderson, and met his wife, Alisha, and my granddaughter, Kelsi, only about four at the time. I hadn't seen or spoken with Jamie since he was four years old. When we all met in a restaurant that afternoon in Glendale, it was like looking at myself 30 years earlier. Now we are in touch regularly, and Jaden – my grandson – is four years old at the time of writing of this book. The family live in England, but we always manage to see each other at least once each year – here in California or over there.

Of course, something unexpected always happens. One night, I took Cynthia out to see my friend, Tom Mclear, who was performing in a club in the valley. Tom decided that I needed to come up and play a few songs. I really didn't want to do this, as the only thing Cynthia knew was that I played a little guitar. I thought it would not do me any good at all, but Tom insisted, so I played 'One Night With You' and 'Unchain My Heart'.

When I got back to our table, Cynthia quietly looked at me and said, 'You are really good. I know you've done this before. Are you going to tell me about it?' She had never heard of The Walker Brothers, so I told her the whole story. Doing that was very awkward for me, because I don't go around telling everyone about my past, and it doesn't sound believable unless you were there. Telling her definitely turned out to be a good idea because the next thing Dave Dee was calling me to confirm that the 2004 Solid Silver Sixties tour was on, and telling me to get in shape.

I got the contracts for that in August. Now I knew it was for real, and that Dave wasn't kidding. The tour had more dates than any I had been on in my entire career. I remembered doing an interview with *Beat* magazine a few years earlier, in which I was asked if I would ever tour again, and I'd said, 'Maybe one day, but not one of those mammoth tours – only about ten dates.' Now there would be more than 50, and over 9,000 miles of travelling. When I looked over the itinerary I almost fainted, but then I remembered one of my favourite sayings: 'What doesn't kill you will make you stronger.' Peter Noone, of Herman's Hermits, who was also on the same tour said, 'They don't pay us to perform, they pay us to show up.'

Dave was in touch soon after I'd looked over the contracts, and then said that of course I needed a souvenir CD to sell on the tour. I was used to taking my time with my music, but now there wasn't just one deadline to be ready for, but two, and I got a little panicky. I knew, once I signed the contract, that I would be on a plane headed for England in mid-February – less than six months away – and embarking on an adventure into the unknown. I didn't feel the least bit prepared, and was suffering anxiety about the reaction I would receive from the audiences. Dave told me that I had to do The Walker Brothers' top hits in my show, which made me really nervous because I felt a lot of pressure at the prospect of performing the songs by myself.

I got to work right away on the souvenir CD, entitled *The Silver Sixties Tour 2004*. I included The Walker Brothers' four most popular songs, some old rock'n'roll I enjoyed doing, and some of my new compositions. I arranged everything the way I wanted, but when it came to the Walkers' songs I didn't base them on our original hits.

Without Cynthia's help and support getting the CD completed and my set rehearsed and ready to go, I think that first tour would have been a disaster. I felt that I had found someone with whom I could share my whole life, not just a part of it, so in the middle of it all I asked her to marry me. I'm sure she had some misgivings, but she accepted, and we were married in December of that year. The best part is that we share each other's interests and dreams, and even though we continue working together on more and more projects, we still find time for ourselves. Between us we have three grown children, and an extended family comprising Cynthia's son, Adam, who has a three-year-old son named Stanly, my daughter Nickole, who is in her mid-20s, and Jamie and his two children, Kelsi and Jaden.

It's important to mention that my values have changed over the years. At one point, the most important issue was where the group was in the charts, or how our latest tour was going. Now, I have a terrific family, and that is the one thing I am most grateful for.

Coming to England early in 2004 was traumatic, and I lost it. I was in a panic to get everything done on time and, again, if it hadn't been for Cynthia I don't know how things would have turned out.

The Dakotas, who (in their original line-up) had backed Billy J Kramer in the sixties, were going to be my backup band, and thankfully they were terrific. But during that first rehearsal with them I went into shock when they told me that it would be best to do the Walker Brothers songs exactly like the records. I protested silently to myself, but readjusted my thinking and did it their way.

The first concert was a matinée at Southend-on-Sea, Essex. I asked Cynthia to watch me from the audience and give me constructive feedback on my performance. I felt awkward to begin with: I was playing guitar, and having to take it on and off between songs; I had to devise choreography, which caused problems. But my biggest concern was how I would be received by the audience. I was extremely tense before I went on. I probably didn't appear at ease on stage, but in fact I got a very warm response.

Afterwards, I listened to the advice Cynthia gave me regarding how I was projecting myself, and that evening I made some changes that improved my act immeasurably and gave me more confidence. You know you're doing it right by the way the audience react – and on that night the response was even better. I continued to work on my performance and eventually, quite early on in the tour, I was receiving standing ovations. I was overwhelmed – I actually didn't know how to react. It was more than I had ever expected.

It wasn't until halfway into the tour that I finally relaxed a little bit. I had put so much pressure on myself that it got in the way of enjoying everything. The audiences were very receptive, and I got

lots of applause and good feedback when I was out signing autographs each night. For the first time in my career I was meeting the fans and signing autographs. Each person expressed their gratitude, and seemed to know what an effort it was for me to come over, get up on stage and perform the songs they loved so much. Over and over, I heard that folks had waited for years, hoping that one or all of us would be back in the public eye, singing the songs they knew so well. I couldn't have been happier with the outcome of what had seemed so daunting and intimidating.

While I was on the tour, I saw countless friends and acquaintances as I travelled throughout the UK. Many came to the shows as well. Gary turned up at the Dartmouth show; it was as though we had never lost contact. He still had that dry sense of humour, and we vowed to keep in touch. Dave Dee was checking in with me by phone, or sometimes in person, every single day of the tour. He had set up everything really well for me. I met up with an old friend, Bill Ansell, who lived near Southampton. Bill also looked after me, even going a step further than that, setting up more PR and television. Bill was a natural entrepreneur, and a great guy; sadly, he passed away from cancer a few years after the tour. Mike Keeley, who had played bass for me during The New Walkers tour many years before, and 'Big' Dave – my guitarist then – came to see me in Manchester. It was a wonderful reunion for the three of us. Sadly Mike, too, has passed away since then. He was such a gentle dude.

I got together several times with Mike Williams and his usual entourage of various friends and acquaintances. Mike always likes to reminisce about the old days, and we end up having a good laugh about some of the daft things we used to do to look cool – like wearing shoes that looked great but were very uncomfortable. I also ran into my good friends from Scotland, Tom Gillespie – who owned the Meadowhead Hotel – and Henry Spurway, who'd promoted the shows up in Scotland many years before. I managed to have a couple of good nights out with them while I was on the tour. Sue Walton, with whom I hadn't been in touch since the mid-eighties, was very enthusiastic about my coming back to the UK – so much so that she started a fan group and website, among other things, on my behalf. I also did a lot of radio interviews and saw some DJs I knew from way back – Richard Cartridge, Dave Cash and David Hamilton.

One of the most important get-togethers I had was with my old friend Mike Gill. Mike had been in the music business for more than 40 years, and knew everybody. At the time he was working on a compilation album of Dusty Springfield hits for Universal; before her death in 1999, Dusty had specified Mike as the person to oversee her archives. Mike and I met, and talked a lot on the phone, with the outcome that he was interested in managing me. He told me that he would bring in a partner – someone he trusted – who had also been in the business for many years, like himself: David Oddie. I liked the idea and felt comfortable with it. The contract was being written up as I was returning to California in the summer of 2004.

It was on a Wednesday morning, a few months after the tour had ended, that I got a call from David. He told me the shocking news of Mike's sudden death the night before. I was actually in my car when I received the call, and had to pull over and just stop in order to take in the news. I was completely stunned. I told David, whom I still had not met, that I'd call him back in a couple of days.

David called me back to see how I was doing, and eventually the subject of management came up. He asked if I had decided what I wanted to do about that situation. After a lengthy conversation, we decided to continue on the same path as before, with David now taking over my management. Although he and I had not met each other, I had trusted Mike Gill's judgement when he'd initially mentioned David as his business partner, and for that reason I felt comfortable working with David.

David and I finally met in the summer of 2005, at a big bash in Hastings. We hit it off immediately: he looked and talked the part of a real pro and had indeed been involved with big agencies like Robert Stigwood – in the early days – in managing the Bee Gees, Eric Clapton, Rory Gallagher and others over the years. I had complete confidence in David and was very excited to see what would unfold in the coming years now that I was re-establishing myself as an artiste.

In early 2005, I was asked to be a special guest artist honouring the Beach Boys in their home town of Hawthorne, California. It was a two-day celebration featuring Al Jardine, David Marks, various surf and tribute groups, artists, producers and old friends.

Carl and Brian Wilson, and other family members, were also in attendance. On the second day, I performed two songs on stage with David Marks's band. This was the first time that Cynthia accompanied me on keyboards at a big event.

In the summer, Cynthia and I flew to the UK to appear in a special show for my fans in Hastings, meticulously organised by Sue Walton. Tiny came over to play drums, while Chris Black and his Black Cats backed us. For our act, Cynthia joined The Black Cats playing keyboards, and Eddie Mooney of The Dakotas played bass and added harmony. Gary and I performed several songs, and Gary entertained the audience with his special humour. We had a wonderful couple of hours entertaining the packed house.

After the Hastings event, I travelled in to London to stay at my favourite hotel, eat at my favourite Italian restaurant, and meet the people at Repertoire Records near Camden Town. They were releasing a CD compilation of all my solo Philips recordings, called *If You Go Away*. Chris Welch, who used to write for *Melody Maker* back in the sixties, was still interviewing people, and we met up after all those years. He was one of the few journalists I liked. For example, he would never insinuate, like a lot of the modern music papers do, that The Walker Brothers were a 'boy band'. When I hear that term, I think of a group that is the product of a record producer, a record company and some very good marketing. We were seasoned musicians before we got to England.

Not long after that, back in California, I was called to do a television interview – in a Beverly Hills hotel – for a British TV show featuring the top 100 break-up songs: 'The Sun Ain't Gonna Shine Anymore' had been voted Number 9. I felt that that was some achievement after 40 years.

I had started working on my new CD, *Just For You*. The theme was love songs. Seven of the ten tracks were my own compositions: 'Just For You', which I originally wrote and recorded in 1986, 'The Road', 'I Can't Let You Go', 'Come Back to My Arms', 'Sweet Dreams', 'Shadow of Night' and an updated version of 'The Ballad'. I also included some covers of songs I had recently discovered and really liked a lot: 'Amazed', which had been an international hit for Lonestar; Amanda Marshall's 'I Believe In You'; and 'Part-time Love' by Kenny Denton. This album forced me to stretch my imagination and skills as an engineer. Cynthia's strings and keyboard parts were an integral part of each song, and the key to the bigger orchestral sound that I wanted. I had a lot of fun – and frustration – during the mix-down sessions, which always took forever before I was satisfied.

In spring 2006, I got a call from Henry DeLuca, a producer for American PBS music shows. He was putting together a special about the Sixties British Invasion, and wanted me to appear. I thought the call was a little odd, and kind of didn't believe him: after all, we were Americans, not British. I pointed that out to him, and he replied, 'Well, yeah, but The Walker Brothers were part of the British Invasion.' We flew to Stoke-on-Trent in England, where it was easy to film Gerry and the Pacemakers, The Tremeloes, Wayne Fontana, Peter and Gordon, The Troggs and a host of other British artists – many of whom were performing in the area on the Solid Silver Sixties Tour that year. I had a quick reunion with Dave Dee and PJ Proby at the Victoria Theatre, and met Gerry Marsden for the first time. What a delightful chap. We spent a lot of time after his show visiting back in the dressing room, chatting away and talking about friends in common from the sixties. We polished off a few bottles of wine as well. The show airs regularly on PBS here in America as a fundraiser for public television.

Our English trip was timely because Universal wanted me to do promotion for a five-CD box set they were about to release. Entitled *Everything Under the Sun,* it is a collection of the entire Walker Brothers back catalogue. Around the same time, Universal also released a 21-track CD called *The Best of Scott Walker and the Walker Brothers,* which made the UK album chart. Along with those, there was an EP with four tracks called *The Walker Brothers,* and a reissued vinyl single of 'The Sun . . .', designed to look like an original Philips 45. Later that year, Universal released a five-CD set called *Scott Walker in Five Easy Pieces.* Then there was *Classics and Collectibles,* a 2006 compilation of Scott's songs featuring an earlier studio take of 'The Sun Ain't Gonna Shine Anymore', as was also featured in the new five-CD box set with the first version, which was in the wrong key and too slow. We had never considered our first recording of 'The Sun . . .' to be the original; it was a practice track that didn't work out.

There were 14 unreleased tracks on the box set – all unfinished.

(I have no recollection of recording the other tracks that Philips are said to have kept in their archives, and suspect that they were Scott solo tracks.) We weren't consulted about these unreleased tracks being included, and weren't at all happy about it. I can't think of any artist who wants their unfinished material released, at least not without their listening to it first and giving permission.

I had completed my CD and was anxious to play live again. My manager David called and asked if I wanted to do an even longer Solid Silver Sixties tour, starting in March 2007. On tour with me this time would be Wayne Fontana, The Merseybeats and The Searchers, with The Dakotas as the backup band. And now I told Cynthia she had to come with me, although she was very reluctant to be part of the show. I convinced her that I needed her to sing with me, or I wouldn't go. She finally gave in, mainly because she knew I wanted to do the shows, but not without her. We began working on our set.

Two new members of David's staff came along for the entire tour: Ann Gwilliam and Joy Ryan. Both have been Walker Brothers fans for many years and were very enthusiastic assets. Joy is the devoted president of my fan club, and Ann is David's personal assistant and runs my MySpace page as well. They both set up lots of promo, and also handled the merchandising every single night, without fail. These ladies work tirelessly for David and me, and also look after Cynthia. I don't know what we'd do without the help of these loyal friends.

During the 2007 tour I was a lot more relaxed and able to enjoy myself. Even though it was a gruelling schedule, Cynthia and I managed to have day trips out and find favourite spots all over the UK, which we visit every opportunity we have. We turned the tour into a working vacation, catching up with lots of folks all over the place, and sightseeing. The funny thing was that I had never done the tourist thing in the UK during all the years I'd lived there, so it was only recently that I went inside Westminster Abbey, Windsor Castle, Arundel Castle, Bath Abbey, Salisbury Cathedral, Lacock Abbey, Lavenham, Chester and the big museums. There are too many more to list.

After the tour, we were hosted in Germany by Lothar and Uschi Drung and their German Walker Brothers' chat-group friends for several weeks. It was a terrific trip, and we loved the German food and old cities. We were taken to Salzburg – a long-time dream for Cynthia, who loves Mozart. We also drove down to Italy and spent several days in the South of France during the Cannes Film Festival, then roamed around Nice and other coastal areas that I had never really visited when I'd lived there many years before. We fell in love with Villefranche and its romantic setting and harbour. On the drive back to Germany we stopped in Strasbourg, and were amazed to see the German and French medieval cities still intact and thriving beautifully side by side.

In Germany we also met Oliver and Richard, the chief members of the experimental group Phallus Dei. Oliver told me that they had been commissioned to write the entire soundtrack for a film called *Sommertag*, and asked if I would be interested in participating in the project. Subsequently, when I got back to California, Richard – the drummer and technical engineer – sent me the their backing track and lyric sheet for a song called 'Will You Come Now'; they wanted me to write the melody and perform it. On first hearing the backing track and reading the lyric, I wondered if I could come up with anything usable. Everything about the piece was so different from anything else I had done before. I was stymied for a few weeks, but the lyric and music haunted me, and soon a melody just flowed. I was quite pleased with the final version, and I really appreciated Oliver and Richard's patience and confidence in me. It was unlike any other project I had been associated with. I'm really happy I was asked to be part of it.

Another tour was in the works, this time with Robin Edwards and David Oddie as promoters. We left America for the UK again in November 2007. This tour was about four weeks long and followed hard on the heels of a trip to Berlin in October for my appearance on a popular German TV show, *Hits Giganten*. The show featured a lot of sixties artists, mostly from the UK. I performed 'The Sun . . .', again with Cynthia on stage with me; I sang to a tape of my own arrangement that I had put together a few weeks before the show, rerecording the song with a further 16 tracks.

While on tour in Scotland, Cynthia and I were guests of honour at the big annual Christmas Scotland Variety Club Ball, held in

Glasgow at the big Hilton. There we met up with my old promoter friend, Henry Spurway.

I had finished recording a CD right before this tour, called *Songs of Christmas and Inspiration*, a collection of old and new favourites, plus an original track that I wrote and really like called *The Promise*. I had wanted to do a CD like this for many years, and managed to get it done just in time for that tour.

Since 2008, I've been writing songs and working in the studio on another CD. It seems to be tinged with a little country, but it keeps evolving – so who knows how it will end up? I've also just completed a souvenir compilation CD called *John Walker – A Collection: Vol. 1*; it has eighteen tracks, including my own arrangements of the four big Walker Brothers hits, and fourteen tracks of assorted solo recordings, which for the most part have been rerecorded and remastered. The songs span my career from 1965 to 2007.

We are also embarking, as I write, on another big Solid Silver Sixties tour. It is wonderful to be back in the UK again, except that I miss seeing my dear friend, Dave Dee, who passed away recently after battling cancer and complications for several years. Every time I walk on stage during this tour, I know I'll feel Dave's presence; he performed in countless shows all over the UK for years, and I know that his devotion to his loyal fans gave him the determination to carry on right up to the end.

Since submitting the manuscript for this book, another important event has occurred in my life. While on the Solid Silver Sixties Tour, David Oddie resigned as my manager. Cynthia has taken over and works with our loyal, hardworking team: our personal representative Ann Gwilliam, president of my fan club and assistant to Ann Joy Ryan, and my webmaster, and son Jamie Andersen. Cynthia and I met with David, Gary and Gary's son Michael at Heathrow on 20 June 2009 – after being away from the US for over four months – to say our goodbyes and have photos taken for this book of Gary and myself... together once again at Heathrow airport after all the years. We wish David and Gary all the best in their future endeavours.

Looking back over the years, I am surprised at the impact I had on so many people. I made a lot mistakes, but I learned from my

experiences. I truly value my wife Cynthia, my family, and the loyal fans and friendships I have today. I also want to thank Scott and Gary, because without them I would not have had this incredible life.

DISCOGRAPHY

THE WALKER BROTHERS

SINGLES

Pretty Girls Everywhere/Doin' The Jerk (1964)
Love Her/The Seventh Dawn (1965)
Make it Easy on Yourself/But I Do (1965)
My Ship is Coming In/You're All Around Me (1965)
The Sun Ain't Gonna Shine Anymore/After the Lights Go Out (1966)
(Baby) You Don't Have to Tell Me/My Love Is Growing (1966)
Another Tear Falls/Saddest Night in the World (1966)
Deadlier Than the Male/Archangel (1966)
Stay With Me Baby/Turn Out the Moon (1967)
Walking in the Rain/Baby Make It The Last Time (1967)
No Regrets/Remember Me (1975)
Lines/First Day (1976)
We're All Alone/Have You Seen My Baby (1976)
The Electrician/Den Haague (1978)

EPs

I NEED YOU (1966)
Looking For Me/Young Man Cried/Everything's Gonna Be Alright/I Need You

SOLO SCOTT, SOLO JOHN (1966)
Sunny/Come Rain or Come Shine/The Gentle Rain/Mrs Murphy

THE WALKER BROTHERS (1978)
Shutout/The Electrician/Nite Flights/Fat Mama Kick

ALBUMS

TAKE IT EASY WITH THE WALKER BROTHERS (1965)
Make it Easy on Yourself/There Goes My Baby/First Love Never Dies/Dancing in the Street/Lonely Winds/The Girl I Lost in the Rain/Land of 1,000 Dances/You're All Around Me/Love Minis Zero (No Limit)/I Don't Want To Hear It Anymore/Here Comes the Night/Tell the Truth

PORTRAIT (1966)
In My Room/Saturday's Child/Just For a Thrill/Hurting Each Other/Old Folks/Summertime/ People Get Ready/I Can See It Now/Where's The Girl/Living Above Your Head/Take It Like a Man/No Sad Songs For Me

IMAGES (1967)
Everything Under the Sun/Once Upon A Summertime/Experience/ Blueberry Hill/Orpheus/Stand By Me/I Wanna Know/I Will Wait For You/It Makes No Difference Now/I Can't Let It Happen To You/Genevieve/Just Say Goodbye

LIVE IN JAPAN (Japan, 1968)
Land of 1000 Dances/I Need You/Everything Under the Sun/Tell Me How Do You Feel/Watch Your Step/Uptight/In My Room/The Lady Came From Baltimore/Living Above Your Head/Dizzy Miss Lizzie/Twinkie Lee/Hold On, I'm Coming/Annabella/Yesterday/

Reach Out, I'll Be There/Make it Easy on Yourself/Saturday's Child/Walking in the Rain/The Sun Ain't Gonna Shine Anymore/Turn On Your Lovelight/Ooh Poo Pah Doo

NO REGRETS (1975)
No Regrets/Hold An Old Friend's Hand/Boulder To Birmingham/Walking in the Sun/Lover's Lullaby/Got To Have You/He'll Break Your Heart/ Everything That Touches You/Lovers/Burn Our Bridges

LINES
Lines/Taking It All In Stride/Inside Of You/Have You Seen My Baby/We're All Alone/Many Rivers To Cross/First Day/Brand New Tennessee Waltz/Hard To Be Friends/Dreaming As One

NITE FLIGHTS
Shutout/Fat Mama Kick/Nite Flights/The Electrician/Death of Romance/Den Haague/Rhythms of Vision/Disciples of Death/Fury and the Fire/Child of Flames

IF YOU COULD HEAR ME NOW (2001)
Compilation album including these unreleased tracks from the 1970s:
Loving Arms/I Never Dreamed You'd Leave In Summer/The Moon's a Harsh Mistress/Marie/Till I Gain Control Again/The Ballad/Tokyo Rimshot

EVERYTHING UNDER THE SUN (2006)
5-CD Box Set compilation including these unreleased tracks from the 1960s:
The Sun Ain't Gonna Shine Anymore (original version)/The Sun Ain't Gonna Shine Anymore (studio take)/Lazy Afternoon/In The Midnight Hour/A Song For Young Love/Let the Music Play/The Shadow of Your Smile/Hang On For Me/I Got You (I Feel Good)/I Got Lost for a While/A Fool Am I/Wipe Away My Tears/Lost One/Looking For Me/Baby, Make It the Last Time

THE WALKER BROTHERS
GARY WALKER

SINGLES

You Don't Love Me/Get It Right (1966)
Twinkie Lee/She Makes Me Feel Better (1966)
Hello, How Are You/Fran (1974)

EP

HERE'S GARY
Twinkie Lee/She Makes Me Feel Better/You Don't Love Me/Get It Right

GARY WALKER WITH THE CARNABEATS
Cutie Morning Moon/Hello Gary

GARY WALKER AND THE RAIN

SINGLES

Spooky/I Can't Stand to Lose You (1968)
The View/Thoughts of An Old Man (Japan, 1968)
Come In, You'll Get Pneumonia/Francis (1969)

ALBUM

ALBUM NO 1
Magazine Woman/The Sun Shines/Doctor, Doctor/I Can't Stand to
Lose You/Market Tavern/Spooky/Take A Look/The View/If You
Don't Come Back/Thoughts of an old Man/Francis/I Promise To
Love You/Whatever Happened To Happy/Francis/Come In, You'll
Get Pneumonia

JOHN WALKER

SINGLES

Annabella/You Don't Understand Me (1967)
If I Promise/I See Love in You (1967)
I'll Be Your Baby Tonight/Open the Door, Homer (1968)
Kentucky Woman/I Cried All the Way Home (1968)
Woman/A Dream (1969)
Yesterday's Sunshine/Little One (1969)
Everywhere Under the Sun/Traces of Tomorrow (1969)
Huellas Del Manana/Quienes Somos (Spain, 1970)
True Grit/Sun Comes Up (1970)
Cottonfields/Jamie (1970)
Over and Over Again/Sun Comes Up (1970)
Good Days/Midnight Morning (1973)
Dark Angel/Remember Me (1982)

ALBUMS

IF YOU GO AWAY (1967)
The Right to Cry/Guess I'll Hang My Tears Out to Dry/Reaching
for the Sun/Good Day/An Exception to the Rule/If You Go
Away/So Goes Love/It's All in the Game/Nancy (With the
Laughing Face)/It's A Hang Up Baby/Pennies from Heaven/I Don't
Wanna Know About You

THIS IS JOHN WALKER (1969)
Sun Comes Up/But Beautiful/Everywhere Under the Sun/I See Your
Face Before Me/True Grit/Here's That Rainy Day/For All We
Know/I'm a Fool to Want You/Traces of Tomorrow/You've
Changed/Who Are We

YOU (2000)
You/Falling For You/If This is Love/So Rare/Never Too Far from
That Dream/Heaven Knows/Inside/What Am I Supposed To
Do/You'll Never Come Back/The Way Love Goes for Me

THE SILVER SIXTIES TOUR 2004 (2004)
Let The Good Times Roll/No Regrets/My Ship is Coming In/Make it Easy on Yourself/Unchain My Heart/The Sun Ain't Gonna Shine Anymore/ Never Too Far From That Dream/My Destiny/I'm Not Gonna Be the One/ Real Love/What Am I Supposed To Do/Just Like the Rain/So Rare/Love's Blind

JUST FOR YOU (2007)
Just For You/Sweet Dreams/I Believe In You/I Can't Let You Go/Come Back to My Arms/The Ballad/The Road/Amazed/Part-Time Love/Shadow of Night

SONGS OF CHRISTMAS AND INSPIRATION (2007)
The Promise/Silent Night/He/(I'll Be) Home For Christmas/Amazing Grace/The Christmas Song/Crying In The Chapel/White Christmas/I Believe/Oh Holy Night

JOHN WALKER: A COLLECTION: VOLUME 1 (2009)
Make it Easy on Yourself/No Other Baby/The Way Love Goes For Me/No Regrets/Inside/I'm Not Gonna Be the One/My Ship is Coming In/My Destiny/I See Your Face Before Me/The Road/Sun Comes Up/I'll Be Your Baby Tonight/You've Changed/Kentucky Woman/Love's Blind/Just Like the Rain/I Can't Let You Go/The Sun Ain't Gonna Shine Anymore